# TWENTY
# ADVERTISING
# CASE HISTORIES

## Second series

*Edited and introduced by*

## Charles Channon

*Institute of Practitioners in Advertising*

CASSELL

**Cassell Educational Limited**
Artillery House, Artillery Row, London SW1P 1RT, England

Case histories originally published in *Advertising Works 3* and *4*, © Cassell Educational Limited 1985, 1987
Compilation and introduction © Cassell Educational Limited 1989

This compilation first published 1989

**British Library Cataloguing in Publication Data**

Twenty advertising case histories, second series.
  1. Advertising
  I. Channon, Charles
  659.1

ISBN 0–304–31722–5

This book has been printed and bound in Great Britain by The Bath Press, Avon

# Contents

# Preface

This book contains twenty case histories about advertising campaigns selected from the best papers submitted for the Institute of Practitioners in Advertising 'Advertising Effectiveness Awards' in 1984 and 1986. It is the second in a series which draws on the Awards to provide, for the benefit of students and others, case histories of the contribution of advertising to the attainment of marketing and business objectives. Fuller details on the background to the Awards and the nature and structure of the cases submitted to them will be found in the Introduction to this book and in the Introduction to the first book in this series, *Twenty Advertising Case Histories*, edited by Simon Broadbent (Cassell, 1984).

It is hoped that this collection will prove a useful addition in an accessible form to the pool of advertising case histories available to teachers and students in colleges and to trainees in companies, as well as to others already in work who feel they can still learn from the thinking and experience of others. The papers are printed as originally published and should be particularly useful for those engaged in courses in business studies, marketing and advertising.

# Acknowledgements

I am grateful to the following individuals whose work directly or indirectly has done so much to encourage this continuing enterprise on the part of the publishers and to promote study of the contribution of the different elements of the marketing mix to the achievement of their common goal. Without this effort the Awards, from which these cases are drawn, would have had less opportunity to be of benefit to a wider constituency than those already at work in advertising agencies themselves.

Professor Michael Baker, Department of Marketing, Strathclyde University
Dr John Bateson, Chairman of Marketing Subject Area, London Business School
Professor Tom Cannon, Manchester Business School
Professor Derek Channon, Manchester Business School
Professor Marcel Corstjens, European Institute of Business Administration, INSEAD
Professor Peter Doyle, Warwick Business School, University of Warwick
Professor Gerald Goodhardt, City University Business School
Professor Stephen Parkinson, Management Centre, University of Bradford
Professor Nigel Piercy, Cardiff Business School, University of Wales
Professor John Saunders, Department of Management Studies, Loughborough University
Professor Ken Simmonds, London Business School
Professor Michael Thomas, Department of Marketing, Strathclyde University
Professor Robin Wensley, Warwick Business School, University of Warwick

# Introduction

## BACKGROUND

As its title makes clear, this book is the second in a series of selected case histories, drawn from the published papers of the Institute of Practitioners in Advertising (IPA) biennial awards for case histories demonstrating the effectiveness of advertising. The first book in this series (*Twenty Advertising Case Histories*, ed. Simon Broadbent, Cassell, 1984) was based on the IPA Advertising Effectiveness Awards of 1980 and 1982. The full published papers from those two Awards appeared in hardback as *Advertising Works* (1981) and *Advertising Works 2* (1983), both edited by Simon Broadbent. This second series, therefore, draws on the Awards of 1984 and 1986, published by Cassell as *Advertising Works 3* and *Advertising Works 4* in 1985 and 1987 respectively, both edited by the present writer. Further details of the Awards and a full discussion of their criteria will be found in those books, which also contain between them a further 19 case histories not included in this present selection.

Simon Broadbent's introduction to the first selection of case histories cannot be bettered as a lucid and insightful summary of the nature of case histories in advertising effectiveness, of the decision structure and process from which they arise and of the ways in which they can be used, in Gordon Wills's words, 'to discover and fix in one's mind productive ways of thinking, ways of feeling, and ways of doing'. This introduction will therefore take that groundwork for granted and should be read in conjunction with it. The one exception is the list of *general* questions Simon Broadbent recommends as a discipline to be followed to get the most out of each case: for ease of reference this is repeated here prior to the *specific* questions listed on a case-by-case basis.

## PROBLEMS SOLVED AND PROBLEM-SOLVING

Entries in the IPA Advertising Effectiveness Awards are, by definition, concerned to demonstrate through evidence and argument the successful solution of a problem or exploitation of an opportunity. More conventionally, a case study is written to describe a problem or opportunity to which the *reader* is expected to propose possible solutions or approaches. This difference in structure and intention has some bearing on how these cases are best used and understood.

To start with, these cases typically have a structure which is more than simply that of narrative and even if they start as a narrative they continue as an argument and end as a reasoned conclusion. Of course, not all the cases are perfect and one would hardly expect otherwise. Real life rarely allows one to tie up all the loose ends, and this is nowhere more true than in the complex interactive world of consumers and goods and services in which marketing and advertising have to operate. Nevertheless, whatever the flaws, these cases have already been judged to have made a *sufficient* argument for their conclusion to be accepted with *reasonable* conviction.

This could suggest that what we have to learn from these cases are 'right answers'. But nothing could be further from the truth. The answers found here were right in their precise marketing environment and competitive context, right for a specific brand or sub-brand at a certain time in a certain situation, given certain consumer needs and attitudes. For another brand at another time in another competitive context or even for the same brand, come to that, the old answer is unlikely to be applicable in the new situation. What is to be learned lies in the principles by which it was arrived at. As case tutors never tire of emphasising, right answers in marketing cannot be learnt, they must always be discovered by right questions. So one way of regarding what we learn from case studies is that we are, by repeated exposure to different cases, learning the principles, techniques of analysis and lines of enquiry that constitute good marketing detective work.

For this reason, it can happen that the cases which leave loose ends here and there and perhaps some pieces of evidence unexamined have even more to teach us than those which are comprehensive and completely buttoned down. Just because the latter cases are structured like arguments they are in a sense harder to get into than the ones which lie open and unstructured before us, as it were, mixing relevant and irrelevant information even-handedly and without guiding emphasis, waiting for us to impose our own analytic structure upon them. In addition, because of the purpose for which they were written, the structure of these cases has a consistent in-built bias which we need consciously to offset in using them for the present purpose. Their argument, quite properly, is designed to culminate in the identification of the contribution of the advertising to profitable sales or share *over and above that of the rest of the marketing mix.*

## MARKETING DETECTIVE WORK AND SALES EFFECTS

There is a sense in which this focus can be quite a narrow one, if still important as any source of additional profit must be. Though concerned with advertising, we will be potentially just as interested in all the other parts of the marketing mix: product (and packaging), price, distribution and forms of promotion apart from advertising. Of course, these papers do not ignore these elements—they have to consider them in order to show that they could not on their own fully account for the whole of the sales effect observed. But our interest is just as likely to be the other way round, and diagnosing the whole of the sales effect (not just some variation above a base level of or underlying trend in sales) may be a very instructive part of our marketing detective work.

Some of the very best papers in this selection, it must be said, do such thorough justice to the whole of the marketing mix and to positioning the advertising as one integral part of it, that this narrowness of focus can scarcely be attributed to them for practical purposes. The TSB school leavers' case is one such and Dulux Natural Whites another.

But when we turn our attention to the dynamics of the total sales picture we are not necessarily or even typically putting advertising on one side, as it were. Thus it is not true to say, for example, that a base level of sales or underlying trend in sales represents the sales effect '*minus* advertising'. This way of talking is not merely careless, it is wrong. When we speak of a sales effect of advertising over and above that of the rest of the marketing mix, 'the rest of the marketing mix' typically *also* includes advertising. The point about the base level of sales or an underlying trend in sales is that we cannot disentangle and separate the contributions of each element to it. But we do know that to a greater or lesser degree all the elements are contributing, whether directly or by interaction or both.

Furthermore, elements which don't change contribute to it as well as elements which do change. Thus distribution may not change but without it there would be no sales. Inevitably these cases are about change—in the advertising and in the resulting sales. Elements which don't change or don't change that much cannot account for the change and yet may still play a major role in the underlying sales position. For the same reason and in the same way the focus in these cases is on the short term, whereas the marketing detective is equally interested in effects which persist even though we cannot go on to say how much each element is contributing. The governing objective of marketing activity is (in most cases) long-term profitable survival and we should care deeply about the marketing principles and decisions that conduce to creating and sustaining that position.

When this is a relevant consideration, to pursue it may well take one *outside* the case as it is presented and the specific questions tend to assume that case tutors will allow this both in this particular regard and elsewhere when it seems pertinent to try to generalise a principle from a particular instance.

## NON-MARKETING CASES

In the present selection, there are one or two cases which are not marketing cases at all in the ordinary sense of the word. In these the ultimate objective is not profitable sales but the minds and hearts of the voter (as in the GLC case) or the habits and disposition of the citizen—in this case the citizen as housewife in the safety campaign concerned with chip-pan fires. The 'competition' in these cases is not another good or service but prejudice or apathy or simply the 'clutter' of all the other things we have to think about as we go about our daily lives. Nevertheless, marketing can learn from these situations and not least from the idea of 'changing the agenda', which was so important a part of the strategy in the GLC campaign. In the event, that campaign did not succeed in its ultimate objective but it did as much as advertising could ever be expected to do in the circumstances. We may regard it as an excellent illustration of a mechanism by which the characteristic priority of marketing, which derives from consumer needs and satisfactions, may be reconciled with the characteristic priority of 'opinion-forming', which derives from the needs of the sender of the message and not from those of its recipients. We can create more common ground between these two very different sets of interests than marketing theory sometimes leads us to expect.

## FURTHER READING

In most cases the likely readers of this book will have been given full guidance on books that might be helpful in their marketing and advertising studies generally and for their case work in particular. But for those who happen to be studying unaided the following list may be stimulating and enlightening:

For understanding what advertising agencies do:

*The Complete Guide to Advertising* by Torin Douglas, Macmillan, 1984.

For understanding branding and its importance to marketing and advertising:

'What is a brand?' by Stephen King, J. Walter Thompson (London), 1971, reprinted in
   *The King Papers*, JWT (London), 1988.
*What's in a Name?* by John Philip Jones, Lexington Books, 1986.
'Advertising' by Charles Channon, Chapter 33 in *Marketing Handbook*, 3rd Edition, edited
   by Michael Thomas, Gower, 1988.

For a classic discussion of the marketing principle:

'Marketing Myopia' by Theodore Levitt, *Harvard Business Review*, 38 (4), July/August
   1960, pp. 45–56.

For a readable introduction to the multiple aspects of marketing strategy and the tools of
marketing:

*Offensive Marketing*, 2nd Edition, by Hugh Davidson, Penguin Books, 1987.

For a checklist of terms, concepts and definitions:

*Macmillan Dictionary of Marketing and Advertising*, edited by Michael J. Baker, Macmillan,
   1984.
*The Pocket Guide to Marketing* by Michael Thomas, Basil Blackwell/*The Economist*, 1986.

For media choice and scheduling:

*Spending Advertising Money*, 4th Edition, by Simon Broadbent and Brian Jacobs, Business
   Books, 1984.

For setting the advertising budget:

*The Advertising Budget* by Simon Broadbent, NTC, 1989.

This selection is partial and personal. Another editor could produce a quite different but equally defensible list. It is deliberately biased towards authors who are directly involved in or very close to the day-to-day practice of advertising in the market-place because these authors can, understandably, get overlooked in the academic pursuit of marketing and advertising studies. Both sides can learn from the other and it is fortunate that on the marketing side most academics have flourishing consultancies. Marketing and advertising in the real world will always be more like an art or a craft than a science. In such a situation *how* you do it and how *well* you do it can be just as important as *what* you do. This is the reason why students can feel the want of understanding just what an agency does in the complex multi-disciplinary practical process which goes from taking a client brief to running an advertisement. For those who have not had in-house experience of working in an advertising agency or in the advertising department of a client, the first book in the list given above can help to compensate for that lack.

## GENERAL QUESTIONS*

Because the case studies all have the same broad structure, they have similar natural breaks at which students should pause. You can then ask yourself the following obvious questions. In addition, each case has its own particular features and further special questions are suggested later.

Read the general and special questions *before* you read each paper. The breaks where you should stop in your reading are when you should ask yourself the questions set. In this way you can tackle the problems facing the people doing the real job, and then compare your answers with the decisions actually taken. Other questions ask you to set down formally, and to try on your own or other data, the techniques used.

After the business background and marketing objectives are explained:

1.  Say whether the objectives are clear to you.
2.  State in your own words the opportunities seen by the company.
3.  Describe exactly the product's advantages and how you think consumers perceive them.
4.  Say what marketing objectives you would have set.
5.  List the changes in consumer behaviour needed to meet the targets.
6.  Describe the other information you would have liked at this stage.

After the campaign plan has been described:

1.  Discuss the advertising budget set.
2.  Say what alternative advertising objectives you would have considered.
3.  Describe the target chosen and other reasonable targets.
4.  Comment on the media choice.
5.  Show how creative research might have improved the advertising.
6.  Draw up a campaign and research plan in which evaluation might have been improved.
7.  Draw up an alternative campaign.

After the evaluation:

1.  Say whether you consider the conclusions justified.
2.  List ways in which a cynic might otherwise explain the results.
3.  List ways in which the evaluation method used could have been made more watertight, or could have explained more.
4.  List other methods which might have been used to measure and explain the results.
5.  Draw up new marketing objectives and campaign plans, with the benefit of hindsight.

It is also useful to go through these examples to draw up for yourself a checklist, set of questions or list of methods in order to:

1.  Write marketing and advertising objectives.
2.  Brief creative people.
3.  Judge creative work.

*This section previously appeared on pages x and xi of Simon Broadbent's first volume in this series. It is repeated here for ease of reference.

4. Write a media plan.
5. Draw up an evaluation scheme.
6. List situations where each method of evaluation might be used—and where it cannot.

## SOME QUESTIONS ON OR SUGGESTED BY THE CASES IN THIS BOOK

### Breaking the Bran Barrier—Kellogg's Bran Flakes 1982–84

1. What does this case mean when it talks of 'positioning' and 'repositioning' and why are these concepts important to its story?
2. In this case market volume share is treated as the key measure of brand performance in the market-place rather than absolute volume of sales. Why is this and what general advantages do measures of market share have? Describe those market situations in which the absolute level of sales might be the more helpful measure.
3. Distribution is obviously tremendously important to Bran Flakes but what is its importance in this particular story? What does this tell you about evaluation exercises?

### Hofmeister: A Study of Advertising and Brand Imagery in the Lager Market

1. Describe in your own words precisely *how* the 'George the Bear' campaign came to increase sales of Hofmeister.
2. Why is *rate* of sale such an important part of the evidence in this case? And what does this tell you about the nature of the marketing task?
3. Explain in your own words why the findings of quantitative research failed to reflect a significant shift in Hofmeister's standing with the consumer.

### ICI Dulux Natural Whites

1. Consider the relationship between added value to the consumer and profitability to the manufacturers in this particular case and describe what each element of the marketing mix contributed to it.
2. Explain the authors' distinction between a 'new product' and a 'new concept'.
3. Describe in detail the different things that could be done to determine *prior* to the launch the appropriate price level for Dulux Natural Whites.

### The Repositioning of Hellmann's Mayonnaise

1. List the principal difficulties this case faces in arguing its case for the effectiveness of the advertising. Evaluate how far each of these difficulties has been successfully overcome.
2. In the event, increased sales came from new users but average weight of purchase has hardly increased. What inferences would you draw from this which might have a bearing on future marketing and advertising policy?
3. If you were marketing manager of Hellmann's, what further questions would you like answered before deciding on future action and why?

### The Relaunch of Cow & Gate Babymeals

1. At the end of this case history it is obvious that one objective of the relaunch has not yet been achieved. What more would you propose to do about babymeals' distribution in grocers?
2. A small budget was all that was affordable for this relaunch. List all the factors you can find or think of that made a small budget workable.
3. In what ways were the change in product formulation and the change in the Cow & Gate range important to the apparent sales effectiveness of the advertising?

### Rebirth of the English Riviera

1. Write an outline brief for the design and content of the English Riviera brochure.
2. Write a memorandum setting out any possible implications of the Torbay Tourist Board's marketing and advertising strategy for the policy and resource allocation of the Torbay Borough Council.
3. Think of six other areas or resorts in the UK (e.g. the Lakes, the Cotswolds, the Highlands, Snowdonia, Cornwall, the Broads, Morecambe Bay, Brighton, Black-pool), and devise for each of them a single image and accompanying phrase or slogan which might sum up its distinctive appeal as a holiday destination.

### TSB's School Leaver Campaign, 1984–85

1. What are likely to be the long-term effects of its 'youth market' recruitment strategy on TSB's positioning and on the profile of its personal banking business?
2. We are told that the bank is the brand and every element of each piece of marketing has to be true to the brand. Based on the evidence supplied in this case, give as complete a picture as you can of TSB as a brand.
3. From your own prior knowledge and the evidence supplied in the case itself, what would be your best guess (and why) as to the real identities of Banks A, B, C and D as they appear in Figures 4 to 6 and Tables 3 to 9? (The actual identities remain confidential and are not known even to the editor. Your reasoning is what counts.)

### The GLC's Anti 'Paving Bill' Campaign: Advancing the Science of Political Issue Advertising

1. Summarise as precisely as you can in your own words just how this campaign came to shift opinion on the issue of the abolition of the GLC.
2. This paper lays considerable emphasis on 'changing the grounds of the debate'. Another phrase for this is 'changing the agenda'. Why is this such an important concept in the political arena and what relevance does it have in the marketing of goods and services?
3. (a) Describe the part played by opinion polls in this particular case history.
   (b) Argue the case for and against banning the publication of opinion polls in the run-up to an election.

## *Promoting the Privatisation of British Telecom*

1. The description of the advertising objectives of the different phases of the BT flotation campaign corresponds with one classic model or theory of how advertising works. What circumstances make this model appropriate in the BT case? And in what other circumstances and markets might it be *in*appropriate, and why?
2. The indexation of the BT image data in Tables 1 and 2 highlights changes over time but in the process conceals other information which could have been deduced from these tables in their original form. What has been lost by indexation and what value might it have had?
3. Some basic information which you would normally expect to find in any advertising case history is not provided in this case. What is it? What could we have learnt from it? And how far does its absence detract from the argument for effectiveness?

## *Chip Pan Fire Prevention, 1976–84*

1. Explain in your own words why prevention is often harder to 'sell' than cure. Think of some commercial products and product fields in which this factor might also be important and make some suggestions as to how the problem might be overcome.
2. Describe a form or programme of research to help test the hypothesis that the decay effect following a burst of such advertising is more likely to be caused by people forgetting about prevention *per se* than by people forgetting the information about the correct containment procedure.
3. Describe the modifications to the use of data and to the argument that would have been necessary if this campaign had been run nationally rather than regionally.

## *Advertising's Part in the Regeneration of London Docklands*

1. Selling London Docklands is a very different task from selling packaged goods, or is it? Analyse the differences and similarities between the role and nature of the advertising task for London Docklands and those typical of packaged goods advertising.
2. What further data would you look for in attempting to explain more fully Corby's apparently outstanding success at this time as an enterprise zone?
3. Figure 7 shows that 'the majority of businessmen move less than 30 miles when relocating'. What further information could have had a bearing one way or the other on the inference the case draws from this statistic?

## *Golden Wonder: A Potted Success Story*

1. The case tells us that during a period of steep decline in this market two chief executives of large multiple food retailers publicly criticised this product category as being the kind of market development that was neither in the manufacturers' nor in the consumers' interest. Presumably, they were better pleased when Golden Wonder started to grow the market again. If this was so, were they right to change their minds? And how would you deflect the charge that the new Golden Wonder Pots advertising was helping to grow and sustain a monopoly in a product field that would cease to exist without advertising?

2. How critical to Golden Wonder Pots' success was the demise of the competition?
3. If you were a potential competitor thinking of entering or re-entering this market, what inferences would you draw from this case about the requirements for a successful challenge to Golden Wonder Pots? And on what conditions would you advise for or against?

### Benylin: Effective Use of Advertising to Increase Sales and Market Share

1. Comparing Benylin's position in 1986 with that in 1984, what seems to have been the effect of the introduction of the Limited List on Benylin's total sales?
2. What information missing from this case could have shed further light on Benylin's success in the over-the-counter cough medicine market?
3. What would you assess to be the long-term threats to and opportunities for Benylin? And what long-term strategy would you pursue in the light of them?

### The New Ford Granada—The Need to Succeed

1. From the evidence given in this case construct a simplified diagram to represent the factors leading from initial awareness to a decision to purchase a new Ford Granada.
2. The case tells us that a change of name to something other than Granada had already been approved for use across Europe. Describe in your own words the reasons for retaining the Granada name in the UK launch.
3. Figures 5 to 8 show trends on key image dimensions for Granada versus the main domestic competition, Carlton and Rover. Supposing that comparable information had been available for the main imported competitor, Volvo, what might it have shown and what would have been the arguments for and against showing it?

### Castlemaine XXXX Lager—The Role of Advertising in Building a Profitable New Brand

1. What in your opinion is the single most important piece of evidence for advertising effectiveness in this case and why is it so crucial in the context of the rest of the evidence?
2. Explain in your own words how advertising seems to work in the standard lager market.
3. From advertising and any other evidence you can think of, compare and contrast the characteristics of the male market for standard lagers with that of the male market for standard whiskies.

### Kensington Palace

1. Table 1 in this case shows substantial year-on-year increases in admissions to Kensington Palace and Table 5 confirms this on a comparative basis. Why is any further information required to demonstrate the effectiveness of the advertising?
2. What does Table 3 add to our conviction of the success of the advertising for Kensington Palace? And what further questions does it raise?
3. Suggest some ideas—uncosted but not obviously unaffordable—for the promotion of the DoE's Osborne House.

### Cymalon—A Successful Relaunch

1. Leaving aside the merits of this particular television advertising execution, explain as specifically as you can how the choice of television as a medium increased the 'credibility' of Cymalon advertising.
2. (a) Why was it important to this marketing and advertising strategy for cystitis sufferers to know that their complaint was more common than they thought?
   (b) What questions would this imply about the advertising and media strategy of the initial launch in women's press?
3. Apart from the direct effect of television on cystitis sufferers, what other factors might have helped Cymalon sales as a result of choosing television advertising? What data would help to confirm or deny that these factors were operative?

### Paul Masson California Carafes: 'They're really jolly good!'

1. Explain in detail precisely how achieving the advertising objectives defined in 1982 would help in the achievement of the market objectives as defined at the same time.
2. The case tells us that the carafe packaging of the Paul Masson range aroused 'some perceived price and disposability problems amongst consumers' in research prior to the launch. What else do you think this carafe packaging may have contributed to the market response to the Paul Masson range? And how important might it be?
3. The case tells us why a presenter route was adopted and retained for the Paul Masson range advertising. What problem can you think of that might arise from this decision later on?

### How Advertising Helped Mazda (UK) to Sell a More Profitable Model Mix

1. Because of the fixed quota on Mazda (UK) sales, this case is concerned with trading up the existing level of sales to improve profitability. What changes, if any, in marketing and advertising strategy would have been necessary or desirable if it had been open to Mazda (UK) to increase its absolute level of sales?
2. In the Appendix we are told that the dealer network has changed 'slightly' over the evaluation period and that the advertising has made it easier to attract new enthusiastic dealers. What differences could this have made to some of the evidence presented in this case?
3. Getting Mazda onto the 'candidate shopping list' is a key objective for the advertising. Apart from automotive and durables, in what other product fields may this be a key objective for advertising? And in what circumstances might it be relevant to product fields with a higher frequency of purchase and much lower unit prices?

### Alphabites: How Advertising Helped Birds Eye Develop the Added-Value Potato Products Market

1. We are told that 'The effectiveness of advertising in this case ultimately rests on the fact that the advertising expenditure has been quickly recouped by the sales generated.' Supposing this had not been so, what criteria would you set for the 'affordability' of the advertising? And in what continuing situation might one justify advertising that did not cover its costs by the *extra* sales that it produced?

2.  What does this case mean generally by *added-value* potato products and what precisely made Alphabites worth its premium to its target market?

3.  In this case the most detailed sales results are given in terms of tonnes ex-factory 'as the most consistent and robust source'. Ex-factory sales data have their limitations. What are they? And how much do you think they matter in this case? What data missing from this case could have been helpful additional evidence of the effectiveness of the advertising?

# 1

# Breaking the Bran Barrier— Kellogg's Bran Flakes 1982-84

## MARKET BACKGROUND

Bran cereals have a long history. All-Bran has been on the market since 1922. Kellogg's added 30% Bran Flakes to their range in 1939, Sultana Bran and Bran Buds in the early 1960s. But for many years demand for bran cereals remained limited, partly because bran is not very palatable (which is one reason why it has generally been removed from processed foods) and partly because of the medicinal and laxative associations created by over 40 years of advertising All-Bran as 'Nature's laxative', associations which people have understandably attached to other brans as well.

Slowly, as public nutritional knowledge improved and a small but increasing number of people began to appreciate the contribution of fibre (or 'roughage') to health, sales of bran cereals increased to the point where it was supply, not demand, that was constraining growth. Recognising the future potential in the developing trend towards healthier eating, Kellogg's made a major capital investment in the bran sector of the cereal market by opening a new plant at Wrexham in 1978, substantially boosting production capacity.

The brakes removed, sector growth accelerated. Bran cereals' volume share of the growing ready-to-eat (RTE) cereal market, which had for long been fairly stable, rose from $8\frac{1}{2}$ per cent in 1977 to 11 per cent in 1981, a volume increase of 35 per cent in four years. Other manufacturers had by now seen the opportunity, and begun to join the bran wagon with manufactured brands or by making stores' own-label brands.

Even so, bran cereals remained minority-appeal products. Consumer attitudes were still largely negative. Many people were not prepared even to try them. Even amongst those housewives who acknowledged the benefits of fibre and recognised bran cereal as a rich source, there was reluctance to serve them to the family.

### The 'Bran Barrier'

The laxative connotations of All-Bran were automatically transferred to other cereals in the sector through the associations inherent in the word 'bran'. However, the use of laxatives was on the wane, and the sales potential of food products bought for occasional medicinal use was not going to keep the Wrexham plant busy. To raise demand we had first to break through the 'bran barrier' of prejudice, by changing the word's associations away from the medicinal aura it had towards that of a healthy, normal food ingredient.

1

Among the many elements of the range of marketing strategies that ensued were: continuing experimentation with TV (print, traditionally, had been the medium for bran cereal advertising) to learn how best to overcome anti bran prejudice and normalise the products; a strong push behind Sultana Bran, concentrating the emphasis of communication on its fruit content; and a major repositioning of Kellogg's Bran Flakes.

## MARKETING STRATEGY FOR BRAN FLAKES

Originally called 30% Bran Flakes, this brand had been positioned as a health product, with advertising centred on its high iron content. But we were convinced that it had much greater potential as a general appeal cereal, both because of the consumer interest we had detected in a wheat flake cereal and because we had a particularly good-tasting product. A research study in which people took home samples of the standard product, but in blank packs, confirmed that consumers, too, thought it delicious. And that a number of them, when subsequently told that what they had been enjoying so much was 30% Bran Flakes, simply refused to believe that it could have been the identical product. Such was the strength of the 'bran barrier'.

Further attitude research confirmed the brand's image as a traditional bran cereal, bought primarily for its medicinal and health qualities, and weak on taste expectation. People just assumed that because it was a bran cereal, it would not taste very good.

Kellogg's and J. Walter Thompson saw an opportunity to use the unrecognised but excellent taste of the product to break through the 'bran barrier'. In 1981, the decision was taken radically to alter the marketing strategy by:

— Dropping '30%' from the name, and redesigning the pack.
— Shifting out of magazines into TV, which had produced encouraging results in previous experiment.
— Adopting an all-family brand positioning as a pleasant-tasting, natural and healthy cereal.
— Concentrating on the *tastiness* of the product, leaving it to the word 'bran' in the product name to supply the health reassurance behind the tasty claim.

The new TV advertising was given two roles:

1. To create an image for the brand which was sufficiently strong to overcome the negative associations of 'bran' in the product name.
2. To make people see the brand in a new way which would make them want to try it.

Its target was all housewives predisposed towards natural, healthy foods, with primary emphasis on the 30–50 age group. Its aim was, firstly, to recruit new consumers and, secondly, to encourage more regular purchase.

The outcome of this brief was 'Tasty', a commercial with a bright and memorable tune and stream-of-consciousness lyrics with the refrain 'They're tasty, tasty, very very tasty', all in a distinctive, colourful and modern style. A scene from this commercial is shown on page 3.

It first went on air, nationally, in April 1982. It had run for one burst when something happened that profoundly altered public opinion about bran.

### The F-Plan phenomenon

Audrey Eyton's *F-Plan*[1] was serialised in the *Daily Express* on 18th–21st May 1982, creating an instant craze. When, shortly afterwards, it was published in paperback, it went straight up the best-seller lists. To date *F-Plan* has sold over 2 000 000 copies. One home in ten has a copy.

For the first time, a mass audience learned about dietary fibre and the importance of its function in the digestive processes. They learned that by maintaining the body's normal intestinal behaviour, high-fibre foods help to protect against some of the more prevalent Western diseases, as well as contributing to general health. They learned that a fibre-rich diet can reduce your weight. And they learned that one of the most accessible sources of fibre is bran cereals.

This produced a dramatic change in public knowledge and opinion. A check in February 1982, before the F-Plan had been heard of, showed that fibre's benefits were then primarily seen as laxative-related. After the F-Plan the emphasis had shifted: awareness and understanding of fibre's contribution to general health and well-being had advanced substantially (Table 1). The proportion of housewives claiming consciously to include fibre foods in the household meals had gone up and so had their recourse to bran cereals as a prime source of fibre (Table 2).

TABLE 1:    FIBRE KNOWLEDGE

| % housewives saying the benefits of fibre are: | Feb 1982 | Jan 1983 |
|---|---|---|
| keeps you regular | 26 | 23 |
| as a laxative | 18 | 19 |
| helps prevent constipation | 13 | 13 |
| | 57 | 56 |
| | | |
| helps keep digestive system healthy/working properly | 22 | 30 |
| provides roughage | 18 | 25 |
| generally good for health/fitness | 12 | 16 |
| helps prevent illness/disease | 1 | 2 |
| | 53 | 74 |
| | | |
| sample base | (546) | (569) |

Source: BMRB Access Omnibus Surveys

TABLE 2:    FIBRE USAGE

| | Feb 1982 | Jan 1983 |
|---|---|---|
| % housewives consciously including bran/fibre foods in diet | 42 | 47 |
| of whom, % buying with fibre in mind: | | |
| All-Bran | 25 | 34 |
| Bran Flakes | 13 | 19 |
| Farmhouse Bran | 3 | 4 |

Source: BMRB Access Omnibus Surveys

Kellogg's marketing response to the opportunity created by this new interest in fibre was swift. The TV campaign for All-Bran, in area test at the time, went national from July 1982. Sultana Bran's advertising funds were increased. And Bran Flakes' national advertising campaign, which had just begun, was extended. Table 3 shows the increase in TV advertising after May 1982. In this table, as in the ones that follow, we show data for years ending May, rather than the usual calendar year. We have divided it this way

TABLE 3:    TV ADVERTISING

| network housewife ratings (TVRs) year ending: | May 1981 | May 1982 | May 1983 | May 1984 |
|---|---|---|---|---|
| Kellogg's Bran Flakes | 400 | 600 | 1800 | 1400 |
| All-Bran | 100 | 300 | 1500 | 1500 |
| Farmhouse Bran | 300 | 1600 | – | 200 |
| Sultana Bran | 1100 | 900 | 1500 | 1400 |

the better to see what happened in the two years after first publication of *F-Plan* (May 1982) compared to the two years before.

## SALES RESULTS

The effect on consumer purchasing was dramatic. In the year immediately before *F-Plan* was published, sales of bran cereals in total rose by 4 per cent. In the year after, they soared by 37 per cent. Kellogg's Bran Flakes' sales rose by 41 per cent, even though they started from a base of marginal decline the year before. More significantly, they have continued to rise by a further 23 per cent in the following year to May 1984, even though growth has slowed in the rest of the sector (Table 4).

TABLE 4:   CONSUMER SALES GROWTH

| annual % volume change year ending: | May 1982 | May 1983 | May 1984 |
|---|---|---|---|
| Kellogg's Bran Flakes | −2 | +41 | +23 |
| other bran cereals | +6 | +35 | + 9 |
| total sector | +4 | +37 | +12 |

Source: AGB Television Consumer Audit

The bran boom lasted for about a year. From the middle of 1983 the craze for fibre in the diet began to wane, and sales began to slow towards a rate of growth similar to the pre-boom rate. But not so Kellogg's Bran Flakes, which has continued to make above-average gains, and shows no signs of reverting to previous rates.

TABLE 5:   FIBRE KNOWLEDGE

| % housewives saying the benefits of fibre are: | Feb 1982 | Jan 1983 | Jan 1984 |
|---|---|---|---|
| keeps you regular | 26 | 23 | 31 |
| as a laxative | 18 | 19 | 17 |
| helps prevent constipation | 13 | 13 | 11 |
| | 57 | 56 | 59 |
| helps keep digestive system healthy/ working properly | 22 | 30 | 23 |
| provides roughage | 18 | 25 | 16 |
| generally good for health/fitness | 12 | 16 | 12 |
| helps prevent illness/disease | 1 | 2 | 2 |
| | 53 | 74 | 53 |

Source: BMRB Access Omnibus Surveys

Thus far it could be argued that the bran boom stemmed largely or entirely from the stimulus of the F-Plan phenomenon, and that advertising played little or no part. Nobody denies the crucial importance of the F-Plan in altering the climate of public opinion towards bran. But as memory of it has faded, so has the salience of the general health-related benefits of fibre; and the laxative benefits are once again to the fore. Table 5 updates Table 1 with more recent figures. This helps explain why sector growth has slowed down. But in that case why has Kellogg's Bran Flakes gone on making headway? The F-Plan boom undoubtedly contributed to its 1982–83 growth; but its 1983–84 growth has some other mainspring.

### Increasing Number of Purchasers

In the two years before May 1982, the average number of homes buying the leading bran cereals was virtually static. (The exception was Farmhouse Bran from Weetabix Ltd, which went national during 1981.) In the following year, the year of the bran boom, they all increased penetration. But only Kellogg's Bran Flakes has continued significantly to gain more users since then, as Table 6 shows.

TABLE 6:    HOUSEHOLD PENETRATION

| % homes buying in average 4 weeks year ending: | May 1981 | May 1982 | May 1983 | May 1984 |
|---|---|---|---|---|
| Kellogg's Bran Flakes | 2.7 | 2.6 | 3.8 | 4.5 |
| All-Bran | 5.5 | 5.3 | 6.3 | 6.3 |
| Farmhouse Bran | .5 | 1.4 | 1.8 | 1.9 |
| Sultana Bran | .9 | .8 | 1.1 | 1.2 |

Source: AGB/TCA

The strong implication of this evidence is that Kellogg's Bran Flakes has, since its new advertising began two years ago, been more successful than other advertised bran cereals in persuading non-users to become users, and occasional buyers to become regular buyers: the essence of our 'breaking the bran barrier' strategy. In the year to May 1983, Kellogg's Bran Flakes' average monthly penetration increased by half, more than any of the others; while the cumulative proportion of homes buying at all in a 12-week period rose from 4.2 per cent to 7.9 per cent between the spring and autumn of 1982. During 1983–84, the number of buying homes increased still further.

But (it may be argued) this still does not prove the effectiveness of the advertising. The bran boom could have induced initial trial and the product's deliciousness could have converted the trialist into a regular consumer, all with little or no contribution from the commercial.

True, the bran boom did encourage trial, and the product itself did help build repeat purchase. So, is there any evidence to demonstrate that the television advertising did affect sales and, if so, how?

## DID THE ADVERTISING AFFECT SALES?

Firstly, sales of Kellogg's Bran Flakes have continued growing, mainly because of an increasing number of buyers each month, when the rest of the sector's growth has slowed down. Something is at work recruiting additional usage that goes beyond the bran boom.

Secondly, it can be seen from Figure 1 that penetration began to rise with the first burst of the new campaign, *even before F-Plan was first published.* Subsequent bursts, moreover, can be seen to have been lifting the numbers of purchasers.

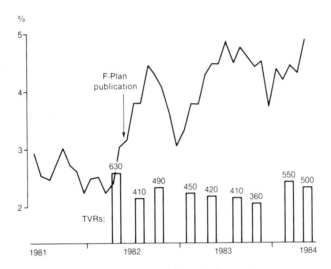

Figure 1. *Percentage of homes buying Kellogg's Bran Flakes. Four weekly*
Source: TCA

Thirdly, we have the findings of extensive econometric analysis. JWT built a model of brand sales, using multiple regression. This technique seeks to explain movements in the dependent variable (in this case Kellogg's Bran Flakes market share) by relating them to coincident movements in a number of other, explanatory factors. It estimates *which* of these other factors have been related to movements in sales, and the size and strength of each of those relationships.

The explanatory variables in the Kellogg's Bran Flakes model are:

— *Relative price:* since the dependent variable we are trying to explain is a relative one (volume *share* of market), we chose similarly to express the brand's price as relative to the RTE cereal market average (pence per kilo, indexed to market average).

— *Advertising:* of which there had been considerable variation, in campaign as well as in quantity: a TV campaign in 1980, a magazine campaign in 1981, the new 'Tasty' TV advertisement in 1982 followed by a further development of that campaign in 1983–84.

— *Close competitors:* the share movements of certain directly competitive brands: other bran flakes, and Special K.

—  *The bran boom:* this had to be allowed for in any model. But there were no figures to quantify the intensity of consumer interest in a high-fibre diet. To approximate to it, we used the combined share growth of other bran cereals as the closest we could get to a description of consumer demand for fibre in general.

Two other explanatory variables were also examined, but in the end discarded, because they did not add significantly to the model. One was brand distribution which, vital though it is, nevertheless varied too little to have any effect detectable through multiple regression techniques. The model is therefore valid only whilst distribution remains steady. The second discarded variable was seasonality: the brand follows the market average, so its market share is seasonally stable. The data used were from the AGB Television Consumer Audit, for the period January 1980 to April 1984.

The result of this analysis was a model that fits the observed data well, with an $R^2$ of 0.91. That is, 91 per cent of observed variation in market share is accounted for by the model. The estimated share line follows the movements in the actual graph closely, as shown in Figure 2. The unexplained residuals, plotted in Figure 3, lie within the 95 per

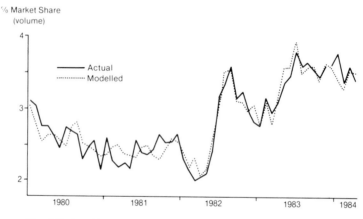

Figure 2. *Market model*

cent confidence limits, are well scattered and show no signs of systematic deviation that would suggest the presence of some other factor beyond those included in the model. The variables that are in the model have good levels of statistical reliability attached to them. The market model is summarised in Table 7.

We can draw the following conclusions:

1.  *The Bran Boom:* as expected, there is a positive correlation between sales of Kellogg's Bran Flakes and other bran cereal products. Had this been fully proportional to market shares the coefficient would have been 0.4 (an increase of 0.4 in Kellogg's Bran Flakes share for every 1 point gained by other brans). The fact that the derived value is 0.2 supports the view that the bran boom explains part of the brand's growth, but is not the only factor.
2.  *Close Competitors:* the negative correlation with other bran flakes denotes a competitive relationship between these very similar products. (It would have been astonish-

% Market Share

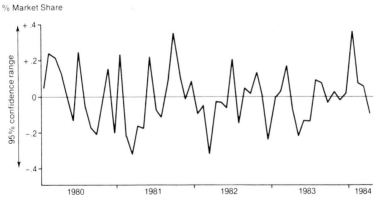

Figure 3. *Residuals*

ing had it been otherwise.) Less predictable was the observation of a competitive relationship with Special K (confirmed by brand switching analyses). On reflection though, Special K's role as a crisp, pleasant-tasting flake for adults who watch their weight can be seen as overlapping that of Bran Flakes.

3. *Price Elasticity:* this is low. Demand for Kellogg's Bran Flakes is fairly insensitive to variations in its relative price. (It is a larger factor in the competition with other bran flakes though.)

4. *Advertising Elasticities:* the effectiveness of the 1980 TV campaign, and of the magazine advertising that ran from the summer of 1981 into the first quarter of 1982, were below average for this market. By contrast, the effectiveness of the new strategy TV campaign, in 1982 and since, is well above average. These are the highest

TABLE 7:    MARKET MODEL

Multiple regression analysis of AGB/TCA data Jan 1980–Apr 1984.
Dependent variable: Kellogg's Bran Flakes volume market share.

*explanatory variables:*
the bran boom
(market share of bran cereals
other than bran flakes)                              + .2 per point

competitor brands
other bran flakes market share               − .5 per point
Special K market share                           − .6 per point

price elasticity                                         − .6

advertising elasticities:
TV 1980                                                 + .1
magazines 1981                                       + .1
TV 1982 ('Tasty')                                    + .3
TV 1983–84 ('Waiters')                            + .4

$R^2 = 0.91$

elasticities we have recorded for any brand in numerous econometric studies of the cereals market.

By weakening the prejudices against bran, the F-Plan naturally made it possible for bran cereal advertising to be more effective. To that extent, the advertising was given a helping hand. But this was equally true for other brans' advertising, with less dramatic effects. It is to the credit of the Kellogg's Bran Flakes campaign that it capitalised more effectively on this change in consumer opinion, and that it has continued to match the public mood.

When we produced 'Tasty' the F-Plan had not been heard of. The commercial worked, and worked well. But consumer knowledge and attitudes were changing, and we had to keep up with the consumer. The evidence from the model is that we succeeded: 'Waiters' - the film that ran in 1983–84 – has been even more effective than 'Tasty'. 'Waiters' won a diploma at the 1983 British Television Advertising Awards.

The model argues strongly that the TV advertising worked. But we do not rely solely on the model. There is other evidence to back it up.

### How did the Advertising Work?

In 1982 the roles of the advertising were to overcome the negative associations of bran and to encourage trial. Helped by the changing climate of opinion, both these aims were quickly and largely achieved. Average monthly penetration rose by half as much again to nearly 4 per cent. Cumulative 12-week penetration doubled to almost 8 per cent. Brand attitudes shifted dramatically (Table 8). Not only did roughage and bran become much more important purchase motivators, but *liking* the product for its tastiness figured significantly more often in respondents' reasons for buying it – exactly on strategy.

In 1983 that strategy was modified for the new 'Waiters' film (see page 11). Qualitative research among consumers had confirmed a move towards greater personal respect and care. People were increasingly trying to improve the quality of their lives by taking more care of themselves. The fashion of jogging epitomised what, at a deeper level, was a more active approach to life, linked to a more relaxed appreciation of it.

The new 'Waiters' film accordingly kept the messages about general enjoyment and product tastiness, but sought to add an even greater air of freshness and activity, allied to a very contemporary expression of discerning choice. The brand's appeal was broadened as a 'healthy' cereal, in a natural and non-cranky way, and particularly enjoyable in its own right. The aim now was to combine a strengthening of the consumption habit among its existing consumers with some further recruitment of new eaters.

Research to monitor attitudes (see Table 8) showed a fall during 1983 in digestion-related reasons for purchase, a maintenance of health and taste-related reasons, and a further rise in secondary reasons: the presence of vitamins (a good measure of consumer perceptions of nutritional value), and the product flavour (which many find needs little or no sugar).

A recent image study found that Kellogg's Bran Flakes is seen – just as much by housewives who have never tried it as by existing users – as a product for modern active people of all ages who like to eat healthy foods, and who are not much in favour of traditional cereals. Only on the all-family appeal of the brand does the 'never-trieds' view

TABLE 8:  REASONS FOR BUYING KELLOGG'S BRAN FLAKES

| % recent buyers who buy because: | Dec 1981 | | Jan + Apr 1983 | | Jul + Oct 1983 |
|---|---|---|---|---|---|
| general health benefits | | | | | |
| plenty of roughage | 38 | ↔ | 50 | | 52 |
| helps keep you healthy | 37 | | 41 | | 37 |
| made from natural ingredients | 16 | | 14 | | 14 |
| rich in vitamins | 8 | | 11 | ↔ | 18 |
| digestive benefits | | | | | |
| contains bran | 38 | ↔ | 44 | ↔ | 31 |
| ensures healthy digestion | n/a | | 29 | ↔ | 20 |
| easy to digest | 10 | | 12 | | 10 |
| other benefits | | | | | |
| I like it | 23 | ↔ | 34 | | 32 |
| tastes nice | 15 | ↔ | 20 | | 20 |
| needs little or no sugar | 9 | ↔ | 14 | ↔ | 21 |
| Purchasing behaviour | | | | | |
| I buy it regularly | 14 | ↔ | 20 | ↔ | 24 |
| Sample base | (120) | | (118) | | (130) |

↔ major changes

Source: Marcos Studies

lag behind. They still see it as mainly a woman's product. This apart, the user image (Table 9) has moved a long way away from that of the elderly, costive bran-eater it used to be.

TABLE 9:    USER IMAGERY

| % housewives saying Kellogg's Bran Flakes would be eaten by: | brand buyers | never tried |
|---|---|---|
| people who like to eat healthy foods | 81 | 87 |
| modern, active people | 66 | 67 |
| people who like traditional cereals | 32 | 31 |
| young adults | 64 | 50 |
| middle-aged | 62 | 50 |
| older people | 54 | 49 |
| women | 68 | 51 |
| men | 44 | 26 |
| children | 43 | 17 |
| all the family | 45 | 26 |

Source: RBL, May 1984

Brand attitudes also show general agreement by 'never-trieds', as much as by users, that Kellogg's Bran Flakes is a particularly healthy, fibre-rich and up-to-date cereal. On the other hand, the 'never-trieds' who are ready to concede that it tastes nice, without ever having tasted it, are a minority still. Yet this itself represents a remarkable advance. Only four years ago, research found a massive expectation among those who had never tried the product that it could not possibly taste nice. Today, some 40 per cent at least are of the opposite opinion (Table 10). It was the advertising that changed their view.

TABLE 10:    BRAND ATTITUDES

| % housewives saying Kellogg's Bran Flakes is: | brand buyers | never tried |
|---|---|---|
| rich in fibre | 96 | 88 |
| a particular healthy cereal | 93 | 86 |
| a modern and up-to-date cereal | 81 | 76 |
| popular | 71 | 55 |
| tastes nice | 84 | 40 |
| appetising | 75 | 38 |

Source: RBL, May 1984

We have seen how the two commercials, 'Tasty' and 'Waiters', have helped to enhance and modify knowledge and opinion about the brand, its taste and its image. There remains one last piece of the jigsaw to fit into place: consumers' perception of the part that the advertising played.

*Advertising's Influence*

As part of the research programme to monitor progress of the brand, we asked buyers of bran cereals to tell us what had encouraged them and their families to start eating bran cereals, or to eat more of them. In January 1983, and again a year later, one respondent in five said she had been influenced by advertisements (Table 11). This, in our experience, is an unwontedly large acknowledgement of the influence of advertising, which ranks remarkably high on this list of stimuli. No less importantly, it is the younger age groups whom the advertising has impressed. Bran cereals had an older consumption profile. The aim of normalising the product required that we introduce it to younger consumers.

TABLE 11:    INFLUENCES ON BRAN CONSUMPTION

| % buyers of bran cereals who were influenced by: | Jan 1983 | Jan 1984 | 15–34 | 35–54 | 55+ | ABC1 | C2DE |
|---|---|---|---|---|---|---|---|
| advertising for bran cereals | 19 | 19 | 29 | 20 | 9 | 16 | 21 |
| newspaper articles | 16 | 22 | 21 | 29 | 16 | 25 | 20 |
| F-Plan book | 12 | 13 | 13 | 20 | 6 | 17 | 9 |
| doctor's advice | 11 | 9 | 9 | 7 | 9 | 8 | 9 |
| articles about F-Plan | 6 | 9 | 11 | 10 | 3 | 11 | 6 |
| radio commentaries | 5 | 10 | 6 | 17 | 8 | 11 | 10 |
| other influences | 26 | 17 | 14 | 16 | 20 | 17 | 17 |
| sample base | (463) | (443) | | | | | |

Source: BMRB Access Omnibus Surveys

Kellogg's Bran Flakes is the second largest brand in the bran sector. Yet it has been the top brand amongst those who acknowledge having been influenced by advertising. Table 12 shows that this supremacy of advertising effect increased during 1983, corroborating the evidence from sales and household penetration data that Kellogg's Bran Flakes pulled away from the rest of the field. Furthermore, there is an indication (though admittedly on small sample sizes) that the evident sales success of this campaign arose not only because it encouraged people to suspend their disbelief about the taste and *try* it, but also because perseverance with the campaign has encouraged trialists and occasional users to become *regular* consumers and purchasers, more effectively than any of its competitors. This is illustrated by Table 13.

TABLE 12:    ADVERTISING INFLUENCE BY BRAND

| % influenced by advertising, who bought: | Jan 1983 | Jan 1984 |
|---|---|---|
| Bran Flakes | 48 | 62 |
| All-Bran | 44 | 41 |
| Farmhouse Bran | 13 | 21 |
| Sultana Bran | 21 | 25 |
| sample base | (93) | (83) |

Source: BMRB Access Omnibus Surveys

TABLE 13:    ADVERTISING INFLUENCE ON CONSUMPTION

| % influenced by advertising who now buy: | Kellogg's Bran Flakes | other advertised brans |
|---|---|---|
| regularly | 63 | 41 |
| occasionally | 37 | 49 |
| don't know | — | 10 |
|  | 100 | 100 |
| sample base | (51) | (83) |

Source: BMRB Access Omnibus Survey, Jan 1984

## CONCLUSIONS

To sum up the evidence:

1.  Since the change in strategy in 1982 and the brand's repositioning as a tasty, natural and healthy cereal for the family, sales have grown faster than the bran-cereal sector average. Sales have continued rising rapidly even though the bran boom and the growth of other brands have slackened.

2.  This has been achieved by an above-average and continued increase in the number of households buying Kellogg's Bran Flakes per month. More homes bought it to try and more homes have become regular and frequent purchasers.

3.  Econometric analysis has uncovered a strong relationship between the 1982–84 TV campaign, and consumer purchases. This was helped by the change in the climate of opinion brought about by the F-Plan diet, but the campaign's effect was not solely due to that: the advertising had begun to work before the F-Plan had been heard of.

4.  The advertising elasticities (0.3 and 0.4) derived from the econometric model are the highest we have recorded in the cereal market. Even after allowing for the bonus effect of the F-Plan, the advertising effectiveness has been remarkable.

5.  Adapting the campaign to keep up with changing consumer needs and attitudes has added even more to its effectiveness. Kellogg's Bran Flakes pulled further ahead of the field in 1983.

6.  The advertising worked by telling people, very credibly and persuasively, that the product really is very tasty – contrary to what most of them previously thought. It has worked, too, by transforming the brand image, which once was that of a traditional, semi-medicinal, older person's product, into that of a healthy food for modern, active people of all ages.

7.  Consumers acknowledge that Kellogg's Bran Flakes advertising, more than that of any other bran cereal, has influenced them and their families to start eating it, or to eat more of it.

The new brand positioning strategy we adopted in 1982, and its execution in advertising, have amply justified our faith in the brand's potential. We may not yet have totally demolished the bran barrier (there still remain some people who have never tried Kellogg's Bran Flakes because they expect it not to taste good), but we have certainly breached it, with the help of some particularly effective advertising. That extra creative effectiveness has a cash value: not one that is calculable with absolute precision, but we can make a reasoned estimate.

Supposing the Kellogg's Bran Flakes campaign had been just as effective – no more and no less – than the advertising for other bran cereals (which are themselves judged to have been successful campaigns)? Then we might reasonably have expected a sales increase in line with other types of bran cereal which, in the latest 12 months, are 35 per cent up on two years ago. In fact, though, Kellogg's Bran Flakes have gone up 73 per cent over the same period. This difference between expected and actual is worth an *additional* £3 million in sales revenue in the latest year alone.

The advertising spend at just average rates of effectiveness would have delivered a satisfactory rate of return. The above-average effectiveness that has brought in an *extra* £3 *million* in sales on top of that is a substantial extra contributor to profit in anybody's book. 'Very very tasty' was the message; very very potent was its effect; and very very profitable the result.

## REFERENCES

1.  Eyton, A., *F-Plan*, London: Penguin, 1982.

# 2

# Hofmeister: a Study of Advertising and Brand Imagery in the Lager Market

## INTRODUCTION

In 1983 brewers spent £44 million advertising lager brands. The market has experienced steady growth for some years, and brands are both big – up to £300 million at retail value – and profitable in relation to ales. Yet the bulk of lager volume goes through the brewers' tied pub trade. People tend to choose pubs as places to drink, rather than for the brands they serve, and even when in the pub will usually ask for 'a pint of lager' rather than a brand by name.

On face value, then, this enormous investment might well appear to be superfluous – why advertise to a captive market? What is the real role and value of all this advertising?

This case history attempts to answer both questions. It looks at Hofmeister, Courage's mainstream lager brand, which came late to the market, suffered a shaky start and subsequently struggled to catch up with the bigger lager brands it was launched to rival.

In simple terms, we will try to demonstrate that a major new advertising campaign for Hofmeister generated profit over and above its costs. In a wider context, we hope to say something more fundamental about the importance of brand imagery, even to a captive market, and the role advertising plays in creating it. We therefore confine ourselves to the tied-pub trade and exclude clubs and off-licences, where Hofmeister is also sold. The pub trade accounts for more than 70 per cent of the brand's sales.

We should make it clear at this point that we are not at liberty in this paper to disclose share or volume figures for Courage brands. These data have therefore been indexed.

## SALIENT FEATURES OF THE LAGER MARKET

For the past two decades lager has been the most dynamic sector of the British beer market, growing to capture one-third of it. Sales of draught lager alone are now worth nearly £2 billion, and even during the recent market recession lager volume has kept increasing. This trend has been to the benefit of the brewers, who derive a 20 per cent higher margin from lagers than from ales.

Lager has achieved this growth through its appeal to young drinkers: 18–34s consume two-thirds of total volume. This further enhances its importance to the brewers: not only is it their market's most dynamic and profitable product sector, it also represents the future. Drinkers tend to carry preferences established when young through the rest of their lives. It is therefore vital to a brewer to have a strong lager brand.

Not surprisingly, the brewers have responded to this opportunity by distributing and promoting a plethora of brands. To ensure the appeal of their pubs, most brewers now offer a portfolio of alternatives on the bar. New contenders frequently appear and some 30 lagers enjoy TV support. Yet, as in most markets, the first brands in have remained the leaders: 60 per cent of draught lager sales are held by the big six brewers' original mainstream brands – Carlsberg, Carling Black Label, Harp, Heineken and Skol.

In part, this persistence is explained by the major brewers' distribution muscle, but the nature of lager and its drinkers' needs also play their part. Mainstream lagers are much of a muchness in product terms, and the low temperatures at which they are served usually mask any differences that may exist between them. In blind product tests, most drinkers cannot consistently discriminate between brands. They differentiate between them on image.

Brand images are crucial in determining choice, a feature of the market highlighted in our qualitative research. And the nature of those images is bound up with the lifestyle of lager drinkers. They tend to be young, sociable and fashion-conscious. They drink in public, amongst their peer group. They prefer lager to bitter not only because its blander taste is more readily accessible, but because it is seen to be a more modern, youthful drink, with a higher price that demonstrates its higher status value.

Successful brands tend to reflect these generic market-place demands. They may have a specific product or heritage story, but they also establish an image around this story. Almost invariably, they demonstrate through the portrayal of their 'ideal' drinkers that they are contemporary, confident and sympathetic to a young man's outlook on life. Drinkers want to be sure that the brands they choose are popular and thus that they themselves are 'doing the done thing'. Big is beautiful.

Media advertising is crucial in creating and sustaining these images of success. Indeed, respondents in lager group discussions often talk of their brands primarily by reference to their advertising. In a market where products are so simple and so similar, advertising-created images provide consumers with the only means to differentiate.

## COURAGE AND HOFMEISTER

Hofmeister was a late entrant to the market. Courage already had a standard lager in Harp, whose ownership was shared amongst a consortium of brewers. Growth in the market and a desire for greater control led to the launch of Hofmeister in 1977, with a 'continental' positioning considered complementary to Harp. By 1981, the new brand had become Courage's main draught lager, replacing Harp in the majority of tied outlets.

During these years, Courage's lager sales performance did not keep up with that of its ales. Thus, on an indexed basis, Courage's 1983 ales market share was 106 compared with 100 in 1977, but its lagers share was 93 compared with 100 in 1977 (see Figure 1).

Courage lagers consistently lost ground in every year except 1981. In that year, ale

Figure 1. *Courage's retail trade share of major brewers market*
*Source:* BMS, Courage

marketing activity increased pub traffic; total pub sales increased, including lager. However, lager sales resumed their downward path thereafter. The movements shown may seem small, but it is worth reiterating their significance for two reasons: the market is huge and the figures, derived from a census of sales returns contributed by each major brewer, are very accurate.

Courage had a problem. In the important lager sector it was losing share. Lagers were 'letting the side down'. Hofmeister was a £100 million brand, available in over 85 per cent of Courage's pubs, but it was underperforming.

The key marketing objective was therefore to reverse Courage's declining lager share. It was the inadequate performance of Hofmeister, the mainstream lager brand with near-universal tied-trade distribution, which had apparently led to the decline; it was up to Hofmeister to bring about its reversal. It was important to discover why Hofmeister was underperforming and, when Boase Massimi Pollitt was appointed to the brand early in 1983, we set out to answer this important question. We needed to explore the nature and position of the brand and to discover whether advertising could play a role in its revitalisation.

## UNDERSTANDING THE BRAND'S PROBLEMS

Qualitative research was illuminating in suggesting reasons for the brand's sales problem. Hofmeister drinkers showed little enthusiasm for the brand. The only reason they gave for drinking it was that it was served in their local. To them the brand was unremarkable, low key and, because they could say little about it, faceless. They even felt that Hofmeister was unpopular amongst men who didn't drink it.

Non-drinkers were indeed critical. The brand was criticised for being 'weak' and 'having no head'. Its symbol – the bear – was mischievously abused, with the brand all too frequently being referred to as 'bear's piss'! All this, when in blind tests it was shown that the brand matched its key competitors. The justification for this criticism was perhaps that the brand had experienced early product shortcomings, but these had been rectified as early as 1981; the real problem lay elsewhere.

Quantitative research added to the understanding of the brand's problems. Hofmeister's weaknesses were apparent in a number of ways.

### Drinker Commitment

Compared with other major lager brands, Hofmeister had the lowest level of drinker commitment (see Table 1).

TABLE 1: DRINKERS' COMMITMENT TO BRANDS

commitment = drink regularly ÷ drink nowadays

|  | % |
|---|---|
| Carling Black Label | 55 |
| Carlsberg | 45 |
| Heineken | 42 |
| Skol | 42 |
| Harp | 38 |
| Hofmeister | 36 |

Source: Millward-Brown Jan–Feb 1983

### Brand Awareness

Hofmeister's prompted brand awareness was comparable with other brands. However, its spontaneous awareness was very low. The brand lacked 'front-of-mindness' (see Figure 2).

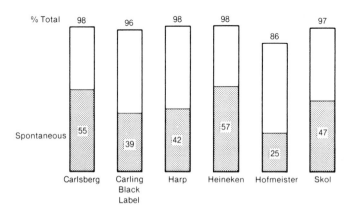

Figure 2. *Hofmeister brand awareness vs. the Big 5*
*Source:* Millward Brown Jan/Feb 1983

*Quantitative Attitude Measures*

The brand had a weak image profile compared to the other leading brands (see Figure 3).

Conventional market research interpretation would suggest that the cause of the brand's problem arose through these image weaknesses, and presumably could be put right by rectifying them. As we shall see, in the real world advertising did not work in this neat way.

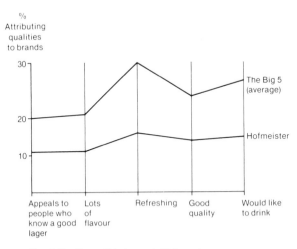

Figure 3. *Brand images: Hofmeister vs. the Big 5 competitors*
*Source:* Millward Brown Jan/Feb 1983

## THE ADVERTISING BRIEF

If Courage's lager performance was to be revitalised, then the new advertising had two essential tasks. In the short term, it had to boost the saliency and appeal of Hofmeister amongst lager drinkers exposed to the brand, primarily Courage pub-goers. In the long term, it had to raise the reputation of Hofmeister alongside that of the market leaders, amongst the wider universe of all lager drinkers.

The initial advertising objective was therefore to raise Hofmeister's profile in the market-place and to increase its franchise of frequent drinkers. Brand loyalty is weak in the standard lager market, but if the advertising could create an aura of popularity and success around Hofmeister, it could bolster the confidence of its drinkers in their choice and thus build their commitment to the brand.

The mechanism by which we believed this could be achieved was the creation of a new brand image for Hofmeister which was not only distinctive, but of genuine appeal and relevance to young drinkers.

The creative brief emerging from this initial research and thinking requested a campaign that would position Hofmeister as 'cool' and fashionable. It suggested a number of guidelines, the most important of which was to bring back 'The Bear'. Our qualitative work had consistently found this to be Hofmeister's only brand asset. Although drinkers were confused as to what the bear did, looked like, or represented, they knew Hofmeister as the 'beer with the bear' and some even claimed to ask for 'a pint of bear'. Despite its two-year absence from Hofmeister advertising, this animal symbol remained potent. What it needed was direction, a purpose and a relevance. If a new bear was to embody the brand or personalise its drinkers, it clearly had to do so in a way that those drinkers found admirable and sympathetic.

A strong character, we felt, could personify the 'cool' aspect of the brand and carry the secondary elements of intended communication, notably Hofmeister's satisfying product qualities and German heritage. It should also provide a long-term brand theme capable of translation into point-of-sale and promotional material – significant elements in drinks marketing.

## MEDIA PLANNING

### *The Reason for Choosing TV*

It was clear from our consumer research that a strong TV presence was an integral part of drinkers' confidence in a lager brand; to compete with the market leaders, we had to match them on that battle ground. More importantly, TV was also the natural choice for the job. Given the need to create a new, confident image for the brand, TV provided the most intrusive and influential way to reach our young drinkers. The budget of £1.7 million set for the draught product was a realistic reflection of the brand's share and less than any of our major competitors' anticipated spend. Rather than dilute this presence further, we therefore decided to put all the money into TV.

### *The Media Strategy*

Although Courage's pubs are distributed throughout England and Wales, 70 per cent of them are concentrated in six TV areas: London, TVS, Yorkshire, Harlech, TSW and Central. We therefore concentrated our advertising in these areas alone. Advertising for canned Hofmeister ran in these areas alongside the draught commercials.

## DEVELOPING THE CAMPAIGN

The development of the new advertising revolved around the development of a character, George the Bear. This took four stages of qualitative animatic testing, during which his personality evolved to meet young drinkers' need for a figure whom they could admire, identify with and be amused by.

The agency's original embodiment of 'cool' was a classically sophisticated, somewhat haughty bear in a dinner jacket; by the final stage, George had emerged as a stylish, 'Fonz'-type, street-smart bear, the leader of his young peer group. Trendy, extrovert, witty, fun to be with and slightly anarchic, George reflected the aspirations of young drinkers. He became at once both brand and drinker and, through this dual role, tied Hofmeister to a set of positive values that the drinkers themselves demanded of the advertising.

*Bear*: Life in a Bavarian forest was boring.
A big event was me and Ronnie Rabbit watching a leaf fall down.
*Rabbit*: (excitedly) a leaf! A leaf!
*Bear*: Hey . . .

*Bear*: Then one day I discovered Hofmeister lager with a picture of my Grandpa on it.
It had a cool cut on the back of the throat that was so good I decided to leave the forest.

And so I found . . .
companionship.

I found the left hand screw to kiss onto the pink. (SFX kiss)
But most of all I found Hofmeister on draught.

The moral is: If you want poetry stand and stare

But if you want great lager – follow the bear, hey!

*Bear*: So the cold Hofmeister is sliding down like a dream

When this girl comes up and asks me what I do.

So I tell her I'm a dispensing chemist, which really impresses her for a bear,

And I'll read her prescription any time.

Sometimes I think the medical profession is misunderstood. I prescribe Hofmeister twice nightly, hey.

Hofmeister. For great lager, follow the bear.

## RESULTS: SALES EFFECT

The year following the launch of the new campaign was a record one for lager: the hot summer of 1983 helped standard lager sales in pubs rise by 9 per cent. Over the same period, Hofmeister's pub sales increased by 25 per cent (see Figure 4). This dramatic

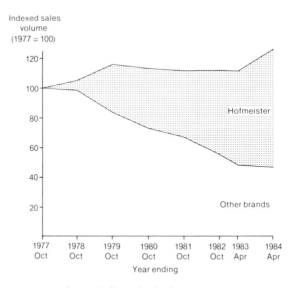

Figure 4. *Courage sales of lager to the pub trade*
*Source:* Courage

growth was not caused by a wider availability of the brand: its pub distribution only grew by 1.5 per cent. Hofmeister's rate of sale thus rose by 13 per cent more than the market. Furthermore, the brand's growth was incremental to Courage's total lager sales, rather than substitutional as it had been before. The company's share of the pub lager market therefore rose after two years of consistent decline, at a time when its ales share was static (see Figure 5). Hofmeister's brand share performance within the standard lager market in pubs was impressive, increasing by 1.24 per cent, worth no less than £10 million in this huge market.

We examined some possible causes of Hofmeister's improved performance:

1.  *Product* There was no change in product specification over the period.
2.  *Price* Hofmeister's price actually increased in relation to its competitors at this time.
3.  *Distribution* As mentioned above, Hofmeister's pub distribution grew by less than 1.5 per cent.
4.  *Promotions* There was no change in the level of below-the-line support for Hofmeister, although new promotions and promotional material were designed to complement the advertising. Indeed, enthusiasm for the advertising led to demand for branded 'George the Bear' T-shirts that surpassed all such previous offers.
5.  *Presentation* The draught fount remained unchanged.
6.  *Pubs* There was no change in pub investment policy over the period.

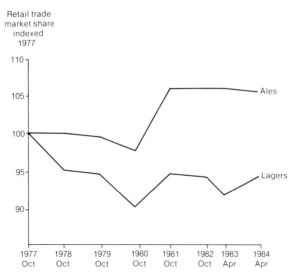

Figure 5. *Courage's retail trade share of major brewers market*
*Source*: BMS, Courage

The reasons for the uplift in sales had to lie elsewhere. The strongest indication as to the cause came from an area analysis of the sales increase, which demonstrated its association with the advertising activity. In those Courage pubs which saw no change in the lagers on offer between the summers of 1982 and 1983, *Hofmeister sales grew at almost twice the rate in the advertised areas as in the non-advertised ones* (see Table 2).

TABLE 2: HOFMEISTER PUB SALES IN UNCHANGED CONFIGURATIONS*

|  |  | 1982 | 1983 |
|---|---|---|---|
| advertised areas | Hofmeister | 100 | 139 |
|  | the market | 100 | 121 |
| non-advertised areas | Hofmeister | 100 | 120 |
|  | the market | 100 | 121 |

period: July–Aug 1983 vs. 1982
* in pubs where the range of lagers on offer did not change
Source: Courage, BMS

## RESULTS: CONSUMER BEHAVIOUR

This uplift in Hofmeister's sales was explained by marked shifts in claimed consumer behaviour relating to the brand. Over the year following the new campaign's launch, claimed trial of Hofmeister rose by 13 per cent in the advertised areas: non-advertised areas showed no rise at all (see Table 3). 'Nowadays' drinkers on the survey also increased, whilst the proportion within those who claimed to be regular Hofmeister drinkers rose as well, indicating a new commitment to the brand. The behavioural data is thus consistent with the observed increase in Hofmeister's sales *in advertised areas*. We will now attempt to explain the link between behaviour and advertising.

TABLE 3:　HOFMEISTER TRIAL AND DRINKING IN ADVERTISED AREAS

|  | Pre % | Post % |
|---|---|---|
| trial | 45 | 51 |
| drink nowadays | 17 | 21 |
| drink regularly | 6 | 9 |
| 'commitment' | 36% | 43% |

commitment = drink regularly ÷ drink nowadays
period: Jan–Feb 1984 vs. 1983
Source: Millward Brown

## RESULTS: CONSUMER ATTITUDES

That advertising had played some part in Hofmeister's improved performance appeared evident from both quantitative and qualitative research. The new campaign was unmistakably noticeable and well branded. Advertising recall shot up in response to the first burst, to levels never previously achieved by the brand (see Figure 6).

This level of awareness, moreover, was greater than for any of the 'Big Five' lager brands' campaigns, despite media expenditure lower than any of theirs. Similarly, brand awareness in advertised areas rose to higher levels than had been seen at the height of the

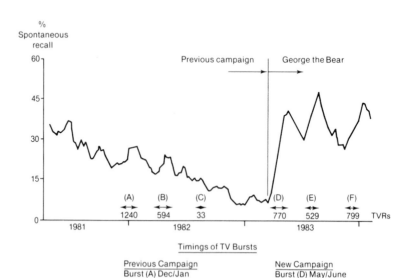

Figure 6. *Hofmeister claimed advertising recall*
*Source:* Millward Brown

1982 campaign, so that Hofmeister's consumer 'stature' came more closely in line with the other major brands (see Table 4).

TABLE 4:   HOFMEISTER BRAND AWARENESS IN ADVERTISED AREAS

|  | Pre % | Post % |
|---|---|---|
|  | spontaneous/total awareness | |
| Hofmeister | 31/90 | 38/92 |
| the 'Big Five' brands | 48/97 | 48/98 |

period: Jan–Feb 1984 vs. 1983
Source: Millward Brown

We sought to establish the link between Hofmeister's new consumer saliency and its observed sales increase, by examining the brand's consumer image. We found this link in qualitative research, but *not* in the quantitative brand imagery data.

### Qualitative Findings

Our findings were based on qualitative research conducted in February 1984. We found that the advertising had altered drinkers' perceptions of the brand. A faceless brand had been given a positive, desirable identity – that of George the Bear: confident, popular and enviable.

'He doesn't have to try'.
'He's cool'.
'He can do anything'.

Drinkers, moreover, had readily identified with George, bear or not:

'I don't really see him as a bear'.
'He's the sort of bloke I'd like to be'.

Drinkers were happy to drink Hofmeister because they perceived it to be popular and trendy, rather than because it was a superior product. Indeed, product perceptions – always low key amongst lager drinkers – had changed little; the advertising, after all, had deliberately provided little more than basic product reassurance. Non-drinkers of Hofmeister, on the other hand, were now reluctant to criticise the brand. Many of them referred to it as second best to their brand.

### Quantitative Findings

When we turned to the quantitative data, however, we were surprised to find that there had been no significant shift in Hofmeister's consumer standing.

To attempt to understand this anomaly, Boase Massimi Pollitt conducted a series of in-depth interviews among lager drinkers who had beforehand completed the lager tracking study questionnaire. We found that brand image and brand usage could not be separated in the way the questionnaire attempted to. This is because when answering a structured questionnaire the majority of lager drinkers will not express an opinion of a brand they have not tried or do not drink regularly. This observation has been made for other product fields.[1]

Regular drinkers of Hofmeister were content with the brand and rated it accordingly. However, because of Hofmeister's relatively small presence in the market, they were swamped by non-drinkers of the brand who were reluctant to rate it. Average ratings were thus low and pegged down by the brand's low absolute availability. Its non-drinkers were now happy with the brand, but still unwilling to praise it extravagantly on *product* grounds against better-known competitors, as they were perfectly well aware that the product was nothing special.

The in-depth interviews supported the earlier qualitative research in suggesting that Hofmeister's new appeal lay in drinkers' perceptions of it as a popular, fashionable lager; thus, the link between the brand's advertising-born saliency and its sales increase was confirmed.

## SUMMARY AND FINANCIAL EVALUATION

In the year following the new advertising, Hofmeister's sales increased at over twice the market rate on a very small distribution increase. This increase was confined to advertised areas; elsewhere the brand's sales simply rose in line with the market. This strong performance almost single-handedly reversed Courage's declining lager share; given no other variables, it seems hard to avoid the conclusion that the new advertising was primarily responsible for Hofmeister's change of fortune, and the achievement of the marketing objectives.

In an IPA competition there may be an expectation for the case history to demonstrate a massive profit payback from advertising investment. Unfortunately the vast majority of advertised brands are not afforded this opportunity. In Hofmeister's case, once the 'natural' market growth has been subtracted from the sales increase (setting aside the fact that the brand had previously performed consistently below the market rate), the incremental wholesale profit on the sales increase achieved was £1.9 million, against an advertising spend of £1.7 million over the same period.

It is worth remembering that the lager market, like many, is one in which heavy expenditure is always expected, simply to *maintain* share, and in which advertisers look gradually to recoup their initial advertising investment in following years. Yet this campaign generated incremental profit greater than the cost of the advertising in the first year alone. Nor have we considered here either the additional effect of the advertising on draught sales in the club trade, which also outstripped the market, or the considerably enhanced retail profit secured by Courage pubs at the same time.

We hope we have shown a 'real world' case where advertising has succeeded in making a significant contribution to sales and a solid contribution to profits.

## CONCLUSIONS

The tied-pub trade is a captive market, yet advertising can be shown to have a significant effect on sales within it. Even where consumer purchase can be guaranteed, advertising has a role to play. Rate of sale depends on consumer commitment to outlet and product, and a key to this is brand imagery; in the absence of any grounds for rational discrimination, advertising must play a crucial part in creating a strong brand image.

This case history suggests that the increased consumer confidence in a brand through a strong brand image *can* bring about a sales increase, even in a captive market, which more than justifies the financial investment involved.

## REFERENCES

1.   Bird, M., Channon, C. and Ehrenberg, A. S. C., *Journal of Marketing Research*, August 1970.

# 3

# ICI Dulux Natural Whites

## INTRODUCTION

This is about the national launch of Dulux Natural Whites, a new paint product range from ICI. The range was sold in from February 1982, and advertised from March 1982. We look at the period 1980–84.

The range fulfilled and exceeded its objectives, and now holds brand leadership of a new market sector. Indeed within the long-established white emulsions market, it has achieved a 17 per cent volume share in the first quarter of 1984, two years after launch.

The launch advertising campaign was wholly original. Consumers identify TV advertising as their prime medium for awareness of and propensity to purchase the range, and its role in the continuing success of the range is demonstrated here.

## THE UK RETAIL DECORATIVE PAINT MARKET

Between 1970 and 1980, the decorative paints market enjoyed dramatic volume growth from 90 million litres to 115 million litres. This is attributable to three key factors:

1.  Consumer expenditure increased, along with a propensity to decorate.
2.  The overall stock of houses grew considerably.
3.  There was a significant move away from wallcoverings to the use of paints, which are seen as more convenient and cheaper to use.

The retail value of the market also increased, but less so. The growth of specialist DIY chains created strong price competition and a consequent reduction in value growth.

Since 1980, whilst consumer expenditure has continued to rise the decorative paint market has remained static in volume. The number of new houses being built has slowed, as has the move from wallcoverings to paints.

### Dulux's Position and Performance in the Market-place

Throughout the 1970s Dulux held brand leadership, averaging 28 per cent market share, and volume sales grew by 35 per cent between 1970 and 1980. In 1980 the Dulux brand as a whole reached 29 per cent volume share, its highest since 1973. However, in whites the share increase in 1980 was only from 25 to 26 per cent, and within that white emulsion had only 23 per cent, a severe decline in the most dynamic market sector.

The dilemma for Dulux was that in a now static market, with its major share product, Brilliant White Emulsion, competing in a heavily price-promoted sector, and with overall pricing being dictated by multiple DIY retailers, share growth through more aggressive pricing would simply lead to a reduction in profit margins. Dulux not only wanted to re-establish dominance in the significant whites area, but also needed to restore profit levels in this specific high volume sector.

### Problems with Dulux Brilliant White Emulsion

However, for some time there had been no product improvements in Dulux Brilliant White Emulsion, so purchasing *Dulux* had become of lower priority, or more commodity orientated. Not only that: reactions to the 1981 Brilliant White TV advertising in qualitative research compared with qualitative findings during the late, as against the early, 1970s showed that whites advertising was beginning to be criticised on the grounds of lack of impact and humanity, and of coldness - positive responses were milder and weaker than in the past.

By 1981, Brilliant White was clearly no longer new, no longer, in its starkest usage, fashionable. Although used on most decorating occasions it was no longer considered to make a marked contribution to the overall effect of the decor, and had become an automatic choice largely based on habit and tradition. Would it be possible to excite consumers about white paint again and if so, how?

Finally an examination of the consumer profile for Dulux highlighted further weaknesses. Dulux's relative strength has always been amongst older, up-market men. The own-label profile countered Dulux's orientation with a bias towards women, the young and the down-market. Long-term business for the brand would have to be ensured by strengthening Dulux's appeal in those specific weak areas.

### ACTION

How, then, in the short term, could Dulux restore brand share and re-establish dominance and profit levels in the significant, high-volume whites area? In the immediate short term (1981) it was planned to achieve this by attacking the competition on price grounds. Secondly, how could Dulux find a way of reducing the price-promoted brilliant whites sector as a market in itself?

It is this second issue to which we turned our attention, for, in the absence of a new product-based story to tell - which would take Dulux out of the commodity arena - any innovation we introduced to differentiate ourselves from the competition would have to come from the creation of an image, *and be advertising-led*. A number of actions were put into effect:

1. In 1981, a major market-research exercise into why consumers used white paint and their attitudes to it.
2. A detailed technical review of potential product improvements: this indicated that whilst there were a number of technical improvements available, none was felt to be

*sufficient* to warrant the consumer paying a *premium*, or to meet the objective of reducing the overall price promoted sector of the market.

3.   A review of Dulux's other paint markets around the world. This provided a clue in the shape of a colour card including a range of *tinted* whites.

4.   Consultations with decor experts.


### The Solution

This action indicated that the concept of a range of *tinted* whites with the exciting feel of *colour* might meet our longer-term objective. Such a range would offer something new, interesting and aesthetic – it would also be unique. More importantly, reassurance that using the shades would lead to successful results would have to be the job of the advertising.


### Towards a Positioning – Whites or Colours?

We had to clarify where such a range of tinted whites should be positioned. Would the role of white paint be upgraded by the juxtaposition of white with colours? Further qualitative research was conducted to investigate this area.

Whilst in research admirers of the new range referred to the paints both as 'near whites' and as 'delicate colours', there was little doubt as to their likely role. The common assumption was that they would be a substitute for brilliant white, ie light and airy, but less stark and harsh – and still a safe option in an integrated colour scheme. Certainly, the lack of courage of the target audience must not be forgotten. We were talking to whites-users, many of whom felt that magnolia was far too dangerous and bold a shade to use. Our target group needed reassurance; what better security than to *know* that the new paints from Dulux would be *white* paints.

However, for two reasons, it was vital that the new range was not felt to be simply an alternative to brilliant white:

1.   Other research revealed indications that consumers were demanding more:

     It's nice to have something that isn't dead white.

     It'd make you want to change your other colours to match, whereas with real white, it just goes with anything.

2.   In strategic terms, we had to move away from the passivity which is involved in the choice of a brilliant white; otherwise the new whites would quickly assume the same unimportant background role.

In 1980 qualitative research identified the most motivating and differentiating proposition for Dulux as an emotional one of 'personal renewal'. The state of consumers' knowledge was that the leading brands offered the same range of paints, based roughly on the same technology. It appeared that any attempt by any manufacturer to lay claim to differentiation on rational grounds would be viewed with active suspicion.

Reinforcing the belief that Dulux paints are superior to others, especially premium brands, would therefore entail an *emotional point of differentiation* which would centre around the assurance of a beautiful end result and the feelings of renewal which accompany redecoration.

### The Creation of the Range

A creative consultant was briefed to produce a range of tinted whites that would meet the criteria set out above. Three whites were produced – Apple White, with a hint of green; Rose White, with a hint of pink; and Fleece White, with a hint of cream.

The agency developed the concept, and also worked with packaging designers to develop appropriate can liveries. When the creative approach was finalised an animatic was produced, together with a number of concept cards and large-scale panels of the paint. These were then qualitatively researched. The tinted whites concept was eliciting encouraging results.

Dulux R&D were briefed to produce three shades of paint, clearly discernible from brilliant white, and yet not pastel colours – colours which would have to be reproducible on a large scale.

Meanwhile, the production of a launch strategy ensued.

## THE LAUNCH STRATEGY

The advertising brief was to develop an approach which would set the range apart from all other paint advertising, which would be distinctive, which would communicate the subtlety of the paint, and which would be more cosmetic and thereby less functional than previous advertising. The point-of-sale (POS) brief asked that material would reflect the advertising idea.

Fleece White had developed into Pearl White and finally into Lily White. Similarly, can designs were refined so their hue indicated the colours of the shades more precisely. Pricing policy was then developed on the basis of research and it appeared that consumers would pay about 15 per cent more for tinted whites than for brilliant whites. This was a fundamental part of the plan in order to meet profit objectives. Volume forecasts were prepared on the basis that these shades would sell along the line of Dulux's previous best selling pale *colours* like Magnolia and Buttermilk.

It was decided that the range would be fully supported, with a spend of £2 800 000 on advertising and £400 000 on POS and display material. The first cans were released on 1st February 1982. Within three months, 75 per cent sterling distribution had taken in the range. The advertising began in March 1982.

## THE ADVERTISING AND MEDIA STRATEGIES

### Marketing Aim

To increase Dulux share of the whites market in the face of heavy promotion from Crown – the main premium competitor – and the continuing threat from the cheaper paints, particularly own-label.

## Advertising Objectives

To reawaken consumer interest in white paint, lifting it from a low-priority commodity area where decisions are taken on the basis of habit and price, to assume a more important role in the decorating process, requiring a more conscious and positive choice.

Within this, to increase interest in and commitment to Dulux white paint by announcing the launch of 'a new range of whites from Dulux'.

## Target Audience

*Users of white paint, whether premium or commodity.* They are likely to feel less than happy about their continued use of white paint, but are not prepared to make a move into the more exciting but far riskier area of colours. In demographic terms this represents a very broad sample - BC1C2, under 55 - but women are likely to play the major role in decision-making.

## Creative Strategy

### PROPOSITION

Now there's an exciting but safe way to transform your home.

### REASON WHY

—because Dulux has developed a new range of whites
—so you can have a white with a touch of pink - Rose White; a touch of green - Apple White; and a touch of cream - Lily White

### TONE OF VOICE

Soft and reassuring.

### CONSUMER RESPONSE

I *know* these paints are whites, so I can feel confident in using them; I *believe* they are colours, so I can take a real interest and pride in their effect in my home.

### EXECUTIONAL CONSIDERATION

The unobtrusive inclusion of the Dulux dog, an extremely effective and emotive branding device, will enable us to concentrate on the overall proposition whilst indisputably linking Natural Whites to the Dulux brand.

## The Media Strategy

To launch Natural Whites at a competitive weight and then to maintain a strong presence. A combination of TV and posters was used to gain high product awareness rapidly (see

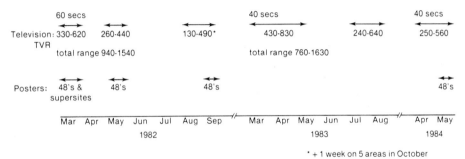

Figure 1. *Natural Whites: Launch Media Plan*

Figure 1). Three factors were essential in the scheduling of TV advertising for Natural Whites:

1.  Because the range is based on an advertising property rather than a product development and is therefore creative-led, the creative requirement for a 60-second time length was paramount, but was not allowed to influence the setting of TV rating targets. Therefore, the campaign was launched at an entirely competitive weight in the market.
2.  The majority of TV exposure would be concentrated just prior to and through the main Easter sales period.
3.  There would be a return to advertising to support the important August Bank Holiday period.

It was also considered that impact would be further increased if Natural Whites appeared in discrete bursts without overlap with other products. The target market was essentially all adults, therefore a time-buying strategy was observed which would ensure a balance particularly across social class.

The decision to support TV with another medium was based on the wish to increase and prolong presence of the campaign. Posters were chosen as the most suitable medium and a mixture of 48-sheets and supersites was used. The campaign ran in March and May to provide maximum impact during the launch period and in September to prolong the campaign period to the end of the major paint buying season. In all cases only high quality poster sites were selected to ensure maximum exposure and the best 'environment' and presentation for the brand.

## THE ADVERTISING

The focus of the work was on the three images created for Rose, Apple and Lily White. These images were used in all creative material, from the can design through to advertising and POS.

The Natural Whites launch commercial follows on page 36. The range was presented through animation – a completely new form of expression for Dulux – which, it was felt, best fitted the need to provide a strong but reassuring emotional point of differentiation for the range.

THE WHITER SHADES OF PALE

*VIDEO*
Open on a display of three new Dulux cans:
Rose White, Lily White and Apple White.

*Title:* WHITE?

Add *title:* NOT QUITE.

Dissolve to continuous animation sequence,
opening on the interior of an elegant
drawing-room.

Pan along the furnishings as far as a lace-
covered table on which a single rose has
been placed.

Freeze and *title:* ROSE WHITE. A RO-
MANTIC WHITE, WITH A DELI-
CATE SHADE OF PINK.

Continue panning through the French win-

*AUDIO*
$1\frac{1}{2}$ seconds silence.

*Sfx* Fade in piano theme: 'A whiter shade
of pale'.

*Sfx* Outdoor: Birds, grasshoppers, bees etc,
under.

*Sfx* Bring up level slightly.

dow to the flower bed, comprising wall-
flowers, delphiniums, then lilies.

Freeze and *title:* LILY WHITE. A RICH
WHITE, WITH A SOFT AND
CREAMY TINT.

Pan along the flower bed, then follow a
butterfly across the lawn – we see a sheep-
dog rise and walk towards camera – to the   *Sfx* Woof!
shade of an apple tree, where a table is set.
On the table is a plate with two apples on
it, with one of the apples cut in two.

Freeze and *title:* APPLE WHITE. WITH
A SUBTLE SHADE OF GREEN.

Dissolve back to the three Dulux cans.

*Title:* THE WHITER SHADES OF   *Mv/o* 'Rose White, Lily White, Apple
PALE and ICI Dulux logo.   White. The whiter shades of pale. Fresh
from Dulux.'

## THE EVALUATION

### Data Sources

ICI's Marketing Research Services group at Paints Division operates a field force of over
300 interviewers and has run a consumer panel of some 4 500 households since 1969. In
addition, this group carries out a Price Distribution and Display check (PDD) in some
700 retail outlets three or four times a year, as well as *ad hoc* studies. These services and
other qualitative and quantitative research data, in conjunction with the media expenditure information, provide the base data for our analyses.

### Historical Trends Prior to Launch of Natural Whites

Figure 2 demonstrates that over the period January 1980 to January 1982 the total
emulsions market remained basically static, although displaying both seasonal and random
fluctuations from month to month. Figure 3 illustrates, for the same period, the Dulux
share within the white emulsions market.

The declining Dulux share was largely caused, as has been stated, by strong price
competition. This is clearly demonstrated by Figure 4, which compares the average price
for Dulux vs. Crown brilliant white emulsions. (This chart runs into the first few months
of the Dulux Natural White launch to further illustrate the extent of the problem.)

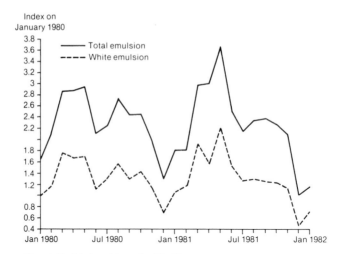

Figure 2. *Trends in the emulsion market 1980-1982*

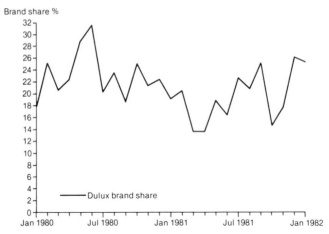

Figure 3. *Dulux share of white emulsion market 1980-1982*

## Evaluation of Results

It is important here to restate a fundamental point made earlier. Natural Whites were not in any structural way a new product. They were a new product concept. As such they would be extremely easy to copy, and indeed lookalikes appeared within nine months. Both for this major reason, and also the dependence on a small number of major national retailers, it was not possible to area-test prior to the national launch.

This fact makes it extremely difficult to isolate the individual contributions to the product's success from all the different factors involved. In particular the correlation between sales and distribution-linked variables is open to debate as to which factor is causal.

As has been explained, *the whole concept relied on the communication of the idea and the reassurance it requires by the advertising.* Therefore, we shall first look at the results in

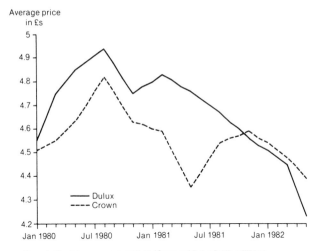

Figure 4. *Trends in average price 1980-82 (Crown and Dulux Brilliant Whites)*

broad terms and demonstrate the success of the launch. Subsequently, we look in more detail at the individual factors involved.

### Overall Launch Success

The launch was successful against all criteria.

1. The dominance of heavily price-promoted brilliant white in the emulsions market was reduced to 51 per cent in 1983 from 58 per cent in 1980–81.
2. Dulux increased its brand share in the white emulsions sector from a low of 18 per cent in 1981 to 36 per cent in 1983, whilst maintaining its share of the colours sector (29 per cent in both 1981 and 1983). The 37 per cent achieved during the first half of 1983 was the highest Dulux share in this sector for a decade.
3. Natural Whites has maintained an average premium of 17 per cent above the Crown Plus Two brilliant white price, and 13 per cent above Dulux's own brilliant white price (the two 'premium brands' in the brilliant white sector).
4. Both share and premium have been maintained despite launches of competitive lookalikes.
5. The product has attracted new and younger users to Dulux emulsions.
6. Above all, the launch was profitable. Over the period 1982–83, Dulux invested £2.9 million more on advertising than had historically been spent in the whites market. However, in 1982 Natural Whites obtained a 13 per cent brand share and in 1983 an 18 per cent share, whilst Dulux brilliant whites lost only 1 per cent. The net effect was a major gain in white emulsion sales over the two years. Compensating for this gain was a small loss of sales for colours caused by a general shift in the emulsions market. Even allowing for the advertising spend, larger profit margin on colours compared to Natural Whites, and non-advertising launch costs, *the resultant benefit in gross profit over the two years is significantly larger than the short-term investment.*

And this ignores the current strength which will maintain very substantial benefits well into the future.

## The Success in Detail

### THE REDUCTION IN DOMINANCE OF BRILLIANT WHITE

Figure 5 plots the annual share of the emulsions market accounted for by brilliant whites and Natural Whites. The former illustrates the declining importance of brilliant whites.

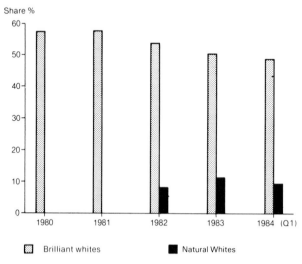

Figure 5. *Emulsion market. Brilliant white & Natural White shares*

### INCREASING DULUX BRAND SHARE

Figure 6 plots monthly and three-monthly moving-average, total brand shares for Dulux in the white emulsions market, along with the Natural Whites brand share. Obviously,

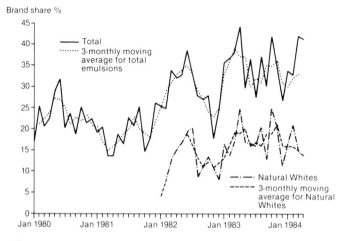

Figure 6. *Dulux White Emulsion brand shares (monthly & 3-monthly moving averages)*

the nature of the data is such that fluctuations can be expected with monthly figures, but the trends are clear. It should be noted that competitive tinted whites were launched, particularly by Crown, during the Summer of 1982. In addition there was heavy discounting on 3-litre and 5-litre brilliant white, by Crown, during the Autumn of 1982. Neither of these activities affected the long-term growth of Natural Whites, although short-term effects were discernible.

NATURAL WHITES PRICE PREMIUM

The aim of achieving a 15 per cent premium for Natural Whites over brilliant whites has been more than met when compared to Crown Plus Two, as shown by the relative price index in Figure 7. Against Dulux's own brilliant white the premium is, on average,

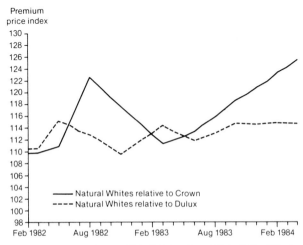

Figure 7. Price premium of Natural Whites (Relative to Crown & Dulux Brilliant Whites)

slightly below 15 per cent, but this is due to the ability to maintain a premium for brilliant white vs. Crown Plus Two on the strength of Natural Whites.

NEW, YOUNGER, FEMALE USERS

During April and May 1982, 295 interviews were undertaken with users of Natural Whites. The findings of this study included the following user-profile comparisons with 1981 Dulux emulsion users shown in Table 1.

TABLE 1:   USER PROFILE COMPARISONS 1982

|          | Natural Whites<br>% | 1981 Dulux Emulsion<br>% |
|----------|---------------------|--------------------------|
| male     | 35                  | 49                       |
| female   | 65                  | 51                       |
| under 35 | 37                  | 28                       |
| 35–54    | 43                  | 38                       |
| 55 +     | 20                  | 34                       |

In addition, of the users questioned only 61 per cent claimed Dulux to be the brand they most frequently purchased *prior* to buying Natural Whites. Importantly also, 84 per cent of users claimed they had decided to buy Natural Whites *before* entering the store, and 79 per cent of users claimed to have first heard of the product through TV advertising.

PROFITABILITY

Table 2 shows the emulsion market breakdown, Dulux brand shares and the Dulux advertising expenditures for the period 1980-83.

TABLE 2:    EMULSIONS MARKET 1980-83

|  | 1980 | 1981 | 1982 | 1983 |
|---|---|---|---|---|
| *all emulsions* | % | % | % | % |
| colours | 42.5 | 42.2 | 37.9 | 38.1 |
| brilliant whites | 57.5 | 57.8 | 53.9 | 50.6 |
| Dulux Natural Whites | – | – | 8.2 | 11.4 |
| *white emulsion* | | | | |
| Dulux Brilliant Whites | 23.3 | 18.4 | 16.6 | 17.4 |
| Dulux Natural Whites | – | – | 13.3 | 18.5 |
| Dulux total whites | 23.3 | 18.4 | 29.9 | 35.9 |
| *colours* | | | | |
| Dulux | 34 | 29 | 30 | 29 |
| *Advertising* | 1980 | 1981 | 1982 | 1983 |
| | £m | £m | £m | £m |
| Dulux Brilliant White Emulsion | 1.2 | 1.4 | 0 | 1.0 |
| Natural Whites | – | – | 2.8 | 1.7 |
| *total* | 1.2 | 1.4 | 2.8 | 2.7 |

From these: the total market volumes and the gross profit margins for Natural Whites, brilliant whites and colours, the approximate gross profit contribution can be calculated. For reasons of confidentiality the precise numbers cannot be divulged. However, as stated earlier, after allowing for the lost share on brilliant whites, the decline of the colours market, and the launch costs, the profit contribution from Natural Whites is still substantial.

*Regression Analyses*

The success of Natural Whites is demonstrated conclusively by the annual results and trends. Inherent in these sales figures is the success of the advertising, since the whole concept revolved around the communication of an emotional stance. However, we have also attempted to quantify the advertising benefit more precisely using some simple modelling techniques. The variables investigated were:

—*Advertising Expenditure* indexed to 1980 levels. This was used rather than some audience measure since the media schedule consisted of multiple media.

—*Share of Shelf Footage* in store.
—*Share of Displays* in store.
—*Relative Price* for both Natural Whites and Dulux Brilliant Whites, relative to Crown Plus Two.

Several analyses were performed which investigated the Dulux share both before and after the Natural Whites launch. For brevity these are not all discussed here, but the key findings are given below and the regression results for the final analysis over the whole data period are shown in the Appendix. The main conclusions were:

1. Prior to the launch of Natural Whites both relative price and Dulux Brilliant White advertising had significant effects on brand share.
2. After the launch Natural Whites advertising and Natural Whites share of shelf footage also showed significant effects.
3. The Dulux Brilliant White price elasticity reduced after the launch from approximately 0.8 to 0.6.
4. Advertising expenditure produced short-term sales effects equivalent to one brand share point for each £100 000 (1980 prices) for both Dulux Brilliant White and Natural Whites.
5. Each 1 per cent of shelf footage allocated to Natural Whites accounts for about $1\frac{1}{2}$ brand-share points.

SUMMARY OF ANALYSES RESULTS

The analyses essentially attribute the sales success to the advertising and shelf footage levels. However, the growth in shelf footage correlates extremely highly with the cumulative advertising levels (as will normally be the case for a successful new product launch). Bearing in mind the research result previously stated, that 84 per cent of purchasers had decided on Natural Whites before entering the store, it seems probable that it was advertising-generated sales which supported the growth of the shelf footage levels, rather than these levels growing independently and leading to sales. However, once established, high shelf-footage produces sales even in the absence of advertising. This could therefore be thought of as a long-term sales benefit from advertising.

Finally, it must be said that these analyses were designed as supporting evidence for the case and not as numerical proof which would have been extremely difficult, given the circumstances of the launch. In this context they are very informative.

## SUMMARY OF EFFECT AND FURTHER DEVELOPMENT

The success of the launch is attributable to three key factors:

1. Thorough analysis and accurate interpretation of the market situation.
2. The identification of a real opportunity.
3. The development of a creative package which was consistent in its approach and highly appealing to consumers.

The launch has succeeded in reducing the brilliant white sector of the market, and with it the move to a commodity type market.

The effect of the UK retail decorative paints market has been considerable. Apart from creating a third major market sector over and above brilliant whites and colours, Natural Whites have enabled manufacturers to improve their profit margins and to bring a new dynamic to the market-place.

Dulux has continued to exploit and develop the Natural Whites range with a number of new activities: these products have subsequently been introduced in both gloss and non-drip gloss finishes. In January 1983, Natural Whites were added to the Dulux Weathershield Exterior Masonry paint range, and to the Dulux Professional Decorator range of paints. The range has been extended by a further three shades: Bluebell, Apricot and Barley White, presented in a similar way to the original three shades. Additionally, to match all the Natural Whites, a range of wallcovering borders has been introduced. The new market will provide yet more opportunities in the future.

## APPENDIX

*Regression Analysis*

| | |
|---|---|
| Dependent Variable: | Dulux Brand Share (White Emulsion) |
| Independent Variables: | Relative Price |
| | Share of Shelf Footage (SSF) |
| | (Natural Whites) |
| | Advertising Expenditure |
| | (Dulux Brilliant White & Natural Whites) |

Results:

| | Coefficient | t-Statistic |
|---|---|---|
| Constant | 79.5 | 3.5 |
| R Price | −56.5 | −2.6 |
| SSF | 1.6 | 7.9 |
| Advertising Brilliant White | 0.01 | 1.3 |
| Advertising Natural Whites | 0.01 | 2.3 |

Goodness of fit: $r^2 = 0.62$

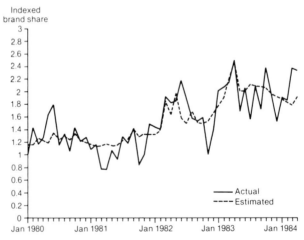

Figure 8. *Regression analysis results (Actual v. estimated Dulux brand share)*

Figure 8 shows the plot of actual brand share and the estimated brand share from this regression analysis.

# 4

# The Repositioning of Hellmann's Mayonnaise

## INTRODUCTION

Most of the classic studies of advertising effectiveness start with a sluggish or declining sales graph, which is then dramatically reversed by the new campaign. Hellmann's is different: it was already a healthily growing brand and the need for a new initiative was not immediately obvious, though we believe and hope to show it was crucially necessary. And, of course, it presents a particular challenge to demonstrate advertising effectiveness under these circumstances.

## BACKGROUND

### *Hellmann's importance to CPC*

CPC Best Foods Division is one of three divisions of CPC (UK) Ltd, the others dealing with catering supply and industrial starch technology. Best Foods (the retail division) currently turns over some £45 million at manufacturer's selling price and the business is comprised of Mazola Corn Oil, Brown & Polson cornflour, Dextrosol, Knorr cubes, soups and sauces, Frank Cooper, and Hellmann's Mayonnaise.

In 1981 divisional strategy was thoroughly reappraised, among other issues addressing the problem of how a finite total marketing budget should be apportioned among a large number of small- to medium-sized brands. One influential tool in the analysis was the matrix originally developed by the Boston Consulting Group, by which each brand is evaluated in two dimensions: market growth and brand dominance.

Dominant brands in growing markets become 'stars' – the opportunities on which the future of the business depends and therefore priorities for investment. Dominant brands in static or declining markets are regarded as 'cash cows', which can be 'milked' to provide investment for the 'stars'. Weak brands in declining markets are described as 'dogs' (for apparent reasons); and weak brands in growth markets must be treated on their individual merits. (This is inevitably an oversimplistic description and the results are rarely as unequivocal as this sounds; it can be, nevertheless, and was here, a useful aid to decision making, as can be seen in Figure 1.)

As a result, Hellmann's (hitherto regarded as a relatively minor part of the portfolio)

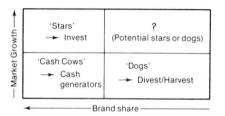

Figure 1. *The BCG matrix*

emerged as a prime candidate for investment: it dominated the mayonnaise market with a 60 per cent volume share, and the market itself had been growing for some years by 10–20 per cent per annum, being worth in 1981 some £7 million (see Figure 2).

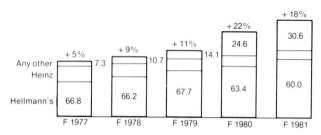

Figure 2. *Mayonnaise market trends (000/jars) & Hellmann's share*
*(NB: F 1977, etc., refers to CPC fiscal years which end*
*30 September. Thus, F 1977 refers to 12 months ending*
*30 September 1977)*

*Source:* Nielsen

### Hellmann's: Early History

Hellmann's Real Mayonnaise, originally an American brand, was launched in this country in the 1960s. At first it was very much a delicatessen product in limited distribution and continued for a number of years to develop a small but discriminating following.

It is important to understand that at the time of Hellmann's original launch, 'real' mayonnaise – ie a thick, spoonable, subtle-tasting emulsion of egg yolks and oil – was virtually unknown to the majority of the British public. The word 'mayonnaise' was widely used, erroneously, as a synonym for salad cream (a peculiarly British product with a pourable texture and highly flavoured with vinegar and sugar). This may be due to the fact that Heinz marketed until 1981 a product called 'Heinz Mayonnaise' which was very similar in taste and texture to salad cream.

Two significant circumstances followed from this. Firstly, mayonnaise became known exclusively as a salad dressing. This may still seem unsurprising to the British reader, until we remember that we are probably the only country in the world where this statement would be true: in the USA or on the Continent, there is no particular link between mayonnaise and salad.

Secondly, the early advertising history of Hellmann's was devoted by one means or another to explaining how the 'real' mayonnaise differed from salad cream expectations. By drawing these comparisons, of course, the salad usage positioning was reinforced.

*Hellmann's Position in 1981*

By 1981, Hellmann's had achieved reasonable distribution throughout the grocery trade (85 per cent £). The brand had been advertised, but not nationally or consistently: the best remembered campaign was that featuring 'Mrs Hellmann' which ran from 1976-79, mostly in London and the South. Penetration was still low and even awareness of the brand continued to be patchy. Year-on-year growth rates were encouraging (see Figure 2); but against this, it could be seen that much of this growth was simply a factor of improved distribution (see Figure 3). Calculating the actual rate of sale, this was much flatter – indeed in certain areas rate of sale could be shown to be in decline.

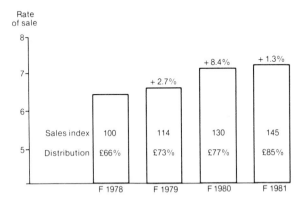

Figure 3. *Hellmann's Rate of Sale (000 jars/% £ distribution)*

*Source:* Nielsen

The original portfolio analysis had taken account of historical growth rates, but had not attempted to predict the future. Yet the logic of investing in the brand depended on the assumption that the market would, or could be made to, continue to grow. At £3.7 million (MSP), Hellmann's was not a large enough brand to justify heavy advertising expenditure simply for maintenance purposes. Its share of market was unlikely to increase, being so high already; indeed, it was almost inevitably foreseen to decline as own-label products became available, retailing considerably cheaper than Hellmann's, yet of highly acceptable quality. Before committing large sums of money, therefore, we had to address the question: what were the prospects of continued market growth?

Our analysis suggested strongly that Hellmann's, as it was at that time perceived and used, could not expect to grow indefinitely and indeed as distribution plateaued, might not grow much further. At its simplest this was predictable from the fact that the amount of salad served, while showing some growth, is finite; therefore Hellmann's would continue to compete with salad cream, and increasingly with other dressings such as French dressing which were – and are – growing from a small base even faster than mayonnaise.

The naive assumption that people would forsake salad cream as soon as mayonnaise became available to them was not borne out by the facts. Loyalty to salad cream was, and is, enormously strong. Most mayonnaise buyers were buying it in addition to, not instead of, salad cream. In fact mayonnaise was seen by the majority of its users as a 'special occasion' salad product, an occasional but not a routine substitute for salad cream.

This 'special occasion' imagery had in the past been recognised by client and agency as an important part of the Hellmann's brand: it grew out of the delicatessen origins of the brand and, in one campaign at least, had been explicitly reflected in an upper-class setting and a suggestion that Hellmann's was 'superior' or 'posh'.

However, we now began to consider whether this imagery was not a limitation as well as a strength. For users it inhibited everyday use of the product, which in any case was unlikely to take the place of salad cream totally. For non-users it was even a disincentive to purchase, especially to the C2D groups: the profile of Hellmann's at this time still being strongly AB (Table 1).

TABLE 1:    HELLMANN'S PENETRATION BY SOCIAL CLASS

| (Base: all housewives) | AB | C1 | C2 | D | E |
|---|---|---|---|---|---|
| Claim to buy Hellmann's nowadays: | 33% | 20% | 10% | 5% | 7% |

Source: TGI

It seemed likely then that once Hellmann's Mayonnaise had achieved a certain share of salad cream occasions, and a certain penetration among ABC1s, and allowing for the fact that about a quarter of all potential buyers reject the product on taste grounds, it would not have much further room to grow. And this point seemed to be not far off. If this were to be the case, it was difficult to justify the level of expenditure which were being contemplated.

## THE NEW STRATEGY FOR HELLMANN'S

All these limitations derived from the fact that mayonnaise was seen exclusively as a salad dressing. This had other limitations as well, in terms of regionality and seasonality. Salad consumption is heavily biased, of course, to the summer. For Hellmann's, with a relatively short shelf-life, this meant plant standing idle in the off-season. Also, salad consumption is greater in the South than the North. Hellmann's historical Southern bias was not a case of the South being ahead of the North; it was largely the same regional pattern as salads, or indeed salad cream.

On the other hand, if it were possible to re-present mayonnaise as a product with a wider range of uses and to divorce it from salad cream, the potential for growth would be very much greater. This would entail consumers seeing mayonnaise more in the way it is seen in the USA or Europe: as a versatile condiment. At the same time, it could be made more accessible and everyday: a condiment for snacks as well as formal meal occasions, associated with good food but not pretension.

Whether or not this aspiration was realistic or not was a difficult question for research to predict before the event. In the end, we decided on a major piece of qualitative research to probe, using individual interviews, people's attitudes to and experience of mayonnaise. This was very encouraging in that it showed little resistance to extending the versatility of mayonnaise usage, though there were clear 'no go' areas such as red meat or meals with gravy. One of the most interesting findings was that the heaviest users of mayonnaise were *already* using it in many different ways, but with considerable guilt because this was not 'proper', and almost disrespectful to a product which had positioned itself on a pedestal.

In addition to this, the new strategy seemed to fit well with some broad trends in eating habits; in particular the long-term growth in all pickles and sauces, the increase of snacking and the decline of the formal meal occasion, and an increasing willingness of the consumer to experiment and try new things.

### Advertising Development

On this basis, we proceeded to a creative brief. The objectives of the new campaign were defined as:

#### ADVERTISING OBJECTIVES

1. To encourage trial of Hellmann's (especially in areas of low salad consumption).
2. To stimulate a wider range of applications among existing trialists.

At the time, we considered two ways of approaching the objective. Either we could maintain our existing salad base and add new suggestions gradually, or we could abandon all the precedents and talk about mayonnaise as if it were a new product, with no salad antecedents. We decided fairly soon that the second approach was the only viable one: we needed to force a complete revaluation of the brand, and to do this we had to be radical, even shocking. The creative strategy was formulated as follows.

#### CREATIVE BRIEF

1. Redefine Hellmann's as a versatile, everyday 'condiment/ingredient'.
2. Divorce Hellmann's from any association with salad cream.
3. Brand Hellmann's strongly.

Guidelines:

— Feature a range of usage occasions (rather than a 'recipe' approach).
— Hellmann's is not just for good cooks - it's idiot proof.
— Hellmann's is a natural, simple product (parallel: whipped cream).

#### TARGET MARKET

1. Current Hellmann's users.
2. Non-users of mayonnaise.

The campaign that was produced was certainly different (see page 52). Not only did burgers and jacket potatoes replace delicate salads: but the black ties and silver candlesticks gave way to a Northern working-class kitchen where Mum was an awful cook and ran off with the coalman, leaving our hero (an overgrown schoolboy) to transform her inedible, boring food with the addition of a little Hellmann's.

Neither the client nor the agency could ignore the dangers of this radical approach if it misfired. Would we jeopardise all Hellmann's traditional brand strengths by debunking it like this? The campaign was extensively researched, both qualitatively as an animatic, and quantitatively as a finished film. The research showed a campaign with great impact which clearly communicated its objective of extended usage, and forced a revaluation of mayonnaise, but which also had no detectable effects on the quality perception of the brand. Indeed, intentions-to-buy scores were improved and the campaign was much liked by users and by non-users (Table 2).

TABLE 2:    INTENTION TO BUY

'How likely would you be to buy Hellmann's Mayonnaise?'

| Base: housewives exposed to: | Previous Commercial % | New Commercial 'Kitchen' % | Control (pack) % |
|---|---|---|---|
| very likely (+5) | 30 | 38 | 34 |
| quite likely | 37 | 31 | 19 |
| neither likely nor unlikely | 6 | 7 | 8 |
| not very likely | 17 | 14 | 9 |
| not at all likely (+1) | 10 | 9 | 31 |
| mean score | 3.62 | 3.74 | 3.17 |
| n = | (161) | (159) | (160) |

Source: Millward Brown

The following verbatims give examples of how consumers responded in group discussions to the new campaign at the animatic stage; the first group are C2D non-users from Cheshire.

'Terrific.'
'Really amusing.'
'It gets you to look at it.'
'Not like some dreary ones.'
'Trying to tell you you can use it on all types of food – more than you think.'
'Some of these things I would never have thought of but I'll try them.'

The second group, from Hampton, Middlesex, are BC1 users:

'I like the Hellmann's brightening the food.'
'Goes with things you would never have dreamt of, like chips.'
'Encouraging other members of the family to help themselves.'
'I like the message that you can use it on things all the year round.'

And the final group, from Oldham, Lancashire, are also BC1 users:

'That's very good.'
'I'd forgotten I'd had it on baked potatoes!'
'There's nothing extraordinary: it's food you eat anyway.'
'Salad cream's just for salad – with that one, it points out that you can use it with all these different things so you get your money's worth.'

*Media*

TV was chosen for its impact, and also because it addresses a family audience; we emphatically did not want a recipe campaign addressed to housewives, but a campaign to stimulate demand from all members of the family. Research suggested, for example, that teenagers making themselves snacks would be part of the opportunity.

Mayonnaise, as we have mentioned, was and still is a market with distinct regional strengths and weaknesses. A number of factors could be identified:

— the historical weight of advertising and distribution in London and the South;
— high salad consumption in the South;
— for an up-market product, the slightly different demographic profile of the South vs. the North.

Given the new strategy, however, we did not feel any of these factors constrained the opportunity. Indeed it was part of our objective to build a broader national brand than we inherited, which would not be limited by regional bias of salad consumption, nor so rigorously confined to AB purchasers.

Accordingly, the campaign was planned nationally and, in fact, the relatively cheaper airtime costs in the North of the country resulted in those areas being upweighted to the consumer. This was in line with our view that a higher weight of advertising was needed to build penetration and awareness in these areas.

The campaign was planned to break around the end of May 1982, the peak season for mayonnaise, followed by another burst in August–September. It was, however, part of our objective to develop counter-seasonal usage for Hellmann's. There had historically been a slight Christmas sales peak associated with cold turkey and seasonal indulgence: we decided to build on this by creating a special Christmas commercial (see page 54) to run for two weeks before and after Christmas, followed by two weeks of the original 'Kitchen' commercial retitled with a new end-line 'Don't save it for the summer'.

This regional pattern was essentially repeated the second year of advertising. To add new life to the campaign we made three new 20-second commercials, each tackling one new type of usage occasion: chips, coleslaw, and sandwiches (one example is shown on page 56).

## THE PROGRESS OF THE BRAND: 1982-84

At the time of writing, (May 1984), exactly two years have passed since the new Hellmann's campaign began. Let us describe first of all what has happened in the marketplace and evaluate Hellmann's progress against our objectives, which may be summarised as:

— *Primary*: major volume growth (while maintaining price).
— *Secondary*: development of weaker areas and development of counter-seasonality to be achieved by increased penetration and increased weight of purchase.

## HELLMANN'S MAYONNAISE
## "KITCHEN"

When I was a lad my mother was a dreary cook.

Her string beans tasted of real string.

Then one day she ran off with the coalman's humper.

Left with a wedge of rubber and one of mother's doorsteps.

I was lucky enough to spot a forgotten jar of Hellmann's.

Quickly I mixed 'em up and bingo!

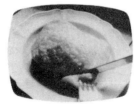

It were stupendous.

I spread Hellmann's on her carpetburgers.

They were magic.

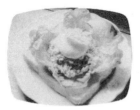

And mixed with tuna thick creamy Hellmann's transformed the limpest cloth lettuce.

Never again would her humble spud taste like it had a woolly on under its jacket.

Hellmann's. Don't save it for the salad.

*Volume Growth*

It is clear that Hellmann's has seen accelerated volume growth (Figure 4). It is true that the brand has also lost some share, but only at the same rate as we have observed for some years previously (about 3 per cent per annum): starting from such a high base this is perhaps not surprising. The share has been lost partly to own-label – in early 1983

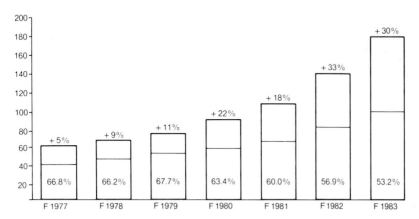

Figure 4. *Mayonnaise market trends (000 jars) and Hellmann's share*
*Sources:* Nielsen, 1977-81, MGS 1982-83

Tesco launched own-label mayonnaise for the first time – and to a lesser extent to Heinz, who relaunched a mayonnaise in spring 1983. This product has taken about 10 per cent of the market, although much of this replaces the share taken by Heinz Slimway Mayonnaise, on sale during 1981 and 1982. Both the own-label and Heinz products are considerably cheaper than Hellmann's, which commands a premium of some 60 per cent by weight at RSP.

Under the circumstances, it is a tribute to the strength of the Hellmann's brand that the rate of share loss has been so low: and for the last 12 months has shown signs of plateauing at around 50 per cent volume share.

What we did not predict was the rate at which the market could grow, with the result that Hellmann's ex-factory sales for the 1983 financial year were considerably in excess of the most ambitious internal forecasts made in 1981. (A 56 per cent increase compared with a 27 per cent forecast increase.)

*Development of Weak Areas*

Here the pattern is less clear cut, and complicated by problems in accurate regional measurement. Progress in Lancashire and especially Yorkshire seems to have been disappointing and all our attempts to explain this have been unsatisfactory; but other areas where mayonnaise was formerly very weak such as Harlech and the West, the Midlands and, in particular, Scotland, have shown very high levels of growth so that the profile of the brand is now more nationally based than it was (see Table 3).

## HELLMANN'S MAYONNAISE
## "TURKEY"

I'll never forget the Christmas we won turkey in raffle...

it were July before we had to feed the cat again...

Luckily Santa left me a jar of thick creamy Hellmans OOH OOH.

It were best Christmas ever.

Gran said if Dad...
ate anymore turkey, he'd end up looking like one.

Hellmanns. Don't save it for the summer.

TABLE 3:    REGIONAL BREAKDOWN OF HELLMANN'S SALES BY VOLUME

|  | 1981 Apr–Oct % | 1983 Apr–Oct % | Population, ISBA regions % |
|---|---|---|---|
| London | 42 | 33 | 20 |
| Southern | 7 | 8 | 9 |
| Wales and West | 6 | 9 | 11 |
| Midlands | 11 | 11 | 16 |
| Anglia | 5 | 7 | 6 |
| Lancashire | 11 | 10 | 13 |
| Yorkshire | 7 | 6 | 10 |
| North-East | 3 | 4 | 5 |
| Scotland | 8 | 12 | 10 |

Source: Mars Group Services

## Development of Counter-Seasonality

This is the most difficult area to evaluate. We have had two winter seasons and two very different experiences. The first winter showed an unprecedented rate of market growth, and one moreover in which Hellmann's participated fully (Table 4). This result is also remarkable for the fact that there is a high correlation between the rate of growth achieved by TV area, and the level of TVRs which our 'net homes' allocation enabled us to buy, making a strong case that this sales peak was in response to advertising (Figure 5).

The second winter, however, shows minimal year-on-year growth. Admittedly, this is starting from a high base, but in view of the continuing high rates of summer growth it means that progress towards making the brand less seasonal has apparently been wiped

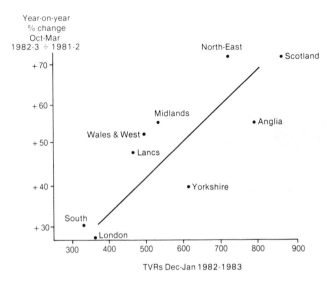

Figure 5. *Hellmann's volume growth: Winter campaign*
*Sources:* MGS, BARB

## HELLMANN'S MAYONNAISE
## "SANDWICH"

In mother's absence

hunger drove me to the four distant corners of the fridge where I discovered a 'ham frisbee'.

With my trustee jar of delicious creamy thick Hellmanns

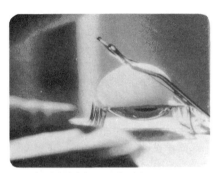

and a trick I learned with an egg...

I fast became expert in the art of the sarnie.
OOH magic.

Hellmanns. Don't save it for the summer.

TABLE 4:    SUMMARY OF HELLMANN'S PERFORMANCE – CHANGE ON PREVIOUS YEAR BY VOLUME

| | Summer 1982 (Apr–Oct) | Winter 82–83 (Nov–Mar) | Summer 1983 (Apr–Oct) | Winter 1983–84 (Nov–Mar) |
|---|---|---|---|---|
| market | +35.8% | +43.0% | +24.5% | +7.7% |
| Hellmann's | +30.7% | +41.5% | +13.6% | −4.2% |

Source: Mars Group Services

out. Weights of advertising each year were similar, but in the second year the campaign did not break until after Christmas, while in the first year it started on 18th December. Whether this made any difference is a matter for debate, but it seems unlikely it could have accounted for such a wide discrepancy.


## THE CONTRIBUTION OF ADVERTISING

As we have seen, our primary objective – major volume growth for the brand – has been achieved. We have yet to make the case that advertising was a major factor in this growth, and that without the advertising it would have been less (we guess the market would have grown, but at a lower rate). Unfortunately the obvious demonstration of this is not available to us as the campaign has been national from the outset and hence no control exists. Given, however, that we have seen an acceleration in the rate of growth, we can build our case on the following evidence:

1.  A discussion of the other factors that might have caused an increased rate of growth.
2.  Measures of the campaign's impact on the consumer.
3.  Changes in usage pattern and user profiles which would reflect the advertising strategy.

### Other Possible Factors in Generating Growth

Let us review and, where possible, discount other factors which might have affected Hellmann's growth.

— Distribution
— Pricing
— Trade stocking and display
— Promotional activity
— Product development


#### DISTRIBUTION

Gains in distribution were a considerable factor in Hellmann's volume growth up to the end of the 1981 financial year. The growth since has, however, come from a much more static distribution base. A calculation of rate-of-sale shows the increase in offtake post-advertising (Figure 6).

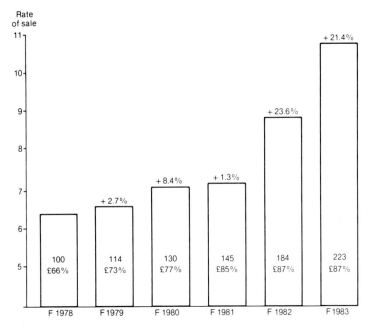

Figure 6. *Hellmann's rate of sale (000 jars/% £ distribution)*
*Sources:* Nielsen, MGS

## PRICING

There was indeed a slight reduction in the retail price between 1981 and 1983, a conse-
quence of increasing volumes being sold through the major multiples (Table 5). However,
while this may well have helped, it did little to reduce the very considerable premium of
Hellmann's over salad cream (Table 6).

Having conducted price elasticity research since, it seems unlikely that these modest

TABLE 5:    HELLMANN'S PRICE APRIL–SEPTEMBER

|        | 1981 | 1982 | 1983 |
|        | £    | £    | £    |
|--------|------|------|------|
| 200 g  | 0.576 | 0.567 | 0.572 |
| 400 g  | 1.04 | 1.00 | 0.982 |

Source: Mars Group Services

TABLE 6:    PRICE PER 100 g: HELLMANN'S AND
HEINZ SALAD CREAM

|                   | 1981 | 1983 |
|                   | p    | p    |
|-------------------|------|------|
| Hellman's         | 28.8 | 28.6 |
| Heinz salad cream | 19.4 | 20.6 |
| premium           | 9.2  | 8.0  |

Source: Mars Group Services

reductions would effect 30 per cent sales increases. The market is clearly not dominated by price: if it were, Hellmann's would hardly be able to command the premium it does over own-label.

With increasing availability of own-label and pressure on the 'salad sector' from other brands, the amount of Hellmann's on-shelf has not increased nearly as much as the actual sales to the consumer. Mars Group Services (MGS) audit the amount of stock in the forward area: taking the period April–September 1981–83 gives us the following figures expressed as indices (Table 7).

TABLE 7: HELLMANN'S PERFORMANCE (INDEXED)

|  | Front Stocks | Sales |
|---|---|---|
| 1981 | 100 | 100 |
| 1982 | 112 | 131 |
| 1983 | 113 | 148 |

Source: Mars Group Services

PROMOTIONAL ACTIVITY

Compared with the considerable advertising spend over this period, there was very little promotional activity and the pack design and copy remained unchanged for most of the period. An on-pack recipe book offer, while it achieved good levels of redemption, does not explain the observed rates of growth.

PRODUCT DEVELOPMENT

During the second year of advertising, in May 1983, two flavour variants of Hellmann's (lemon and garlic) were launched and had achieved a 6 per cent share of the market by September. The rationale behind the flavours is to differentiate the brand from own-label and to stimulate re-trial among lapsed users who find ordinary mayonnaise too 'bland'. As such, they may be expected to have contributed something to the brand's growth, though the extent of straight substitution for the base product is very hard to estimate. It is worth noting also that the launch of flavours has not been reflected in increased total Hellmann's facings in the retail trade. Our best conclusion must be that the addition of flavours to date has been a contribution – but not *the* major factor – in the growth picture, and this in any case applies to the last 12 months only.

We conclude that no other factor or combination of factors can conceivably explain Hellmann's rate of volume growth.

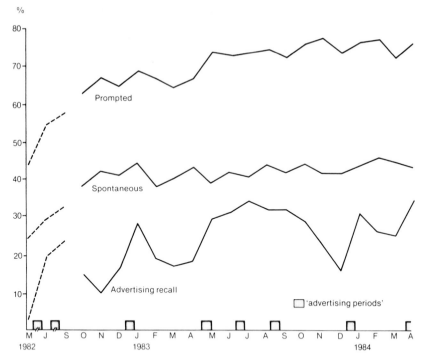

Figure 7. *Awareness & advertising recall of Hellmann's Mayonnaise*

*Sources:* ---- NOP
        ——— Millward Brown

## Consumer Reactions to the Advertising

While the following data does not necessarily equate to purchasing behaviour, there is considerable evidence that the campaign has been widely seen, recalled, understood, and liked by the consumer (see Figure 7).

— Brand awareness has improved significantly since the campaign began.
— The campaign has achieved consistently high recall levels. (To put these figures into context, the high points are the highest figures (with one exception) recorded on the CPC tracking study, which includes not only all CPC's own brands but heavily and successfully advertised competitors such as Heinz and Oxo.)
— Related recall is accurate and recall of the main message is on strategy (Table 8).

TABLE 8:    RELATED RECALL OF HELLMANN'S CAMPAIGN

| (average 11 months to April 1984) | % |
| --- | --- |
| use of different things/not just salad | 38 |
| livens up boring meals/revives them | 24 |
| makes things taste better | 24 |
| adds flavour to ordinary food/makes more interesting | 27 |

Base: all recalling Hellmann's advertising
Source: Millward Brown

TABLE 9: PROMPTED COMMENTS ON HELLMANN'S
CAMPAIGN

| (average 11 months to April 1984) | % |
|---|---|
| it gave the impression the product would be very good | 40 |
| I liked it | 38 |
| it made me more interested in buying the product | 15 |
| it was no different from most other commercials | 7 |
| it was hard to believe | 9 |
| I'm getting fed up seeing it | 3 |
| it put me off buying the product | 1 |
| I don't like it | 2 |

Base: all recalling Hellmann's campaign
Source: Millward Brown

On a standard set of statements, the campaign is clearly liked and appreciated. Again, these figures are high compared with company norms (Table 9). These types of responses are also found in qualitative research where the campaign is characteristically received with recognition and enjoyment.

> He was lovely ... human ... you really felt sorry for him ... it's just how men are on their own.
> He's a bit scruffy ... the lazy type ... had his mum to run around for him and in a bit of a mess until he found the Hellmann's.
> He is quite nice ... down to earth type ... it somehow makes you think that anyone can have Hellmann's ... it's not just for posh people.
> It's the versatility of the product – it's not like a salad cream, you can use Hellmann's on anything ...
> It's quite stunning with him in it.

— Image ratings over time have shown increases in 'versatility' and 'everyday usage' without any loss in traditionally high-quality ratings (Table 10).

These quantified image ratings also reflect a profound change in the way people talk about mayonnaise in qualitative research. Two years ago mayonnaise was widely seen as having strong class connotations which, for many, were a real inhibition to trial. The following statements from C2 non-users in Cheshire illustrate this point:

> My husband's boss – he wouldn't have salad cream, only mayonnaise.
> We buy salad cream, they buy mayonnaise.

These barriers are now very much a thing of the past, and there is now a much more relaxed acceptance of mayonnaise as an accessible product among all social classes. This is reflected in consistent figures that show the new market entrants in the last two years to come increasingly from C2s and Ds (Table 11).

So much for the accessible image of the product, but how have usage patterns actually changed? We measured this in July 1983 and were able to make some comparisons with a survey conducted in 1980 (Table 12). While it is clear that salad remains a common denominator (though to a lesser extent than for salad cream), there have been increases in most non-salad uses. Also, the specific uses shown in the advertising (eg burgers,

TABLE 10:    IMAGE STATEMENTS

| | agree % | |
| | disagree % | |
| Accessibility: | 1980 | 1983 |
| --- | --- | --- |
| 'I would only serve mayonnaise on special occasions' | 25 | 13 |
| | 63 | 83 |
| 'Mayonnaise is too expensive to use all the time' | 34 | 27 |
| | 51 | 68 |
| 'There's no point in giving mayonnaise to children, they wouldn't enjoy it' | 15 | 17 |
| | 55 | 66 |
| | Hellmann's buyer | own–label buyer |
| Versatility: (*not asked in 1980*) 'Mayonnaise is something the family will help themselves to for snacks' | 48 | 43 |
| | 41 | 47 |
| 'I think of mayonnaise mainly as an ingredient' | 37 | 38 |
| | 54 | 56 |
| 'Mayonnaise has more use than salad cream' | 57 | 55 |
| | 27 | 31 |

Source: ICI

TABLE 11:    INCREASE IN PENETRATION 1980-83

| AB | C1 | C2 | D | E |
| --- | --- | --- | --- | --- |
| +3% | +12% | +22% | +117% | +15% |

Source: TGI

potatoes, cheese on toast), while not comparable with 1980, have attained respectable levels. Also, it can be shown that while in 1980 mayonnaise was less versatile than salad cream, the positions are now reversed (Table 13).

A more sophisticated analysis segments mayonnaise users into four categories: traditionalists, combination salad makers, 'new' types of users, and combination plus 'new' users. This indicates that 40 per cent of Hellmann's users are using the product in at least one of the ways shown in the advertising. Interestingly, too, this proportion is significantly higher among Hellmann's users than it is among users of own-label mayonnaise (Table 14).

TABLE 12:    HELLMANN'S USERS: WAYS OF USING MAYONNAISE

| | (mayonnaise) | (mayonnaise) | (salad cream) |
|---|---|---|---|
| | 1980 | 1983 | 1983 |
| | % | % | % |
| with a lettuce type of salad | N/A | 84 | 97 |
| with tomatoes | N/A | 57 | 69 |
| salad sandwich | 24 | 51 | 63 |
| egg mayonnaise | 52 | 64 | 36 |
| prawn cocktail | 34 | 46 | 30 |
| cold meat without salad | 16 | 19 | 24 |
| chips without salad | 5 | 14 | 18 |
| hot meat without salad | 8 | 14 | 3 |
| fish without salad | 8 | 15 | 11 |
| savoury dip | 8 | 23 | 15 |
| bread & butter without salad | 0 | 12 | 18 |
| with: | | | |
| hamburgers | N/A | 11 | 7 |
| tuna fish | N/A | 34 | 23 |
| cheese on toast | N/A | 10 | 8 |
| jacket potatoes | N/A | 20 | 15 |
| potato salad | 47 | 46 | 43 |
| coleslaw | 42 | 41 | 41 |
| cucumber salad | 10 | 14 | 11 |
| rice salad | 14 | 15 | 8 |
| Russian salad | 8 | 10 | 5 |
| Waldorf salad | 6 | 10 | 4 |
| prawn salad | 1 | 27 | 18 |
| mixed vegetable salad | 2 | 22 | 24 |
| sweetcorn salad | 0 | 11 | 8 |
| other made salad | 9 | 12 | 8 |

Source: 1980–PAS
      1983–ICI

TABLE 13:    AVERAGE NUMBER OF CLAIMED USES PER RESPON-
DENT

| | 1980 | 1983 |
|---|---|---|
| salad cream | 3.1 | 6.1 |
| mayonnaise | 2.8 | 6.7 |

Source: 1980–PAS
      1983–ICI

(Note: The increase 1980 to 1983 is considerably exaggerated by a
longer list of uses: the object of the chart is the relative position
of salad cream vs. mayonnaise.)

TABLE 14:    TYPES OF USE MEASURED

| salad | combination salad | new uses |
|---|---|---|
| lettuce type | cucumber salad | cold meat without salad |
| tomatoes | rice salad | chips without salad |
| salad sandwich | Russian salad | hot meat without salad |
| | Waldorf salad | fish without salad |
| | prawn salad | bread & butter without salad |
| *traditional recipe* | mixed vegetable salad | hamburgers without salad |
| | sweetcorn salad | cheese on toast without salad |
| egg mayonnaise | savoury dip | jacket potatoes without salad |
| tuna fish | | |
| potato salad | | |
| coleslaw | | |

MAYONNAISE USAGE SEGMENTS

| | all | Hellmann's users | own-label users |
|---|---|---|---|
| | % | % | % |
| 1.  salad/traditional only | 31 | 27 | 30 |
| 2.  salad/traditional + combination salad | 23 | 23 | 28 |
| 3.  salad/traditional + 'new uses' | 17 | 19 | 11 |
| 4.  salad/traditional + combination salad + 'new uses' | 27 | 29 | 28 |

Source: ICI

# CONCLUSION

In summary then we can show that the advertising has made an impression; that perceptions of mayonnaise have been changed in the way we intended: that ways of using the
product reflect that change. These findings, and the otherwise unexplained acceleration
in volume growth from a static distribution base, lead us to conclude that the advertising
has been effective in achieving our main objective.

We hope to have shown that the growth we have seen would not have taken place
without the advertising. It would be wrong, however, to leave the argument there without
admitting that the nature of that growth has not been entirely what we anticipated, and
that more remains to be achieved in the future.

We expected growth to come from two sources – from attracting new users to the
market, and also from increasing the average weight of purchase which, for most mayonnaise users, has always been very low. In the event, as extensive TCA analyses have
shown, the weight of purchase has hardly increased: the brand and market growth has
instead largely come from new trialists including, as we have seen, many from social
classes hitherto unfamiliar with mayonnaise. Inevitably, not all these trialists will become
regular users: hence our strategic focus for the future will be increasingly on creating
more weight of purchase.

What, then, have we achieved? We have taken mayonnaise off its pedestal and made it
accessible to a whole new market; we have reduced its exclusive association with special
occasion salads and encouraged experimentation and a more relaxed attitude towards it.
This has increased penetration for the brand: it has also, without a doubt, endorsed the

existing behaviour of a core of heavy, versatile users who have always been important to our sales. At the same time, we have not devalued the brand, which retains very high loyalty among its users even at a considerable premium price (TCA shows very little direct switching to own-label or to Heinz).

# 5

# The Relaunch of
# Cow & Gate Babymeals

## INTRODUCTION

This paper describes a genuine sales success story for Cow & Gate babymeals. Against a background of disappointing sales and an absence from consumer advertising of over two and a half years, the brand reacted strongly to advertising in support of a relaunch in summer 1983.

The case for advertising's contribution to this success is demonstrated by isolating the effect of other brand and market variables. This examination leads us to conclude that the placing of a persuasive advertising message in carefully selected media was the major contributor to Cow & Gate's sales growth.

The sales effect of the advertising is all the more interesting in that the media spend was at a low level throughout the campaign.

## BACKGROUND

### The Company

Charles Gate founded a dairy in Guildford in 1850, and in 1910 began producing baby-milks. Cow & Gate expanded to produce other babyfoods, with babymeals produced from 1965. Today, Cow & Gate is exclusively a babyfeeding company and is now the largest manufacturer of babyfoods in the UK. It produces products in all sectors – milks, meals, rusks and juices, as well as specialist foods for the treatment of infant feeding disorders – to meet all a baby's feeding needs up to the age of one year.

### The Brand

Cow & Gate babymeals are packed in jars and are produced in two stages. Stage 1 is for babies beginning mixed feeding from about three months; it is a very smooth product with no lumps, and it is presented in 78 g jars. Stage 2 is for babies aged from about six months; it has a thicker texture and contains small pieces, and is sold in 113 g jars. Both stages are produced in a range of breakfast, dinner and dessert varieties. In addition, Cow & Gate produce a single-stage range of baby yogurt desserts in 113 g jars.

*The Market*

The babymeals market was worth £52 million in 1982. However, the market had declined in real terms since 1974 to only 90 per cent of its value, as Table 1 shows.

TABLE 1:   BABYMEALS MARKET VALUE (RSP)

|  | 1974 | 1976 | 1978 | 1980 | 1982 |
|---|---|---|---|---|---|
| £m | 18 | 27 | 31 | 45 | 52 |
| Index | 100 | 150 | 172 | 250 | 289 |
| Index at 1974 prices | 100 | 95 | 87 | 95 | 90 |

Source: EIU/trade estimates

The size of the babymeals market and its potential for growth are closely related to the annual birth rate. In 1983, for the first time since 1980, the decline in the birth rate stopped (see Figure 1). The birth rate, and hence the market, shows no seasonal differences.

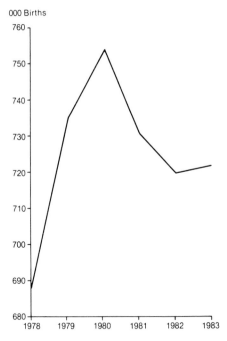

Figure 1: *The annual birth rate*
*Source:* Office of Population, Censuses and Surveys (England and Wales), Scottish Office, Northern Ireland Office

The babymeals market consists of two basic product sectors: 'wet' meals, which are sold in jars and cans ready to heat and serve, and 'dehydrated' meals, which are sold in a powder or granulated form and are reconstituted by adding water or milk. From 1979, the dehydrated sector of the babymeals market grew at the expense of the wet.

Because the various brands of babymeals are available in widely differing sizes, the shift in balance between wet and dehydrated is best shown on a servings basis. Table 2 shows that in independent chemists by the end of 1982 dehydrated babymeals accounted for seven out of ten of all manufactured meals served compared with five out of ten in 1978.

TABLE 2:   INDEPENDENT CHEMISTS: SHARE OF SERVINGS BY WET AND DEHYDRATED BABYMEALS

|  | 1978 % | 1979 % | 1980 % | 1981 % | 1982 % |
|---|---|---|---|---|---|
| wet | 47 | 37 | 32 | 31 | 30 |
| dehydrated | 53 | 63 | 68 | 69 | 70 |

Assumptions:    One pack Cow & Gate, Heinz and Gerber    = one serving
One pack Robinsons and Heinz weaning    = three servings
One pack Milupa    = twelve servings
Source: Nielsen/AMV estimates

## Competitive Situation

Prior to the relaunch, Cow & Gate were in a weak position competitively. The position as shown in Table 3 represented a loss of one share point in volume and two share points in value for Cow & Gate since the beginning of 1982.

TABLE 3:   BABYMEALS BRAND SHARE

|  | Volume % | Value % |
|---|---|---|
| Cow & Gate | 9 | 7 |
| Heinz cans | 54 | 37 |
| Heinz jars | 9 | 8 |
| Gallia jars | 1 | 1 |
| *Total wet meals* | 73 | 53 |
| Milupa | 8 | 18 |
| Robinsons | 11 | 17 |
| Heinz weaning food | 2 | 2 |
| Boots own label | 6 | 10 |
| *Total dehydrated meals* | 27 | 47 |

Source: RSGB Baby Panel, 12 weeks ending 18th June 1983

# STATE OF THE BRAND PRIOR TO RELAUNCH

## The Trend to Dehydrated Products

Cow & Gate is a wet brand and was therefore suffering in the trend in the market towards dehydrated products.

Qualitative research conducted by AMV in 1981 revealed that mothers saw real product benefits in dehydrated babymeals, which accounted for their popularity. Like all manufactured babymeals, they were seen as being convenient, but they were also seen to have additional benefits over wet meals: they could be made up in small quantities and various textures to suit each baby's individual needs.

### Distribution

Although Cow & Gate were building distribution in the grocery trade, sales opportunities were being missed through very low distribution in this sector (see Table 4).

TABLE 4: STERLING PROFILE BY SOURCE OF PURCHASE

|  | total market | | Cow & Gate | |
|---|---|---|---|---|
|  | 1982 % | 1983 % | 1982 % | 1983 % |
| grocers | 37 | 35 | 5 | 9 |
| Boots | 42 | 42 | 62 | 63 |
| other chemists | 20 | 21 | 33 | 26 |
| other outlets | 1 | 2 | – | 2 |

Source: RSGB Baby Panel, 12 weeks ending 16th June 1982 and 18th June 1983

### Price

The brand leader, Heinz cans, is seen to be the definitive brand in the wet meals market, with the definitive price against which other brands are compared on a unit-by-unit basis (not price per gram).

Cow & Gate was perceived by mothers as being the most highly priced brand. Twenty-seven per cent of mothers felt that Cow & Gate babymeals were highly priced, as compared with only 12 per cent for Heinz (PHL, May 1983).

In fact, in spring 1983 Cow & Gate jars were up to 30 per cent per unit more expensive than Heinz cans (Table 5).

TABLE 5: INDEX OF AVERAGE RSP PER UNIT

|  | Index |
|---|---|
| Heinz cans (128 g) | 100 |
| Cow & Gate 1 (78 g) | 118 |
| Cow & Gate 2 (113 g) | 129 |
| Cow & Gate yogurt (113 g) | 121 |
| Heinz jars (128 + 170 g)* | 135 |

* Nielsen reports two sizes together as average
Source: Chemist Nielsen, March–April 1983

## *Lack of Support*

Cow & Gate received no advertising support from January 1981 until the relaunch in August 1983. In contrast there was significant activity from competitors, especially in the dehydrated sector. Heinz weaning food was launched in May 1981 with national advertising support on TV, and in July 1982 Robinsons relaunched their product with new packaging and heavy advertising support. Then in June 1983 Heinz launched their Pure Fruit range, again with significant spend on TV.

Milupa, who had successfully launched their range in the early 1970s, continued to build their franchise by extensive sampling through clinics, health visitors and the 'Bounty Bag' (sampling of mother and baby products to mothers in hospitals). Then, in summer 1982, Boots repackaged their dehydrated product and significantly extended the range of varieties offered. Table 6 summaries competitive activity.

TABLE 6:    SUMMARY OF COMPETITIVE ACTIVITY

|  | Year ending | | | | | |
|  | Dec 1981 | | Dec 1982 | | Jun 1983 | |
|  | £000 | % | £000 | % | £000 | % |
| Total | 1010 | 100 | 1926 | 100 | 2546 | 100 |
| Heinz | 856 | 85 | 970 | 50 | 1565 | 62 |
| Robinsons | 74 | 7 | 908 | 47 | 954 | 37 |
| Others | 80 | 8 | 48 | 3 | 27 | 1 |

Source: MEAL (TV and Press Expenditure)

## *Product Formulation Problems*

Following product placement (PHL 1983), it was found that Cow & Gate's texture was being criticised for being too thin and runny; texture problems were likely to be adding to the brand's sales deficiencies.

# THE CONSUMER AND BRAND DECISION-MAKER:
# USAGE AND ATTITUDES

## *The Consumer*

The ultimate consumer is, of course, the baby, and the success or failure of a brand will depend on his or her acceptance of it. The mother, though, is the brand decision-maker, and there are important differences between first-time and subsequent mothers' attitudes to feeding their babies (AMV Qualitative).

First-time mothers are generally less confident about how to feed their babies, especially babies under six months. They are driven by an underlying concern that their baby should behave normally, yet they have no real benchmark of their own by which to judge what is normal. Therefore they will turn to others for advice: to their mothers, their peers, the clinic and the health visitor.

The subsequent mother tends to take a more pragmatic approach to feeding, as she has been through it all before and so can rely on her own experience more than on the advice of others. She will often replicate the brand choices established with previous babies.

### Attitudes to Manufactured Babymeals

Manufactured babymeals are generally considered to be second best to real food, but because they are so convenient their use is heavily rationalised, and almost all mothers use them to some extent. There is also a very clear underlying belief that all babyfoods will be safe, as manufacturers are totally trusted to produce appropriate products.

Mothers stressed the need for variety in babies diets, for several reasons: so that babies can be educated to different tastes, so that they don't become faddy eaters, so that they get a nutritionally balanced diet, and so that they do not become either flavour dependent or brand dependent. This results in an almost total absence of solus brand usage in the market, and a pattern of brand choice influenced by availability of varieties.

### Cow & Gate Strengths and Weaknesses

Prior to the relaunch, awareness of Cow & Gate was lower than that of Heinz, Robinsons and Milupa.

Qualitative research (AMV 1983) revealed that competitive brands had developed strong images. Heinz was viewed very positively as expert in all manufactured foods, including babymeals. Robinsons was seen as a reliable, long-established company, and Milupa, although relatively new to the UK market, had already built up a reputation as a producer of delicious products.

Cow & Gate's brand imagery was almost entirely generic. Apart from some positive values gained from the use of Cow & Gate babymeals, positive imagery tended to emanate from the benefits of the glass jars which were considered the preferred mode of packaging for wet meals (clean, hygienic, easy to open, resealable) (PHL 1983). There was some praise for Cow & Gate as a user of natural ingredients, but generally the brand had no real benefits, as all manufactured babyfood has to be reliable. Thus there was felt to be no real reason to purchase.

Cow & Gate's user profile had become progressively more upmarket until 1983; usage was biased towards ABs (see Table 7).

| TABLE 7: | CLASS PROFILE | | |
|---|---|---|---|
| | housewives % | babymeals all users % | Cow & Gate users % |
| AB | 16 | 18 | 24 |
| C1 | 23 | 22 | 18 |
| C2 | 28 | 31 | 33 |
| DE | 33 | 29 | 25 |

Source: TGI 1983

*Product Usage Problems*

Babymeals are recommended to be served from the age of three months. Stage 1, or strained meals, are served from this age, and Stage 2, or Junior meals, are introduced from age six to eight months. Table 8 shows that Cow & Gate usage was disproportionately concentrated among younger babies.

TABLE 8:   USAGE OF WET BRANDS BY AGE OF BABY

|  | total wet % | total Cow & Gate % | total Heinz cans and jars % |
|---|---|---|---|
| under 3 months | 3 | 7 | 2 |
| 3– 6 months | 22 | 27 | 21 |
| 6– 9 months | 31 | 34 | 31 |
| 9–12 months | 22 | 18 | 22 |
| 12–18 months | 18 | 11 | 19 |
| 18–23 months | 5 | 3 | 4 |

Source: RSGB Baby Panel, 12 weeks ending 18th June 1983

Table 9 shows that the problem was prevalent in both stages of the brand. Looking at the Stage 1/strained products, nearly twice as much of Cow & Gate's product volume is served up to six months old compared with the brand leader, Heinz. And whereas 40 per cent of Heinz Junior is served to babies over one year old, only 33 per cent of Cow & Gate's Stage 2 reaches older babies.

TABLE 9:   USAGE OF STAGES OF WET BRANDS BY AGE OF BABY

|  | Cow & Gate | Heinz | | Cow & Gate | Heinz | |
|---|---|---|---|---|---|---|
|  | Stage 1 % | Strained jar % | Strained can % | Stage 2 % | Junior jar % | Junior can % |
| Under 3 months | 18 | 3 | 4 | – | – | – |
| 3–6 months | 60 | 43 | 38 | 10 | 4 | 4 |
| 6–9 months | 17 | 27 | 38 | 44 | 18 | 27 |
| 9–12 months | 3 | 9 | 14 | 25 | 33 | 29 |
| 12–18 months | 3 | 19 | 6 | 17 | 42 | 31 |
| 18–24 months | – | – | 1 | 5 | 2 | 9 |

Source: RSGB Baby Panel 12 weeks ending 18th June 1984

## SUMMARY OF COW & GATE'S POSITION PRIOR TO RELAUNCH

1.  Cow & Gate was suffering in the trend towards dehydrated babymeals.
2.  There were missed sales opportunities due to low distribution in the grocery trade.
3.  Cow & Gate was significantly more expensive than Heinz cans, the definitive wet brand.

4. Cow & Gate had received no advertising support since 1980, compared with significant activity by competitors.
5. There were product texture problems.
6. There was a lack of brand awareness and brand values, so no reason to purchase Cow & Gate.
7. Usage of Cow & Gate was disproportionately concentrated among younger babies.

## THE RELAUNCH: PROBLEMS ADDRESSED

Four problem areas were identified to be addressed prior to the relaunch: the product formulation and range, chemist-only distribution, Cow & Gate's price, and the low levels of consumer awareness and interest in the brand. These were the only areas that were addressed in the relaunch: all other aspects of the marketing mix remained static.

## THE RELAUNCH: MARKETING ACTIVITY

### Product Formulation and Range

The product was reformulated to address the criticisms on consistency that had been made by mothers. Both the Stage 1 product and the Stage 2 product were made thicker. The range of varieties offered was rationalised, with the withdrawal of the less popular varieties and the introduction of new varieties. Whereas before, some varieties were available in one stage only, several were now produced in both stages. Prior to the relaunch the range consisted of 45 main meals/desserts and five yogurts; after it there were 46 main meals/desserts and five yogurts, with a further four yogurts added in February 1984.

The improved products were introduced in their existing packaging with no indication that the recipes had been improved. Since the target market of mothers is constantly changing and experiencing the product for the first time, there was no need to alert them to the change.

The products are now continually re-evaluated and will be improved as required.

### Chemist-Only Distribution

Prior to the relaunch, Cow & Gate had a single sales force which dealt with hospitals as well as with the chemist and grocery trade. The sales force was restructured to split the medical (hospital) sales force from the retail sales force, so that each could develop its own special area of expertise. In addition, the national account team was strengthened in order to capitalise on the growing importance of the grocery multiple.

### Price

While it was recognised that the premium price over Heinz cans which existed prior to the relaunch was too high to encourage sales, it was considered important to maintain some price premium to add value to the product.

After an initial price reduction in May 1983, the price was held in the face of a competitive price increase from Heinz cans.

### Low Levels of Consumer Awareness and Interest

Sampling activity was improved with the introduction of Cow & Gate products into the Bounty weaning pack alongside Heinz, Gallia and Milupa. This pack was available in Boots from July 1983 and is estimated to reach 40 per cent of mothers.

Advertising was developed to begin in August 1983.


## THE ADVERTISING

### Development of Advertising Strategy

Qualitative research was conducted with mothers (AMV, January 1983) to aid development of the advertising strategy; in this a number of conceptual areas were explored. These included statements of reassurance about the balance of the baby's diet, the use of wholesome ingredients with no added salt, artificial colouring, flavouring or preservatives, descriptions about the extent of the range and Cow & Gate's experience in babyfeeding.

This survey concluded that there is a requirement to reassure consumers that Cow & Gate babymeals meet all a baby's nutritional needs, are made from natural ingredients and contain no additives. But this would form only part of the task, as all manufacturers are trusted to provide nutritionally sound products, so a distinctive identity for Cow & Gate babymeals was required.

Despite the product improvements, the characteristics of the products were not considered sufficiently distinctive on their own to differentiate Cow & Gate from its competitors. The new Stage 2 formulation was generally seen to bring Cow & Gate into line with competitors, rather than make it superior to them.

However, a strong positioning did emerge in that Cow & Gate help babies grow up to adult food. This claim was believable and meaningful, as adult food is the objective towards which mothers are working. Cow & Gate was seen to help with the transition from milk, through early solids, to eating with the family, and therefore gained both practical and emotional benefits. This strategic route was felt to be campaignable, as there are several stories that can be told about the products: taste education, texture education etc.

Importantly, this approach was found to be particularly relevant to our prime target market: first-time mothers who require support and guidance in feeding education. However, subsequent mothers were also sympathetic to this proposition.


### The Role of Advertising

Mothers have to be given a reason to purchase Cow & Gate babymeals when other brands have high awareness levels, high trial and repeat purchase and also previous consistent advertising support. Awareness of Cow & Gate was poor, the brand was known to be expensive and there was satisfaction with other brands. The role of advertising was thus to capitalise on the warm and positive reactions to the new superior formulations and varieties.

*Target Audience*

The primary target audience was defined as mothers with babies aged two to four months who are thinking about starting their babies on solid food, especially those who are first-time mothers. (Overall the advertising was addressed to all mothers with babies aged two to nine months.)

*Advertising Objectives*

1. To build rapid awareness of Cow & Gate babymeals among a constantly changing pool of mothers (purchase cycle only 12–16 weeks).
2. To associate Cow & Gate with expertise in baby feeding: the most advanced in understanding the needs of babies and how to develop their taste for adult food.
3. To re-establish the brand values with which Cow & Gate has traditionally been associated: the manufacture of high-quality, natural food for babies.
4. To establish Cow & Gate babymeals as a regular part of the repertoire of mothers who are feeding babies.

*Creative Strategy*

Cow & Gate help your baby to grow up to adult food.

*Support*

1. The Cow & Gate babymeals range includes a complete range of varieties in breakfasts, dinners, savouries, desserts and yogurts.
2. Cow & Gate prepare their babymeals to take into account the need to learn to cope with food of a thicker consistency and varied texture.
3. Protein, vitamins and minerals are balanced to ensure that the nutritional needs of babies are met.
4. No salt, artificial colour or preservatives are added.

Four advertisements were produced. In research they were very favourably received by mothers, and worked well together as a campaign. 'Three big steps' encompassed the role of Cow & Gate overall, helping the baby grow up to adult food. 'Liver and bacon' was specifically appropriate and relevant to starting out on Cow & Gate both practically and emotionally, a position encroached upon by the dehydrated sector. 'Mother Nature' communicated texture education, and 'Varieties' communicated that Cow & Gate could aid in taste education and the extent of choice offered.

The unusually long copy was welcomed by the mothers who were hungry for relevant and supportive information (see pages 77; 79; 83).

(Creatively this campaign has been extremely well received with 'Liver and Bacon' winning the 1984 DADA gold award for the most outstanding colour consumer magazine advertisement, and the Campaign Silver Award for Best Food and Non-Alcoholic Drinks Advertisement 1984.)

*Media Choice*

The key criteria influencing the choice of media was the need to have, as far as possible, all-year support. This was very important because of the rapidly changing target audience. In addition qualitative research had clearly shown that as well as the period of purchase of the category being very short (only 12–16 weeks) mothers tended not to think of the category much in advance of the first purchase.

National support was also required, on a limited budget of only £200 000 per annum.

The rapidly changing pool of mothers meant that it was possible to reach the core of our target audience via a relatively small list of specialist titles: *Parents*, *Mother & Baby*, *Mother* and *Maternity and Mothercraft*. Coverage was built up by adding a small group of mass market magazines including *Living*, *Family Circle*, *Good Housekeeping*, *She* and *Woman & Home* which all have sympathetic editorial including children's sections which were keyed into whenever appropriate.

A mix of full-colour spreads and single-colour pages was selected to increase impact and improve the brand's standing.

From August to December 1983 the campaign delivered 47 per cent coverage of housewives with children aged 0–23 months at 4.9 OTS. The 1984 (12 month) schedule is designed to deliver 61 per cent coverage of the same target audience at 7.1 OTS (NRS).

## EVALUATING THE RELAUNCH

Figure 2 shows the increase in Cow & Gate's volume sales ex-factory as moving annual totals. Following an overall decline to a low at the end of June 1983, after the relaunch, sales recovered and were still increasing at the end of the latest sales period ending mid-May 1984.

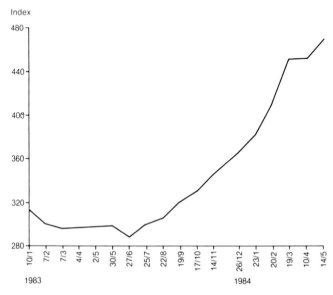

Figure 2. *Cow & Gate MAT volume sales indexed*
*Source:* Cow & Gate Ltd. Ex-factory sales

This increase in sales ex-factory is not due only to retailers stocking up with product, but is due to an increase in consumer off-take. The Nielsen data in Table 10 shows that in the independent chemist trade following an initial stocking up in May–June 1983, stocks decreased over the period following the relaunch with sales increasing steadily.

TABLE 10:    COW & GATE STOCKS AND SALES TRENDS IN INDEPENDENT CHEMISTS

|  | Mar–Apr 1983 | May–Jun 1983 | Jul–Aug 1983 | Sep–Oct 1983 | Nov–Dec 1983 | Jan–Feb 1984 | Mar–Apr 1984 |
|---|---|---|---|---|---|---|---|
| **Stocks** | | | | | | | |
| months' supply | 3.7 | 3.5 | 2.9 | 2.9 | 2.7 | 2.7 | 2.3 |
| stocks year on year % change | −11 | +2 | −6 | −9 | −11 | +2 | +6 |
| sales year on year % change | −17 | −4 | +3 | +10 | +21 | +51 | +68 |

Source: Nielsen

Cow & Gate have increased their sales volume ahead of the market. Figure 3 shows Cow & Gate's sales performance against their major market (as monitored by Nielsen), the chemist trade (excluding Boots), and we can see that although the market has shown

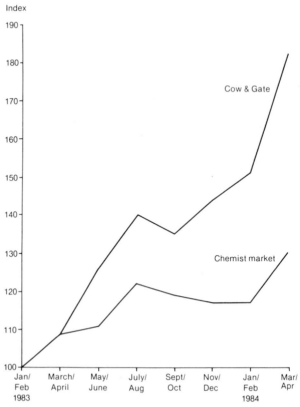

Figure 3. *Index of volume sales for Cow & Gate and babymeals chemist market  Source:* Nielsen

# May we recommend the liver and bacon to follow?

During the first few months of life, breast milk is the perfect baby food.

Then, at around 3 or 4 months, something a little more substantial is called for, or even cried for.

But liver and bacon?

Are we mad?

On the contrary. We're one of the country's longest-established makers of baby food.

Experience has taught us that most mothers prefer their breast or bottle fed babies to move from the breast or bottle to real grown-up food as naturally and smoothly as possible.

So our baby meals are designed to help you do just that.

### Learning to eat in easy stages.

Cow & Gate baby meals aren't simply little glass jars of baby food.

They're a two-stage training programme that gently paves the way to adult food.

Stage 1 meals are for babies starting out on solids, and still getting much of their nourishment from breast or baby milk.

Since your baby will only be able to suck and swallow, they're finely sieved or puréed.

Then, about 3 months later, it'll be time to move onto our Stage 2 meals.

But more about that later on.

### The first step.

If you're still troubled by the thought of a young baby tucking into liver and bacon, let us explain.

Sooner or later your baby will have to get used to adult food tastes.

And there's really no reason why it shouldn't be sooner rather than later.

That's why our Stage 1 range includes lots of grown-up tastes.

There are cereals, meats, vegetables, puddings, fruits and even artificial additive-free yogurt desserts.

So during those first few months of weaning, your baby's palate will be in for quite an education.

After 2 or 3 months, it'll be complete. And your baby will be ready to graduate to our Stage 2 meals.

### Grown-up tastes. Grown-up textures.

The next stage is to develop your baby's ability to chew.

For this reason, our Stage 2 meals are thicker, and have either meaty or fruity pieces in them.

With a little practice your baby will soon realise that food needs to be chewed before it can be swallowed.

(And knowing that babies don't like coping with too many changes at once, most of our Stage 2 meals are available in the same varieties as Stage 1.)

You wouldn't take too kindly to eating the same food day in, day out.

And neither do babies.

That's one reason why we make 23 different Stage 1 varieties, 23 Stage 2 varieties and 9 yogurt desserts.

But it isn't the only reason.

Perhaps more importantly, your baby grows so fast in the early months that a varied and well-balanced diet is essential.

What's more, it should help you avoid trouble in the years to come.

By educating your baby's palate to accept all sorts of different tastes and textures you should forestall 'food fads' later on.

### The best for your baby.

When it comes to feeding young babies, you can't be too careful.

That's something that we at Cow & Gate never ever forget.

So we buy only the best foods.

All our suppliers must meet the rigorous standards we set.

Every item of food that comes in is checked by our inspectors.

Then our chemists carry out checks of their own.

And the same thing happens all through the cooking process.

In fact, over 20% of our staff do nothing else.

### It tastes like adult food...

If you think all baby meals are bland and flavourless, you've obviously not tasted ours.

We've recently altered our recipes so our meals now taste much more akin to grown-up food.

The fact is, we've found that babies prefer them that way.

And so do mothers.

Because when the time comes to move onto adult food, the switch will be that much gentler because your baby will already be used to its taste.

### ...but it isn't adult food.

Compared to adult food, our baby meals have some very important differences.

We add a little extra vitamin C to some of our desserts to replace the amount lost in cooking.

But we don't add any salt whatsoever to any of our meals.

And none of them contain any artificial colourings, flavourings or preservatives.

But we do, however, make sure they supply protein, vitamins and minerals a growing baby needs.

### Gently does it.

We hope we've shown you how our baby meals make the journey to adult food in short, gentle steps.

If you have any queries, have a word with your Health Visitor.

Or by all means write to us at Cow & Gate, Trowbridge, Wilts BA14 8YX.

But it's worth remembering that no two babies are the same.

While you can encourage progress, never force the pace.

And be prepared for some little dramas and setbacks on the way.

But don't lose heart.

If it's a Cow & Gate meal on it shouldn't be too long before it's real liver and bacon with the rest of the family.

Two short steps to grown-up food.

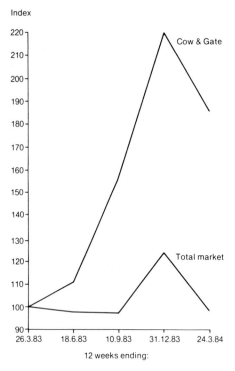

Figure 4. *Index of volume sales for Cow & Gate and babymeals market*
*Source:* RSGB Baby Panel

growth since June 1983, Cow & Gate sales have increased at a much more rapid rate. Similarly, Figure 4 plots Cow & Gate's sales against the total market, and again we can see Cow & Gate's successful growth pattern.

TABLE 11:    BABYMEALS BRAND SHARE

|  | Volume | | Value | |
|---|---|---|---|---|
|  | June 1983 | March 1984 | June 1983 | March 1984 |
|  | % | % | % | % |
| Cow & Gate | 9 | 14 | 7 | 11 |
| Heinz cans | 54 | 49 | 37 | 33 |
| Heinz jars | 9 | 11 | 8 | 9 |
| Gallia jars | 1 | * | 1 | 1 |
| Total wet meals | 73 | 74 | 53 | 54 |
| Milupa | 8 | 7 | 18 | 16 |
| Robinsons | 11 | 11 | 17 | 18 |
| Heinz weaning food | 2 | 1 | 2 | 1 |
| Boots own-label | 6 | 7 | 10 | 12 |
| Total dehydrated meals | 27 | 26 | 47 | 46 |

* Less than 0.5 per cent.
Source: RSGB Baby Panel 12 weeks ending 18th June 1983 and 24th March 1984

*Brand Share*

Again looking at Nielsen data for the chemist trade, Cow & Gate had increased their sterling brand share to a record 24.5 per cent by March–April 1984 (see Figure 5).

Cow & Gate also improved their performance within the market overall, achieving a 14 per cent share of volume and 11 per cent of market value (see Table 11).

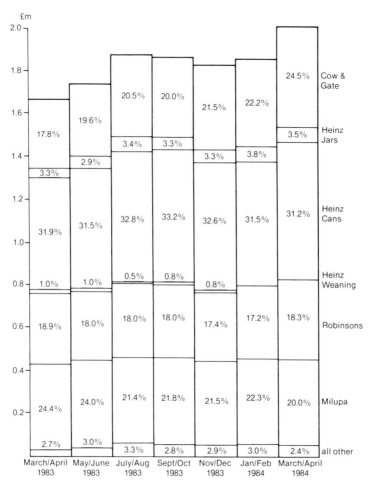

Figure 5. *GB consumer sales value share — independent chemists*
*Source:* Nielsen

*Awareness and Attitudes*

Spontaneous awareness of Cow & Gate babymeals increased by six percentage points over the year to May 1984 following nine months of advertising support. Cow & Gate showed the most improvement of all the brands monitored (see Table 12). Image measurements

TABLE 12:     SPONTANEOUS RECALL OF BABYMEALS MANUFACTURERS

|  | May 1983 | Nov 1983 | May 1984 | May 83–84 Change |
|---|---|---|---|---|
| base: | (241) | (244) | (253) |  |
|  | % | % | % | % |
| Heinz | 87 | 87 | 86 | −1 |
| Robinsons | 73 | 66 | 66 | −7 |
| Milupa | 69 | 74 | 71 | +2 |
| Cow & Gate | 60 | 64 | 66 | +6 |
| Boots | 44 | 42 | 44 | = |
| Gerber | 9 | 11 | 9 | = |
| Gallia | 8 | 13 | 6 | −2 |

Source: Audience Selection Ltd

were included in the monitor. Respondents were read out a series of statements and asked to indicate how strongly they personally felt each applied to Cow & Gate and competitive brands by awarding a mark out of ten. Cow & Gate improved their standing on the key dimensions that the advertising had aimed to address (see Table 13).

TABLE 13:     IMAGE OF COW & GATE

|  | mean rating out of 10 | | |
|---|---|---|---|
|  | May 1983 | Nov 1983 | May 1984 |
| They make products to cater for all baby's feeding needs up to the age of one year. | 7.3 | 7.4 | 7.6 |
| They are a brand you see around a great deal. | 7.2 | 7.6 | 7.7 |
| A brand I can really trust. | 7.4 | 7.3 | 7.8 |
| They are clearly the babyfeeding specialists. | 6.9 | 7.2 | 7.4 |
| They really do help your baby grow up to adult food. | 6.4 | 6.8 | 7.2 |

Source: Audience Selection Ltd

Whilst it is early days for shifting the image of Cow & Gate, the brand does appear to be moving in the right direction. This movement becomes more apparent when we look at the performance of other brands on these dimensions as a control (see Table 14). Cow & Gate consistently shows a more positive trend.

TABLE 14:    COMPETITIVE IMAGERY OF BABYMEALS MANUFACTURERS CHANGES IN MEAN RATING
OUT OF 10 MAY 1983 TO MAY 1984

| | Cow & Gate | Heinz | Milupa | Robinsons |
|---|---|---|---|---|
| They make products to cater for all baby's feeding needs up the age of one year. | +0.3 | +0.1 | +0.2 | +0.1 |
| They are a brand you see around a great deal. | +0.5 | +0.3 | +0.3 | +0.1 |
| A brand I can really trust. | +0.4 | +0.2 | +0.1 | +0.2 |
| They are clearly the baby-feeding specialists. | +0.5 | −0.7 | +0.2 | +0.3 |
| They really do help your baby grow up to adult food. | +0.8 | +0.2 | −0.2 | 0 |

Source: Audience Selection Ltd

### Penetration

Cow & Gate improved their penetration of mothers with babies aged 0–2 years from June 1983, particularly among those with older babies, the weak group prior to the relaunch.

TABLE 15:    PENETRATION OF BABYMEALS BY AGE OF BABY

| | all wet meals | | Cow & Gate | |
|---|---|---|---|---|
| | Jun 1983 % | Mar 1984 % | Jun 1983 % | Mar 1984 % |
| Total | 44 | 42 | 16 | 19 |
| 0–3 months | 34 | 33 | 16 | 16 |
| 3–6 months | 75 | 75 | 38 | 38 |
| 6–9 months | 74 | 81 | 31 | 41 |
| 9–12 months | 61 | 57 | 24 | 29 |
| 12–18 months | 35 | 30 | 6 | 10 |
| 18–24 months | 13 | 10 | 2 | 3 |

Source: RSGB Baby Panel 12 weeks ending 18th June 1983 and 24th March 1984

## EVALUATING THE ROLE OF ADVERTISING

The relaunch of Cow & Gate babymeals only commenced ten months ago. However, all data sources monitoring the effect of the relaunch have shown consistent improvements since that date.

We have already listed the four areas addressed in the relaunch: product formulation and range, distribution, price, and low levels of consumer awareness and interest which were addressed through advertising and sampling. We now assess the role of each of these areas in contributing to the success of the relaunch.

### Product Formulation and Range

Cow & Gate's product range was rationalised and new varieties were added. The increase in Cow & Gate sales was not due to a significant add-on effect of sale of new varieties;

the top-selling varieties after the relaunch were mostly those that had been favourites before; only Spaghetti Bolognaise was a top-selling newcomer (see Table 16).

TABLE 16: INDEX OF SALES INCREASE FOR TOP SIX VARIETIES MARCH–JUNE 1984 ON MARCH–JUNE 1983

|  | Index |
|---|---|
| Stage 1: | |
| 1. Chicken Dinner | 213 |
| 2. Lamb Dinner | 180 |
| 3. Chocolate Pudding | 142 |
| 4. Beef Dinner | 119 |
| 5. Peach Melba* | 206 |
| 6. Fruit Delight | 157 |
| Stage 2: | |
| 1. Spaghetti Bolognaise | new |
| 2. Beef Dinner | 162 |
| 3. Chicken Dinner | 236 |
| 4. Cherry Treat | 167 |
| 5. Lamb Dinner | 196 |
| 6. Peach Melba* | 149 |
| Yogurts: | |
| 1. Strawberry | 172 |
| 2. Banana | 193 |
| 3. Raspberry | new |
| 4. Pear | 173 |
| 5. Apple and Blackcurrant | new |
| 6. Apricot | 174 |

*Renamed from Peach Teatime Treat with Vitamin C (stage 1) and Peach Delight with Vitamin C (stage 2).
Source: Cow & Gate Ltd. ex-factory sales.

## Distribution

We mentioned earlier that Cow & Gate restructured their sales force, and aimed for an increase in grocery distribution. Although Cow & Gate have been building the drugstore

TABLE 17: STERLING PROFILE BY SOURCE OF PURCHASE

|  | total market | | Cow & Gate | |
|---|---|---|---|---|
|  | Jun 1983 % | Mar 1984 % | Jun 1983 % | Mar 1984 % |
| grocers | 35 | 32 | 9 | 8 |
| Boots | 42 | 45 | 63 | 55 |
| other chemists | 21 | 22 | 26 | 36 |
| other outlets | 2 | 1 | 2 | 1 |

Source: RSGB Baby Panel 12 weeks ending 18th June 1983 and 24th March 1984

sector, this still accounts for only a tiny proportion of the total market. Attempts to build distribution in grocers are still at an early stage and have yet to prove effective.

The increase in Cow & Gate sales has not been due to significant improvements in distribution since the increased share of purchases in other chemists (see Table 17) has been secured from a static distribution base.

*Price*

Cow & Gate's price has been reduced, but a price premium over brand leader Heinz cans has been maintained (see Table 18). If Cow & Gate's price had gone below Heinz we would have expected price to be a major influence on the recent sales success. But as

TABLE 18:    INDEX OF AVERAGE RSP PER UNIT

|  | Mar–Apr 1983 | Mar–Apr 1984 |
|---|---|---|
| Heinz can (128 g) | 100 | 100 |
| Cow & Gate 1 (78 g) | 118 | 108 |
| Cow & Gate 2 (113 g) | 129 | 119 |
| Cow & Gate Yogurt (113 g) | 121 | 115 |
| Heinz jars (128 + 170 g)* | 135 | 128 |

* Nielsen reports two sizes together as average
Source: Chemist Nielsen March–April 1983 and 1984

already stated. it was policy to maintain some price premium to add value to the product. So although the pricing was adjusted to a more realistic differential, apart from a brief initial undercutting at the early stage of the relaunch to aid rapid sales of old product, Cow & Gate did not undercut Heinz cans (regarded by the consumer as the definitive price in the market) and so is not considered to have had the major effect on sales.

*Low levels of consumers awareness and interest*

SAMPLING

Increased sampling activity brought the brand to the attention of more mothers, but the Bounty pack (estimated 40 per cent coverage) also includes competitive products which are known to be popular among mothers. Whilst an important component in the relaunch, sampling can not build brand values and is not considered to have had the major effect on sales.

THE ADVERTISING

Competitors continued to support their brands during Cow & Gate's activity and Cow & Gate only achieved a minor share of voice overall, being heavily outspent by both Heinz and Robinsons. (see Table 19.)

Figure 6 shows the relationship between the commencement of advertising activity and Cow & Gate's increase in sales. Our hypothesis for the success is that the advertising has drawn attention to the brand in it's new preferred recipe format and has added emotional

TABLE 19: SUMMARY OF COMPETITIVE ACTIVITY

| | Jul–Sep 1983 | | Oct–Dec 1983 | | Jan–Mar 1984 | | total year ending March 1984 | |
|---|---|---|---|---|---|---|---|---|
| | £000 | % | £000 | % | £000 | % | £000 | £ |
| total | 395 | 100 | 197 | 100 | 392 | 100 | 1644 | 100 |
| Cow & Gate | 55 | 14 | 102 | 52 | 55 | 14 | 212 | 13 |
| Heinz | 217 | 55 | 87 | 44 | 66 | 17 | 1021 | 62 |
| Robinsons | 119 | 30 | – | – | 257 | 66 | 376 | 23 |
| others | 4 | 1 | 8 | 4 | 14 | 4 | 35 | 2 |

Source: MEAL (TV and Press Expenditure)

values. As stated before, the packaging had not changed and so there was no reason why the consumer should realise it had improved, nor would they notice the difference as the target market is constantly changing. The advertising constantly encourages a new target group of mothers to try the brand; they are satisfied with the new formulation, repeat purchase occurs and sales continue to increase.

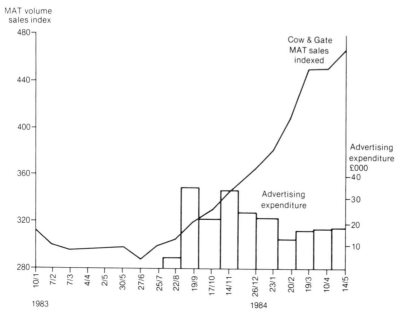

Figure 6. *Cow & Gate MAT volume sales indexed and advertising expenditure*
*Source:* Cow & Gate Ltd. Ex-factory sales actual advertising expenditure

## EFFECT OF RELAUNCH ON PROFIT

The relaunch has significantly increased profitability on Cow & Gate babymeals. In real terms, it is estimated that profit will have increased by 65 per cent on 1982 levels, representing notable return on advertising investment. (See Table 20.)

TABLE 20:    INDEX OF PROFIT CHANGE ON BABYMEALS

|        | index | adjusted index** |
|--------|-------|------------------|
| 1982   | 100   | 100              |
| 1983   | 114   | 109              |
| 1984*  | 182   | 165              |

Source: Cow & Gate Ltd
* 1984 profit estimated on first six months.
** Index adjusted to RPI at January each year.

## CONCLUSIONS AND IMPLICATIONS FOR THE FUTURE

Cow & Gate were in a weak position prior to the relaunch in August 1983. Deployment of the £200 000 advertising budget for the relaunch demanded careful attention as the advertising needed to create awareness and build brand imagery and reason to purchase among a target audience that changed every 12–16 weeks.

The low budget needed to work particularly hard for Cow & Gate in the face of being heavily outspent by competitors. By utilising specialist and selected women's colour press, the campaign efficiently reached our target audience all year round.

So overall, the success of the advertising has been due to the identification of a motivating strategy, a persuasive creative message and the placement of advertisements in relevant and efficient media.

The advertising has been identified to be the major contributor to the relaunch of Cow & Gate babymeals. It is judged to have stimulated trial of the improved product which has resulted in repeat purchase.

The relaunch activity has boosted sales to a level whereby profits generated by Cow & Gate babymeals have increased. Confidence in the contribution of the advertising to the relaunch is demonstrated by the increased budget allocated by Cow & Gate to advertising their babymeals in the remainder of 1984.

# 6
## Rebirth of the
## English Riviera

### INTRODUCTION

The 'English Riviera' and its prime resort, Torquay, have had a long history as one of the leading holiday areas in Britain.

Tourism is vital to the people of Torquay, Paignton and Brixham. Tourists spend £130 million (November 1982 figure) in this area (Torbay) and at the height of the season at least a third of Torbay's workforce are deriving their employment from tourism.

The Torbay Tourist Board is in effect a committee of Torbay Borough Council, including 12 councillors and four co-opted commercial members. Staff resources include a tourism officer, his deputy, a marketing officer and clerical assistants.

### MARKETING BACKGROUND

#### Adverse Trends

In 1982 tourism in Britain was faring poorly. The number of tourist visitors to the Torbay area had dropped from 1.3 million in 1976 to 1 million in 1982. The travel industry generally had been hard hit by the recession with fewer of the British planning to take any holiday.

Trends towards later booking of holidays were evident as people waited to see whether they could afford a holiday at all (for most, the largest single purchase in an average year) and whether by leaving booking till later they could achieve one of the 'last-minute bargains' often heavily promoted by overseas tour operators.

TABLE 1:   HOLIDAY INTENTIONS 1979-82

|  | 1979 | 1980 | 1981 | 1982 |
|---|---|---|---|---|
| base: all adults | 1971 | 2010 | 2150 | 1989 |
|  | % | % | % | % |
| intending a holiday of 4 + nights |  |  |  |  |
| yes | 64 | 66 | 62 | 58 |
| no | 28 | 29 | 29 | 35 |
| don't know | 8 | 6 | 9 | 7 |

Source: ETB Holiday Intentions Survey

The English Tourist Board's annual Holiday Intentions Survey, carried out in March each year, revealed the trends shown in Table 1: a considerable decline 1980–82 in the numbers intending to take a significant holiday. Thus, for those in the holiday business, May 1982, when the survey results were published, was a traumatic time. Not only had the number of people intending to take a holiday dropped by four percentage points for the second year in succession but there was also a hardening of attitudes *against* taking a holiday that year. People were not just unsure; 35 per cent expressed the definite view that they would *not* be taking a 'long' (4 + nights) holiday.

Over the same period, intentions to take a holiday in Britain declined sharply whereas holidays abroad were still being planned and intentions even rose between 1980 and 1981 (see Table 2).

TABLE 2:    INTENDED HOLIDAY DESTINATIONS 1979–82

|                            | 1979 | 1980 | 1981 | 1982 |
|----------------------------|------|------|------|------|
| base: all adults           | %    | %    | %    | %    |
| in Britain                 | 40   | 42   | 35   | 32   |
| in England (specifically)  | 28   | 29   | 25   | 22   |
| abroad                     | 19   | 20   | 23   | 22   |
| don't know where           | 4    | 4    | 4    | 4    |

Source: ETB Holiday Intentions Survey

Holidays abroad are most popular among the AB social groups who in 1982 were suffering less than others from economic constraints.

Holidays in Britain are particularly popular among the C2 social classes and to a lesser extent C1s and DEs, and hence were more vulnerable to the effects of adverse economic conditions on the skilled and semi-skilled worker. And as the English Tourist Board (ETB) said in 1982:

'Regional intentions to holiday show exceptionally severe decreases since last year by residents of Northern England and the Midlands while intentions have kept up much better in the relatively better-off Western and Southern parts of Britain, especially in London. Such results reflect regional variations in economic conditions.'[1]

### Effect on Torbay

As mentioned earlier the number of holiday visitors to the Torbay area had declined and in 1982 there was a considerable amount of press and TV coverage given to the problem of 'empty beds' in English resorts, with the public being urged to travel to the West Country and other tourist areas where vacant accommodation was said to be plentiful.

It was at this time (August 1982) that Pictorial Publicity[2] was appointed to handle the advertising for the Torbay Tourist Board.

However, although trends were adverse, the market for English holidays was (and is) substantial. It was estimated by the ETB that in 1983 over 25 million people would each take a week's holiday in England. The task was thus to increase the numbers coming to Torbay.

## DEFINITION OF MARKETING AND ADVERTISING STRATEGY

*Research Findings*

Research conducted by the Torbay Tourist Board and by Pictorial Publicity during the course of its 'pitch' revealed several interesting points.

1. There were two major types of Torbay holiday-makers. The first saw Torbay as the best resort area in Britain and was not interested in foreign travel; the second, while preferring to go abroad – to be sure of good weather – could not afford it at the time and saw Torbay as the closest approximation to a continental holiday available in Britain.
2. Visitors to Torbay were generally satisfied with their holidays: the beaches, the scenery, the friendly pubs, nightlife and general cleanliness all scored highly.
3. Repeat visitors constitute a high proportion of holidaymakers in Torbay. In 1981 nearly two-thirds of visitors had stayed in Torbay before.
4. There were fewer visitors than might be expected from the AB social groups, especially when compared with other West Country resorts. (These are also, of course, the type of people most likely to take second holidays.)
5. There were fewer visitors than might be expected from London and the South East. Particularly adverse economic conditions in other parts of Britain made it vital to attract holidaymakers living in London and the South East.
6. Although the Torbay area has one of the best climates in England, awareness of this was limited and it appeared that the good weather had not been effectively presented and exploited.
7. Perhaps most important of all, the name 'Torbay' was not helping the area. Even people who had visited Torquay, Paignton or Brixham had not heard of 'Torbay' and, when asked what it meant to them, thought it was a separate resort.
8. The term 'The English Riviera' on the other hand, though it had fallen out of 'official' use, was associated by many respondents with the resorts of Torquay, Paignton or Brixham and also engendered associations of a warm climate, attractive beaches, beautiful scenery and the famous palm trees.

Thus 'The English Riviera' and what it symbolises is what people would be looking for in the better type of English holiday.

*Implications and Opportunities for the Torbay Tourist Board*

Economic trends and the research data available thus indicated that:

1. Regular visitors would keep coming back to Torbay. The urgent need was to attract the first-time visitor.
2. Specific opportunities for 1983 lay with:

   (a) The holidaymaker who prefers to go overseas but in 1983 could not afford to do so. To these, Torbay offered something of the style and quite a lot of the weather associated with a continental holiday.

    (b)   The second holiday market: especially in the upper social groups, there was a burgeoning market for the shorter/second holiday, for which people are often prepared to consider destinations completely different from those preferred for their main annual holiday.

    (c)   The more affluent, especially in London and the South East.

## ADVERTISING ROLE AND OBJECTIVES

How could advertising help to achieve these marketing objectives? The advertising budget available was small – around £100 000, to include production. Its deployment had to be carefully considered to contribute towards the following objectives:

— to create (or recreate) the image of the Torbay area as the most stylish English resort area, comparable with the better continental seaside resorts;

— to widen awareness of it as a top-class seaside resort with the facilities and weather for a highly enjoyable holiday, so as to attract, in particular, more first-time visitors.

— to help Torbay reach its potential among the higher social classes and the more prosperous areas of London and the South East.

## THE ADVERTISING ROUTE

When the advertising tasks are defined as creating a wider awareness and better image of a product, the media planner's mind turns primarily to TV, the most powerful medium for achieving such tasks. However, on a small budget such as Torbay's there was obviously no question of producing a full-scale TV commercial or of buying adequate airtime to achieve the necessary coverage. The chosen route was therefore as follows:

— to produce a stylish brochure, with details of Torbay's facilities and accommodation, which would also make a significant contribution to the image-building task.

— to advertise by inviting the public to send for this brochure, deploying the advertising budget to buy a large number of relatively small spaces in appropriate publications and partial TV coverage of the country using a very simple and low-cost ten-second commercial.

To make advertising work in such modest spaces and in a very short commercial it was absolutely essential to develop a distinctive 'branding' device for Torbay which would economically and effectively convey the identity of the area and something of its characteristics.

## AGENCY'S ADVERTISING RECOMMENDATIONS

### Creative

The agency's creative recommendation was based on the opportunity to use two special 'properties' that were unique to Torbay in order to create an easily recognisable identity device which also communicated the desired image of the area.

## THE ENGLISH RIVIERA
TORQUAY · PAIGNTON · BRIXHAM

Send for our free 208 page colour brochure.
The English Riviera, Dept. No. DE1, Torquay TQ2 5JG.
Telephone 0803-211211 (24 hours).

The first of these 'properties' was the name 'The English Riviera' which was already understood by the public to denote the Torbay area. The word 'Riviera' clearly also invites the comparison with the resorts of other, continental, 'rivieras' – a comparison that we were not afraid to encourage.

The second 'property' was the palm tree image. This had been used before in a humorous way and was closely associated with the Torbay resorts. The agency planned to represent it so that it projected the panache and climate of a stylish continental resort.

Thus it was recommended that for the purpose of communicating with the holiday-taking public the name 'Torbay' should be dropped, as it appeared to be meaningless, and that 'The English Riviera' should be revived as the name for the area. This name in conjunction with the palm device would neatly and economically express the values we wished to associate with the area: those of being a warm, sunny resort which, though in England, offered much that was comparable with the continent.

These recommendations were accepted, and after the agency's appointment John Gorham was commissioned to produce the definitive expression of this identifying combination. Subsequently, this device was used for the cover of the 1983 brochure, and throughout the 1983-84 advertising.

For the 1984 Brochure and poster, the palm tree device was used in a different way to provide continuity of imagery while avoiding mere repetition.

*Media*

The agency's media recommendations for 1983 were to use a combination of appropriate national press, and TV, in regions of particular importance. In brief, the rationale for this combination was that while national TV could not be afforded, national press obviously provided a certain level of national coverage. However, there were good marketing reasons for using TV regionally, particularly since a key objective was to attract more interest in Torbay from London and the South East. TV achieves high audience coverage and generates awareness quickly, and for the holiday advertiser it has the added advantage of a telephone answering service for brochure requests.

The media schedule for December 1982–March 1983 can be summarised as follows:

PRESS

| | |
|---|---|
| 10 cm × 2 cols: | *Daily Mail* |
| | *Daily Express* |
| | *Sunday Mirror* |
| | *Sunday People* |
| | *News of the World* |
| | *Sunday Express* |
| | *Sunday Times* |
| | *Mail on Sunday* |
| various sizes up to ¼ page: | *Radio Times* |
| | *TV Times* |

# Which Riviera has 22 miles of unspoilt coastline?

Send for our free 248 page colour brochure. There's something for every-one from grand hotels to campsites, apartments to caravans.

Name_____

_____

Address_____

_____

_____

NW/2

Send to:
The English Riviera, Torquay TQ1 3EY.
Telephone: 0803-211211 (24 hours).

THE ENGLISH
RIVIERA
TORQUAY · PAIGNTON · BRIXHAM

| single buyline: | *Readers Digest* | |
| approximate total press cost: | | £60 800 |

| | TV | |
| 10 seconds | London | |
| | Midlands | |
| | South | |
| achieving 250 adult TVRs over 3 weeks | | |
| approximate TV cost | | £37 400 |

| Total advertising cost for December 1982–April 1983 (excluding production) | £98 200 |

The success of this advertising activity will be expanded upon later but first we will discuss how the campaign was continued and modified for 1984.

Based in detailed coupon response analysis of publications used in 1983, a 1984 media plan was drawn up. Budget constraints ruled out TV in London and the South and so in 1984 TV was concentrated on Central (Midlands) and on Yorkshire.

To provide some extra coverage of holidaymakers in prime target areas, national press was supplemented by posters in the London Underground in March 1984 to coincide with the English Riviera display at the Ideal Home Exhibition, and posters were used again in London in July 1984 to pick up this major late-booking market, made even more important with the impact of the miners' strike in the North and Midlands.

The media used for the 1983–84 peak booking season were:

PRESS

*Radio Times* – Christmas edition
*Radio Times/TV Times* English Tourist Board feature
*Sunday Express Magazine* (colour)
*Readers Digest*
*TV Times*
*Daily Mail*
*Daily Express*
*Sunday Express*
*News of the World*
*Sunday Mirror*
*Daily Mirror*
*Sunday People*
*Mail on Sunday*
*Sun*

*Woman, Woman's Own, Woman's Weekly,*
*Woman's Realm,*
*Mother*

*Summertime Special*
*England Holidays 1984*

Local Press: a number of local and regional newspapers, mainly in the North and West Midlands, to tie in with local exhibitions featuring the English Riviera.

approximate total cost                                              £ 87 000

TV

10 seconds:                    Central (Midlands)
                               Yorkshire
achieving 300 adult TVRs over 2 weeks
approximate TV cost                                                £ 22 000

LONDON UNDERGROUND

4-sheet posters
approximate cost                                                   £  6 000

total advertising cost for December 1983–March 1984 (excluding production)                                                £115 000

## RESULTS OF THE ADVERTISING

*Introductory Note*

There are a variety of possible ways of measuring the success of an advertising campaign. Ideally, in the case of the Torbay Tourist Board, we would have liked to have had:

— *tracking* studies of awareness of Torbay, attitudes towards taking holidays there, and

awareness of the advertising spanning the seasons before and after the adoption of the new approach recommended by Pictorial;
— estimates of the *'fullness' of the resorts* (such as bed occupancy rates);
— an analysis of *bookings by source of enquiry* to assess the effectiveness of the advertising in placing the brochure in the hands of the most appropriate target groups.

However, one of the problems often encountered when working with relatively small advertising budgets is that the cost of market research surveys can be wholly disproportionate to the size of the marketing budget and is hard to justify, given that it represents money deducted from the funds available for advertising space or brochure production.

In this case, estimates of resort 'fullness' would not prove the effectiveness of the advertising, since 1983 saw relatively good summer weather and this will have boosted the holiday trade. However, Torbay does appear to have outperformed other English resorts in 1983 according to comments made by UK Tourism Resort Officers.

More feasible in theory would be an analysis of accommodation bookings by source of initial enquiry. Possibly a panel of hotels, guest houses, proprietors of holiday flats, and so on, could be set up, but this has not been done so far. It would require a considerable amount of effort on the part of the small team of marketing professionals employed by the Torbay Tourist Board, plus commitment from the hoteliers, landlords and landladies on such a panel.

These observations are made because by the standards of large national advertisers with multi-million pound budgets, the data available to prove the effectiveness of the advertising for the Torbay Tourist Board may well appear rather 'thin'. It consists of brochure enquiries resulting mainly from *direct response* to the advertising. We cannot *prove* that any particular proportion of these brochure enquiries resulted in bookings, and therefore directly benefited Torbay. But it is worth noting that brochure enquiries are a pure, if limited, measure of the *advertising's* effectiveness. There is no 'interference' such as can be caused by distribution difficulties or competitive activity as in the case of sales of a retail product.

Further, since we are dealing with enquiries during the winter–spring booking season, the results are unaffected by the weather which obviously has a crucial effect on the business in a total holiday season and could, whether good or bad, mask the effects of the advertising campaign.

*Analysis of Response to Advertising*

PERIOD COVERED

This analysis deals with the peak winter–spring holiday booking season, that is, from December to April each year. In all years, efforts have been made to attract 'late bookers' by further bursts of activity in early and mid-summer. Activity during these late booking periods has been diverse and we do not feel that valid year-on-year comparisons can be made. Hence, we have confined the results analysis to the peak December–April booking season in each year:

(a)   1981–82   Prior to appointment of Pictorial Publicity

(b)   1982–83 ⎫
             ⎬ Pictorial's tenure of account
(c)   1983–84 ⎭

RESULTS ACHIEVED

Response analysis is based on two sources of enquiry: first, coupon response to advertise-ments, and second, enquiries to the 24-hour Ansaphone number included in the adver-tisements, and to the TV answering services. It *excludes* enquiries made directly to the Tourist Board's information centres. (Some of these might have been attributable to the advertising but it would not be valid to assume that *all* would be so attributable.)

TABLE 3:   TORBAY TOURIST BOARD—ADVERTISING RESPONSE 1981–82
           TO 1983–84

|                                    | 1981–82 | 1982–83  | 1983–84  |
| ---------------------------------- | ------- | -------- | -------- |
| December–January                   | 28 805  | 32 078   | 51 025   |
| February                           | 10 840  | 14 913   | 23 805   |
| March–April                        | 8 399   | 14 038   | 8 830    |
| total December–April               | 48 044  | 61 029   | 83 660   |
| Percentage change year-on-year     |         | +27.0%   | +37.1%   |
| index (1981–82 = 100)              | 100     | 127      | 174      |

Source: Torbay Tourist Board Statistics

Table 3 shows that the levels of response in 1982–83 were 27 per cent up on the previous year's figures; and in 1983–84 a further 37 per cent increase was achieved.

### Results in Relation to Advertising Budgets

It would hardly be fair to claim that advertising had been more effective than in previous years if the budget had substantially increased. To prove that it is the advertisements themselves that have succeeded, it is necessary to analyse cost per response and/or response per pound spent. This is the subject of the following analysis.

Different agencies can obtain different levels of media discount, so to avoid distortions from this source the analysis is based on advertising spend as reported by MEAL (hence discrepancies occur with the budgets given on page 99).

Two analyses have been conducted; the first uses quoted MEAL figures, the second quotes expenditure at 1982 media costs with subsequent years adjusted for media cost inflation (using the Advertising Association's inflation estimates).

UNADJUSTED EXPENDITURE

Table 4 shows that Pictorial's campaign not only achieved increases in response but did so in spite of lower expenditure in 1982–83 and a relatively modest increase in 1983–84 over 1981–82. Further, the cost per response was reduced by more than a third with corresponding increases in the returns per pound spent.

TABLE 4: ADVERTISING EXPENDITURE AND RESPONSE 1981-82 TO 1983-84

|  | 1981-82 | 1982-83 | 1983-84 |
| --- | --- | --- | --- |
| advertising expenditure | £108 800 | £86 400 | £125 300* |
| percentage change on 1981-82 |  | −21% | +15% |
| responses | 48 044 | 61 029 | 83 660 |
| percentage change on 1981-82 |  | +27% | +74% |
| responses per £ spent | 0.44 | 0.71 | 0.67 |
| percentage change on 1981-82 |  | +61% | +52% |
| cost per response | £2.26 | £1.42 | £1.50 |
| percentage change on 1981-82 |  | −37% | −34% |

* MEAL plus posters not recorded by MEAL

### ADJUSTED FOR INFLATION

The increased response rate per pound and reduced cost per response become more dramatic when expenditure is adjusted for media cost inflation (see Table 5.)

TABLE 5: ADVERTISING EXPENDITURE AND RESPONSE 1981-82 TO 1983-84— ADJUSTED FOR INFLATION

|  | 1981-82 | 1982-83 | 1983-84 |
| --- | --- | --- | --- |
| advertising expenditure (MEAL) at 1982 prices | £108 800 | £77 481* | £102 800* |
| percentage change on 1981-82 |  | −29% | − 6% |
| responses | 48 044 | 61 029 | 83 660 |
| percentage change on 1981-82 |  | +27% | +74% |
| responses per £ spent | 0.44 | 0.79 | 0.81 |
| percentage change on 1981-82 |  | +80% | +84% |
| cost per response | £2.26 | £1.27 | £1.23 |
| percentage change on 1981-82 |  | −44% | −46% |

* adjusted by Advertising Association press inflation factors. 1983-84 also includes posters not recorded by MEAL to which inflation factor has not been applied.

### Holiday Intentions 1984

As a final note, it is worth quoting from the 1984 English Tourist Board Holiday Intentions Survey. Overall, the numbers intending to take a holiday of four or more nights rose to 61 per cent in 1984 from the 58 per cent and 57 per cent recorded in 1982 and 1983. But intentions to holiday in *Britain* have remained *level* in 1982-84 and England's popularity remains in long-term decline (see Table 6).

'Britain in general and England in particular are no more popular as holiday destinations in 1984 than they were in 1983 and the year before.'[3]

The success of Pictorial Publicity's advertising in arousing interest in holidays in Torbay – 'The English Riviera' – has thus been achieved against a background of continued British apathy towards holidaying in Britain.

TABLE 6:    HOLIDAY INTENTIONS 1981–84

|  | 1981 | 1982 | 1983 | 1984 |
|---|---|---|---|---|
| base: all adults | 2150 | 1989 | 1978 | 2189 |
|  | % | % | % | % |
| intending a holiday of 4+ nights | 62 | 58 | 57 | 61 |
| in Britain | 35 | 32 | 33 | 32 |
| in England (specifically) | 25 | 22 | 24 | 23 |
| abroad | 23 | 22 | 22 | 26 |
| don't know where | 4 | 4 | 2 | 3 |

Source: ETB Holiday Intentions Survey 1984

## CONCLUSION

Although the marketing objective was complex, the role of advertising for the Torbay Touring Board could be reduced to two tasks.

1. To create a distinctive identity and image for the area – an image which evoked the right associations of weather and style.
2. To put the Torbay Tourist Board's brochure into the hands of the right target audience.

Because of prohibitive cost, no consumer survey data was available to show whether or not the British holidaymaker's view on 'The English Riviera' had changed. However, the response figures, particularly when analysed in terms of cost per response and response per pound spent, indicated that the advertising created by Pictorial had proved highly successful and cost effective in meeting the needs of the Torbay Tourist Board and reviving interest in 'The English Riviera'.

## REFERENCES

1. *Holiday Intention Survey*, English Tourist Board, 1982, page 5.
2. Now Travis Dale & Partners.
3. *Holiday Intention Survey*, English Tourist Board, 1984, page 6.

# 7

# TSB's School Leaver Campaign, 1984–85

## BACKGROUND

The TSB has its origins in the Industrial Revolution and in the development of independent trustee savings banks operating as small savings institutions. From the early informal links between these banks, which at one time numbered over 600, the movement coalesced by association and amalgamation into the TSB Group as it is today, with just four banking companies: TSB England & Wales, TSB Scotland, TSB Northern Ireland and TSB Channel Islands.

The pace of change accelerated in the 1960s, in response to consumer needs for wider and more flexible money services. TSB introduced cheque accounts in 1965, in addition to its previous savings accounts, followed by personal lending and overdrafts, a credit card (Trustcard), mortgages, life, household and motor insurance, and the development of commercial and corporate services. Today's TSB offers the full range of services of a major banking and financial group and competes on equal terms with other major High Street banks.

This case history deals with one particular marketing operation out of the many that the TSB conducts: the recruitment of new customers among school leavers, by TSB England & Wales.

## RECRUITMENT STRATEGY

The TSB Group handles more than 13 million accounts on behalf of some 6 million customers. The profile of this customer base is less middle-class oriented than the other High Street banks, which is understandable given the origins of the TSB and its reputation as the 'people's bank'. Less understandable – and a source of concern – is the fact that the customer profile is also older than the other banks.

All the High Street banks compete intensely for share of new accounts opened. Since the main opportunity to recruit new customers is to catch them when they first come to need banking services, this competition is directed chiefly at the youth market. Half the new cheque accounts opened each year are owned by people under the age of 25.

To redress the imbalance in its customer age profile, the TSB needed to gain an above-average share of new youth accounts. But there was a severe problem. The other banks had traditionally directed most of their activity towards the student market: those going on to higher education at university and polytechnic, and subsisting on a student grant. These young people, it was judged, would become valued customers in the future. But TSB's share of the student market was weak, largely because of a lack of conveniently accessible on-campus branches. These had become very expensive both to establish and to operate.

In 1983, when reviewing their recruitment strategies, the TSB decided that the heavy investment needed to raise their share of the student market could not be justified. Instead, they decided to focus attention on the remaining three in four school leavers who were not going on to higher education and were available for full-time employment. Individually, members of this group might not present as good a potential source of profitable business in the future as the higher-flying students (though that point is debatable), but in quantity they amply made up for any shortfall in quality. Moreover, much less marketing activity from the banks as a whole had been addressed specifically to school leavers. They presented a relatively untapped opportunity.

Table 1 shows banks' advertising expenditures in TV and press, as reported by MEAL, on campaigns directed at the various parts of the youth market. Most is spent on student recruitment. TSB has concentrated on school-leavers.

TABLE 1:  BANKS' ADVERTISING EXPENDITURES FOR YOUTH MARKET (TV AND PRESS)

|  | 1983 £000 | 1984 £000 | 1985 £000 | 1985 Media |
|---|---|---|---|---|
| Barclays: |  |  |  |  |
| School leavers | 464 | 339 | 603 | TV |
| Students | 622 | 212 | 781 | TV/Press |
| Young adults | – | 839 | 1222 | TV |
| Lloyds: |  |  |  |  |
| Students | 341 | 448 | 266 | Press |
| Midland: |  |  |  |  |
| School leavers | 303 | 347 | – |  |
| Students | 347 | 342 | 615 | Press |
| Young adults | – | – | 88 | Press |
| Nat West: |  |  |  |  |
| 'On Line' savings a/c | 633 | 751 | 149 | Press |
| School leavers | 246 | – | – |  |
| Students | 672 | 708 | 966 | Press |
| Young adults | – | – | 1168 | TV |
| TSB: |  |  |  |  |
| School leavers | – | 453 | 1316 | TV/Press |

Source: MEAL

The marketing strategy for youth recruitment in 1984/85 was therefore defined as follows:

*Target Audience*

15 to 19-year-old school leavers:

— Going into full-time employment (primary target).
— Going on to higher education (secondary target).

*Objectives*

1.  Increase the number of new cheque accounts opened by school leavers with the TSB. (Progress in 1984 led to a more specific target of 79 000 new accounts in 1985.)
2.  Increase total awareness and, in particular, the salience (unprompted awareness) of TSB, among the target audience.
3.  Enhance the TSB's image as efficient, warm, friendly and welcoming to school leavers.

It should be borne in mind that this was just one of several simultaneous strands of marketing activity. Each campaign had its own strategy and objectives. At the same time, each campaign also had to contribute towards the corporate whole. The bank is the brand. And every element of each piece of marketing activity has to be true to the brand.

## COMMUNICATIONS STRATEGY

Within the 15 to 19 target age range, this new strategy had shifted the primary emphasis away from the student (18 to 19) to the school leaver (16 to 18). Purely in years, the difference is small. But, as any parent of grown-up children will confirm, the difference in experience, in maturity and in outlook is enormous. Our communications strategy had to be appropriate to the new younger target.

Research confirmed that these school leavers are tugged in two different directions. On the one hand, they need to demonstrate their new independence (from school and parental 'authority') by publicly rejecting the mores of the previous generations. This is clearly visible in how they present themselves (dress, hairstyle, make-up), in the music styles they go for, and in the way they use language and slang. On the other hand, having money of one's own, and being able to handle it sensibly, are also outward symbols of being adult and independent. So there is less rejection of expert advice on money matters, provided it is neither authoritarian nor too overt. In this respect, banks are regarded with a mixture of respect (they are experts) and fear (they appear forbidding and difficult to approach).

We needed a communications strategy that would dissipate the fear without damaging the respect.

We had one advantage. The TSB image was less firmly fixed in the traditional bank mould than its competitors. It was already less unapproachable. We could capitalise on this *if* we could find a means of communicating with school leavers in a style of language that struck a chord with them, and which avoided being either patronising or false.

The solution adopted was a carefully tailored mix of a promotional package, conventional media advertising and a new and unconventional medium. Each of these elements had a different and specific role to play. But each was dovetailed in with the others to work as a whole.

The component parts were as follows (and see Table 2 on page 106)

*Promotional Package*

A package of incentives when you first open a cheque account is usual in this market. Aimed primarily at students, such incentives have typically included, for example, free student rail-cards, temporary overdraft facilities at special student rates of interest, and discounts on appropriate merchandise. For school leavers a different package was devised.

In 1984 this package consisted of a promise of three years' free banking (while in credit) plus discounts on top LP or cassette albums and on personal hi-fi equipment and keyboards, as well as all the usual banking services.

For 1985 the package was further expanded to include, in addition to free banking, a discount card for use in Virgin music stores, a mail order programme offering savings on records, cassettes and videos, and discounts on Yamaha and other musical instruments.

*TS Beat*

Continuing the music theme that was central to the operation, TS Beat was devised as a free magazine for specific and carefully targeted circulation. Copies were distributed to secondary schools, to sixth form and further education colleges, to youth clubs, leisure centres and YMCA clubs, to careers officers, youth advisers, leisure officers in local authorities, and to universities, polytechnics and teacher training colleges. All of these were distributed in the quantities requested by the recipients when they answered a prior mailing shot. In general, the response to this mailing was gratifying: about 35 per cent of schools, for example, wrote back requesting copies. TS Beat was also made available at rock concerts and dispensed, in large quantities, through TSB branches.

The magazine runs to three editions a year, distributed during March, June and September, and is now in its third year of publication. Each edition consists of up to 1 million copies, and total distribution has been 2.3 million in 1984 and again in 1985.

Primarily devoted to 'chart' music matters and written in the popular music magazine idiom, TS Beat also carries articles on financial matters for the school leaver. And it carries advertisements for TSB banking services and the TSB promotional offers.

*Conventional Media Advertising*

The primary medium in 1984 and 1985 was television, with a commercial in the style of the overall 'The bank that likes to say Yes' campaign, but recognisably addressed to the youth market (see opposite). It emphasised the free banking offer, the availability of cheque guarantee and Speedbank cash dispenser cards, and the music and Virgin discount card offers. It also cross-referred to TS Beat and its availability in bank branches.

In 1984 TV advertising was concentrated into bursts: in June, September and (to a lesser extent) December. The results in terms of accounts opened led to a different timing in 1985: a continuous low-level campaign from July to September. This difference in timing played a significant part in evaluating advertising's contribution to the success of this marketing pro-gramme, as will be discussed later. Supporting media used were cinema, teenage and music magazines, and radio in selected areas.

The advertising's 'tone of voice' was adjusted to fit the medium. Just as TS Beat adopted the popular music magazine idiom, so the magazine and radio advertisements were written in the language of the teenage culture, whereas for the TV and cinema media, with their wider audiences, the commercials were in TSB's usual brisk, modern and youthful (but not teenage) style.

A scene from the 'youth' commercial

'The bank that likes to say Yes'

TABLE 2: TSB AVERTISING

|  | 1984 | | 1985 | |
| --- | --- | --- | --- | --- |
| Television (adult TVRs) | June | 280 | | |
| | | | July | 220 |
| | | | Aug | 280 |
| | Sep | 180 | Sep | 50 |
| | Dec | 90 | | |
| Teenage/music magazines | June–Sep | | July–Sep | |
| Cinema | June–Aug | | July–Sep | |
| Radio (selected stations) | July | | Aug–Sep | |
| TS Beat (000 distributed) | Mar | 800 | Mar | 1000 |
| | Jun | 1000 | Jun | 1000 |
| | Sep | 500 | Sep | 300 |

## RESULTS: ACCOUNTS OPENED

Results exceeded expectations. From a total of 33 000 new youth accounts opened in 1983, when no advertising was specifically addressed to school leavers, the number doubled in the first year of the campaign to 66 000. The target then set for 1985 (79 000) was handsomely exceeded, with 126 000 new accounts. Figure 1 graphs the monthly results. It is noticeable that the largest increases in both years coincided precisely with the start of television advertising.

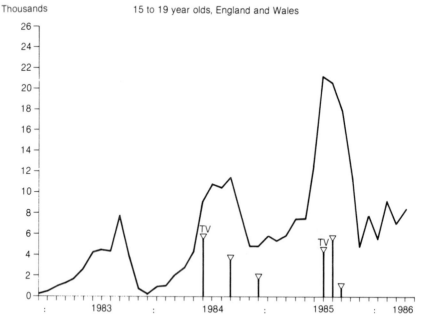

Figure 1. *TSB youths accounts opened*
Source: TSB

There is one complicating factor in the data. A new monthly reporting system for youth market accounts was introduced at the start of 1985, and there is evidence that this improved the correct classification of new accounts at branch level. But by no stretch of the imagination could this account for more than part of the recorded rise in new youth accounts in 1985. And even if 1983/84 were somewhat under-recorded, this does not detract from the 1985 performance. In a year when 783 000 youngsters left school in England and Wales, of whom perhaps half would open a bank account, a recruitment score of 126 000 represents a very large share.

Consumer research evidence confirms this. Since 1983, TSB's share of accounts opened by 16 to 20 year olds in the past year has trebled to reach 22 per cent (Figure 2), which has raised the bank's overall share of a market sector that has itself been growing (Figure 3).

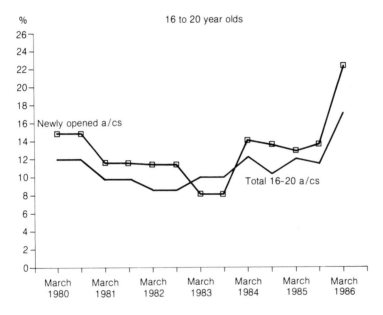

Figure 2. *TSB share*
Source: NOP Financial Survey

Analysis by TSB of their internal 1985 youth market statistics shows that at the time of account opening, approximately:

— 18 per cent were still at school.
— 50 per cent were in full-time employment.
— 10 per cent were in full-time further education.
— 15 per cent were neither studying nor in employment.
— 7 per cent insufficient data to classify.

This is confirmed by market research data (Table 3). TSB's share of new accounts opened by the student market remained weak at 5 per cent. But share among those who had gone into employment was no less than 32 per cent, nearly twice as high as the next best bank. The strategy of going for the school leaver market worked, and worked very successfully. TSB

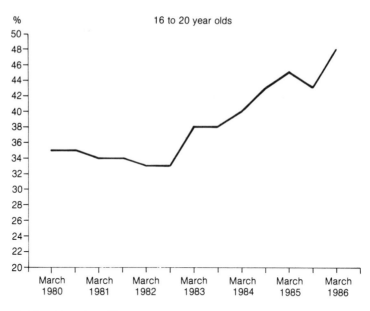

Figure 3. *Cheque account ownership*
Source: NOP Financial Survey

gained the largest share and, by implication, contributed substantially to the growth of the banking habit among these youngsters.

TABLE 3:   BANKS' SHARES OF SCHOOL LEAVERS' ACCOUNTS, 1985

|  | In first year of full-time employment (%) | In first year of further education (%) |
|---|---|---|
| Have current account with: | | |
| TSB | 32 | 5 |
| Bank A | 18 | 27 |
| Bank B | 14 | 18 |
| Bank C | 13 | 34 |
| Bank D | 12 | 23 |

Source: Millward Brown School Leavers' Study; RSL Student Banking Survey

## HOW DID IT WORK?

### Awareness

Consumer awareness and knowledge of TSB has not kept up with its remarkable metamorphosis over the last two decades into a major full-service bank. Spontaneous awareness of TSB, for instance, has lagged behind the other High Street banks: it does not spring as readily to mind as do Barclays, NatWest, Midland or Lloyds.

Among school leavers, however, there have been marked changes during 1984–85. Spontaneous awareness of the bank is catching up (Figure 4). Awareness of TSB advertising has overhauled the field and is now ahead of all four competitors (Figure 5). And, similarly, awareness of TSB's promotional schemes for school leavers has risen higher than any of the competitors (Table 4).

Comparing all three indices (Figure 6) shows the close correlation between the rise in spontaneous awareness of TSB and the rises in awareness of its advertising and promotional activity. Correlation, of course, does not prove causation. But it is difficult to see how awareness of the bank could have risen except as a result of its advertising and promotions, which are its public face. Few 'unbanked' school leavers ever go into bank premises, except perhaps with their parents. And, as we shall see, the majority of TSB's new young customers came from homes which did not previously bank at the TSB.

We concluded that the second objective, that of raising the awareness and salience of the bank, had been successfully achieved by the campaign.

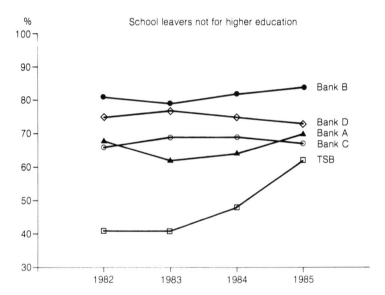

Figure 4. *Spontaneous awareness of banks*
*Source:* Millward Brown

TABLE 4:  AWARENESS OF SPECIAL SCHEMES FOR SCHOOL LEAVERS

| | *School leavers not going on to higher education* | | |
| | 1983 | 1984 | 1985 |
| | % | % | % |
|---|---|---|---|
| Aware of schemes offered by: | | | |
| TSB | 35 | 45 | 56 |
| Bank A | 20 | 22 | 28 |
| Bank B | 22 | 46 | 46 |
| Bank C | 10 | 16 | 21 |
| Bank D | 16 | 21 | 21 |

Source: Millward Brown

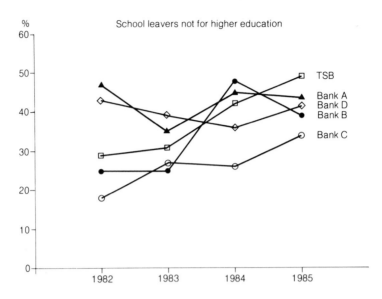

Figure 5. *Advertising awareness*
Source: Millward Brown

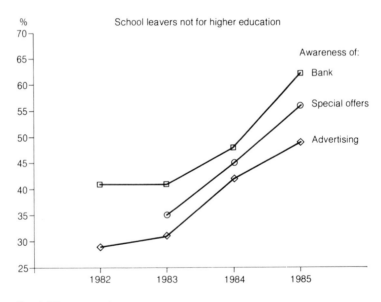

Figure 6. *TSB awareness growth*
Source: Millward Brown

*Why School Leavers Chose TSB*

The expansion in recruitment brought in new customers from sections of the population where the TSB would not traditionally have been the first choice. We took the largest share of those from ABC1 homes, as well as C2DE (Table 5). Whilst successfully retaining the loyalty of most of the teenagers whose parents banked with the TSB, we also succeeded in breaking down, to a markedly greater extent than any other bank, the second generation loyalty of those whose parents banked with the competitors (Table 6).

TABLE 5:   SHARE OF NEW ACCOUNTS, BY CLASS

| | School leavers in first year of full time employment, 1985 | | |
| | All | ABC1 | C2DE |
| | % | % | % |
| Have current account with: | | | |
| TSB | 32 | 28 | 35 |
| Bank A | 18 | 20 | 17 |
| Bank B | 14 | 14 | 14 |
| Bank C | 13 | 19 | 9 |
| Bank D | 12 | 11 | 13 |

Source: Millward Brown

TABLE 6:   SECOND GENERATION BANKING

| | School leavers in full-time employment, with current account, 1985 | | | | |
| | TSB | Bank A | Bank B | Bank C | Bank D |
| Parents bank with: | % | % | % | % | % |
| School leavers bank with: | | | | | |
| TSB | 68 | 24 | 24 | 26 | 19 |
| Bank A | 7 | 47 | 20 | 15 | 21 |
| Bank B | 4 | 9 | 28 | 20 | 9 |
| Bank C | 7 | 6 | 11 | 31 | 7 |
| Bank D | 6 | 6 | 7 | 8 | 34 |

Source: Millward Brown

Recommendation by parents or friends is probably the single most important factor affecting choice of bank. It is also a relatively weak point for TSB because of the older customer base. Research (Table 7) showed that we had overcome this weakness, by:

— Appearing more helpful and approachable than any other bank, and offering appropriate and desirable incentives;
— registering the free banking offer clearly;
— and communicating these facts and impressions through the advertising, more effectively than most other banks.

It is clear that the reason why so many teenagers chose TSB is because of the *combination* of all these factors: they noticed the communications, they liked what the bank was offering them and they felt more at ease about approaching the TSB than they did about the other banks.

The latter point, about the TSB's approachability, is easily demonstrated by looking at the images of banks among those recent school leavers who, at the time of the research (August 1985, at the height of the campaign) had not yet opened a bank account. This was the group from whom we were aiming to recruit. And in their opinion the TSB was at least the equal of

TABLE 7:   MAIN REASONS FOR CHOOSING BANK

| *School leavers in full-time employment, 1985* | | | | | |
|---|---|---|---|---|---|
| (Total mentions) | TSB | Bank A | Bank B | Bank C | Bank D |
| | % | % | % | % | % |
| *Contact/recommendation* <br> Family/friends/employer recommended <br> Previously had other account there | 87 | 114 | 111 | 119 | 98 |
| *Help young people* <br> Helpful, approachable <br> Special offers for young <br> Magazine for young | 70 | 33 | 33 | 32 | 14 |
| *Offered free banking* | 45 | 61 | 22 | 27 | 16 |
| *Convenience* <br> Branch nearby <br> Cash dispensers <br> Saturday opening | 43 | 55 | 69 | 55 | 68 |
| *Saw/heard advertising* | 23 | 22 | 8 | 11 | 5 |

Source: Millward Brown

any other bank on all the dimensions checked in research (Table 8), and markedly superior on friendliness, being interested in people even if they did not have much money, and being a good bank to save with. The third objective had been achieved.

TABLE 8:   IMAGES OF BANKS

| *School leavers, without a bank account, not going to higher education, 1985* | | | | | |
|---|---|---|---|---|---|
| | TSB | Bank A | Bank B | Bank C | Bank D |
| | % | % | % | % | % |
| Up to date | 51 | 38 | 54 | 28 | 36 |
| Interested in helping school leavers | 46 | 18 | 45 | 16 | 17 |
| A good bank to save with | 46 | 17 | 31 | 15 | 18 |
| Understand the needs of school leavers | 44 | 16 | 41 | 13 | 15 |
| A very friendly bank | 38 | 31 | 29 | 12 | 14 |
| Sort of bank I'd be happy to join | 38 | 19 | 38 | 15 | 19 |
| Treat young people like responsible adults | 36 | 19 | 35 | 12 | 16 |
| Interested in people even without much money | 33 | 20 | 24 | 18 | 13 |
| Good at explaining things | 32 | 21 | 34 | 15 | 15 |
| Sympathetic to customers' problems | 29 | 18 | 24 | 10 | 13 |

Source: Millward Brown

The image is clear; that of a bank that is genuinely sympathetic to, and understanding of, the teenager's problems and needs, without condescension. It is seen to treat young people like responsible adults – and that is something they respond to warmly.

This image appears to have been built up by all elements of the marketing programme working together, in content and in style, as a whole. Awareness was high for TSB's special magazine (TS Beat) and for the discounts on records and tapes, as well as free banking and the booklet of money-handling advice for school leavers (Table 9). All these confirmed their relevance to this target market, a relevance which will have demonstrated – better than any words could – the bank's understanding of the teenager's interests and needs. The promotional package combined desirable incentives and desired help.

TABLE 9: AWARENESS OF SPECIAL OFFERS

*School leavers, without a bank account, not going to higher education, 1985*

|  | TSB % | Bank A % | Bank B % | Bank C % | Bank D % |
|---|---|---|---|---|---|
| Special magazine for young people | 43 | 10 | 20 | 6 | 8 |
| Discounts on records and tapes | 42 | 4 | 7 | 3 | 1 |
| Booklet with practical help for school leavers | 35 | 15 | 30 | 7 | 11 |
| Free banking | 31 | 25 | 27 | 8 | 12 |
| Free banking for 2 years | 17 | 12 | 17 | 6 | 8 |
| Cash dispenser card | 23 | 23 | 35 | 17 | 22 |
| Cheque card if employed | 21 | 13 | 29 | 14 | 16 |
| Starting work kit | 13 | 7 | 17 | 4 | 5 |
| Cheaper insurance on personal goods | 9 | 2 | 6 | 4 | 5 |

Source: Millward Brown

TS Beat itself had been seen by no less than 38 per cent of school leavers, an impressive level of coverage (Table 10). Comparison of other indices among those who had seen the magazine, and those who had not, showed that it contributed significantly to raising awareness of the bank, its advertising and, in particular, its special offers, and in encouraging the choice of TSB

TABLE 10: THE TS BEAT CONTRIBUTION

*School leavers not going on to higher education, 1985*

|  | TS Beat seen % | TS Beat not seen % |
|---|---|---|
| All school leavers | 38 | 62 |
|  | (= 100) | (= 100) |
| Awareness of: |  |  |
| TSB | 71 | 56 |
| TSB offers | 66 | 50 |
| TSB advertising | 55 | 45 |
| Attitude to TSB: |  |  |
| Already have current a/c at TSB | 16 | 4 |
| Bank most likely to open account with | 16 | 6 |
| Bank would consider opening account with | 20 | 14 |

Source: Millward Brown

to open an account with. It did an excellent job of communicating information about the bank and what it had to offer and, through its tone of voice as a music magazine, in conveying a sense of empathy and understanding.

Television advertising contributed strongly to making the bank seem less forbidding and easier to walk into (Table 11), reminding school leavers about the services and incentives that the TSB offered, and raising overall awareness of the bank, in particular through association with the 'Bank that likes to say Yes' slogan (Table 12).

TABLE 11:   OPINIONS OF TV ADVERTISING

| *School leavers not going on to higher education, 1985* | | | | |
|---|---|---|---|---|
| TSB % | Bank A % | Bank B % | Bank C % | Bank D % |
| Made the bank seem friendly and approachable    44 | 44 | 26 | 25 | 19 |
| Will give people a better opinion of the bank    28 | 21 | 35 | 26 | 14 |
| Told me something about the bank I didn't know    12 | 16 | 20 | 11 | 20 |

Source: Millward Brown

TABLE 12:   SLOGAN IDENTIFICATION

| *School leavers, without a bank account, not going on to higher education, 1985* | | | | |
|---|---|---|---|---|
| TSB % | Bank A % | Bank B % | Bank C % | Bank D % |
| The bank that likes to say Yes    89 | | | | |
| Competitors' slogans | 76 | 40 | 33 | 62 |

Source: Millward Brown

All these elements combined to build a more rounded and attractive image for TSB than for any other bank. On their own, none of the elements is likely to have been as effective. Collectively, they worked extremely well. But could we in some way disentangle and separate out their respective contributions?

## WHAT EACH ELEMENT OF THE MARKETING PROGRAMME CONTRIBUTED

We formed a working hypothesis that the elements combined together as follows:

1.   TS Beat was the initial medium of communication. It reached a large audience, carried interesting and relevant information, especially about the incentive package, and began to build a sympathetic image for the TSB.

2.    The music-related incentive package was particularly appealing to the target market, combining desirable special offers with the most-needed banking services (free banking and practical advice for the new customer).

3.    The advertising raised awareness of the bank among the target market, reminded them of the services and incentives offered, and reinforced the friendly, approachable image.

4.    The sharp rise in numbers of accounts opened coincident with the start of TV (a different month in each year) indicates that the television advertising in particular acted as an action trigger. Seeing the TV commercial, after previous exposure to TS Beat, led many youngsters who had been considering opening an account (and probably putting it off out of nervousness) to take the plunge.

To investigate this further we turned to econometric modelling. This presented particular difficulties, because the 'independent' variables are not in fact independent but closely correlated one with another, in time and in function. Furthermore, the effects were lagged, but lagged differently for individual elements of the mix. Hence we found that various models could be specified, with slightly different permutations of variables and lag factors, each of which fitted the data statistically. The model finally chosen (and explained in more detail in the Appendix) was the one we judged to make the best *marketing* sense.

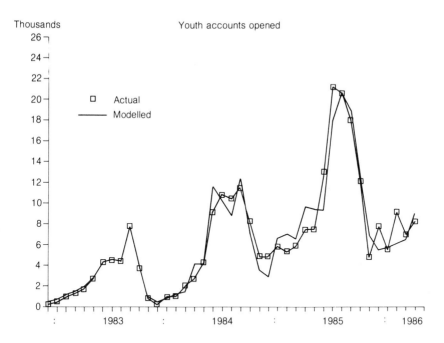

Figure 7. *Econometric model*

The model fits the data very closely ($R^2 = .930$, and see Figure 7). Its main implications are:

1.    The direct effects of TS Beat on opening new accounts were, not surprisingly, lagged. Most of the effect was felt in the month *after* distribution, the balance coming a further

month later. This makes sense. Opening a bank account for the first time is a step that requires a measure of forethought and self-preparation.

2. Most of television advertising's effect occurred in the month of transmission, supporting the hypothesis that TV was acting as a trigger mechanism. The balance of effect carried over into the two following months.

3. Given the simultaneity of all the media advertising (as well as the difficulty of expressing the *exposure* of other media schedules with anything like the accuracy of TV ratings data) we were unable to disentangle the effects of cinema, teenage press or radio from those of television. The TV variable in the model almost certainly represents the effect of the total media mix.

4. The 1984 music-based incentive package was similar in effect to previous years' offers. The expanded 1985 package, with its Virgin store discount card and Yamaha musical instrument discounts, pulled much more strongly. But because the 1985 offer started at the same time as the new monthly reporting system for youth accounts, it is not possible to separate the gains achieved by the incentive package from the effects of the improved classification of new accounts.

5. There are indications of a cumulative advertising effect, which the model fails to capture, but which is visible in Figure 7. In June 1984, when TV began, the actual number of accounts opened fell short of the model's predicted figure. In July 1985, however, the start of television produced an excess over prediction, implying that advertising's contribution to the mix had further increased in effectiveness.

6. The relative contributions of the various elements of the school leaver campaign were as follows (given the problems of specification and correlation mentioned above, these can only be taken as approximations, but we believe they are realistic estimates):

|  |  | *Accounts per year* |
|---|---|---|
| Base level (including effect of 1983/84 offers) |  | 33 000 |
| TS Beat (1984/85) |  | 10 000 |
| Advertising (TV and other media) | – 1984 | 23 000 |
|  | – 1985 | 27 000 |
| 1985 incentive package<br>New account reporting system<br>Long term cumulative advertising effect<br>(These 3 factors are inseparable) | } 1985 | 56 000 |

## CONCLUSIONS

We concluded that the expanded incentive package in 1985 had been a considerable success and the prime cause of the huge growth in new accounts. But it would not have worked anything like as effectively had the contents of the offer not been widely and attractively communicated to the target market.

To that extent, the estimate (in the previous section) of how much each element of the campaign contributed is specious. Without the special offers, the incentive would have been absent. Without TS Beat, the advertising would have been less successful in triggering action. Without advertising, the special offers would not have been widely known about. Without all the communication elements, the bank's image and salience would not have seemed so approachable and sympathetic to the school leaver.

Each element had its own role and carried it out successfully. The evidence points to the following conclusions:

1.  The incentive package, particularly in 1985, was one main discriminating factor governing school leavers' choice of bank.
2.  The second main discriminating factor – the TSB image for approachability – stemmed from the content and, especially, the style of the communication elements.
3.  Television advertising, with its coverage and visibility, was the main channel of communication. It contributed decisively to the bank's more approachable image. It reminded school leavers of the special offers. It converted interest into action.
4.  TS Beat helped school leavers to begin thinking about the benefits of a bank account, and demonstrated the TSB's interest in, and understanding of, the teenager.
5.  The supporting media also reminded school leavers of the special offers and contributed to the bank's image.

The campaign fulfilled all its objectives and surpassed its targets. It gave TSB the leading share of new accounts opened by school leavers. And it won share even from households who had no previous contact with the TSB.

Total expenditure on TSB youth marketing (advertising, brochures and TS Beat) was £1.7 million in 1985. This worked out at rather less than £14 per new account. The profitability of a new account is not usually measurable before some years have passed, but in this case it seems predictably certain that, when the final assessment of this campaign's profitability is made, the bank will say 'Yes'.

## APPENDIX: ECONOMETRIC MODEL

The model was built using monthly data from December 1982 to April 1986, 41 observations in total. The dependent variable was the monthly number of new youth accounts opened with the TSB.

Independent variables were:

*Seasonality* There is a markedly seasonal pattern, peaking in the summer months, with an additional peak in September from the student market. We took 1983 to represent the normal pattern of market seasonality in the absence of advertising support.

*TS Beat* Data used were circulations of each edition, lagged and weighted as follows (these lag factors were derived empirically from the data):

|                              |      |
| ---------------------------- | ---- |
| 1 month after distribution   | .64  |
| 2 months after distribution  | .36  |
|                              | 1.00 |

*TV Advertising* Data used were monthly adult TVRs (for England and Wales), lagged and weighted as follows (also empirically derived):

| | |
|---|---|
| month of transmission | .56 |
| 1 month later | .23 |
| 2 months later | .21 |
| | 1.00 |

Because subsidiary media appeared at the same time as the TV, it was impossible to separate their effects from that of the main medium. The TV variable is therefore almost certainly a surrogate for the total advertising effect.

*1985 Incentive Package* This was entered as a dummy, from January 1985 onwards. This, however, coincided with the introduction of the new monthly reporting system, which appears to have increased the number of youth accounts reported. It was impossible to separate these two factors, both of which are included in this variable.

Other variables examined but not included in the final model, because no significant *separate* effect could be discerned, were the 1984 incentive offer, and the supporting campaigns in teenage magazines, cinema and radio.

Because of the level of correlation that exists between the explanatory variables, the final model is just one of several possible 'best' solutions, all of them equally valid statistically, but with slightly different combinations of lag factors and variables. The final model chosen was the one that made most marketing sense. Its specifications are:

Monthly new youth accounts =

| | | *t value* |
|---|---|---|
| Constant | 301 | |
| + Seasonality: 1983 data | × .96 | (7.5) |
| + TS Beat (millions, lagged and weighted) | × 43.4 | (3.8) |
| + TVRs (lagged and weighted) | × 45.6 | (8.3) |
| + 1985 Incentive, etc. (dummy variable) | 4944 (per month) | (10.2) |
| | $R^2$: .930 | |

# 8

# The GLC's Anti 'Paving Bill' Campaign: Advancing the Science of Political Issue Advertising

## INTRODUCTION

This paper seeks to demonstrate the effectiveness of a GLC advertising campaign which aimed to counter the Government's Local Government (Interim Provisions) Bill. The Bill became known as the 'Paving Bill' because it 'paved' the way for abolition of the GLC by cancelling the GLC elections scheduled to take place in May 1985, provided that the main abolition legislation had by that time passed into law. The Bill sought to place control of the GLC in the hands of councillors nominated by the Government from May 1985 until the following year, when the authority would cease to exist and new arrangements for London's local government came into force.

The paper will attempt to demonstrate that the advertising stimulated widespread opposition to the proposed legislation – among the public, within the media, and within Parliament. Partly through the mechanism of public opinion polls, it will be shown that the advertising stimulated and influenced media coverage of the issue, thus consolidating and intensifying opposition to the Bill. The paper will hopefully demonstrate that this created the climate in which the Government's original proposals were overturned by Parliament.

For, although the Bill reached the statute book in July 1984 and thus secured the abolition of the GLC elections, it did so in amended form. The interim provisions, whereby control of the GLC was to be placed in the hands of nominated councillors, was defeated by the House of Lords and the Government was forced to grant the elected Council a stay of execution for an additional year.

In one sense this achievement may seem 'small beer'. Yet it will be shown that the scale of what the advertising achieved in stimulating public and media opposition to the Government's proposals, in transforming the issue from one of obscure local government administration into a matter of genuine and popular concern, in pushing the issue up the political agenda and in undermining confidence in the Government's local government reforms, was unique. Its effectiveness in achieving all the above is without parallel; the advertising must surely be regarded as one of the most significant campaigns in British advertising history.

## DEVELOPING A ROLE AND STRATEGY FOR ADVERTISING

To demonstrate the effectiveness of the anti 'Paving Bill' advertising it is necessary to understand how it was intended to work, and what it was designed to achieve.

When Boase Massimi Pollitt started to work with the GLC in January 1984, there was an urgent need for a judgement on what advertising might accomplish. From the beginning, qualitative research proved vital. Throughout the period from January to July 1984, the agency conducted 38 group discussions among Londoners of all political persuasions. This proved invaluable in understanding popular attitudes to the issue, in developing a strategy, and later advertising executions. In January quantitative and qualitative research revealed that abolition was of low interest to Londoners and that attitudes towards it largely reflected party political loyalties[1]. Negative perceptions (for long fostered by the press) that the GLC was synonymous with 'Red Ken', the squandering of money on dubious minorities and irresponsible meddling in national politics as demonstrated by the invitation of IRA leaders to County Hall, were both more salient and widespread than knowledge of the body's technical functions and responsibilities[2].

Against this background a number of advertising objectives were agreed.

1.  Given the Government's massive majority of over one hundred in the Commons, the strategy would have to persuade the Government that the political costs of the unpopularity that would result from pursuing its policy would outweigh any benefits of getting the proposed legislation on to the statute book without amendment[3].

2.  In order to popularise and enliven the 'Paving Bill' issue, advertising would have to demonstrate to people that 'democratic rights' lay at the heart of the debate. In January 1984, Boase Massimi Pollitt's qualitative research identified that 'democracy' had the potency to popularise the debate in a non party-political manner and to outweigh existing prejudices against the controversial Labour-controlled council[4]. The agency's qualitative research proved invaluable in 'hot-housing' arguments, and facilitating assessments of the various strategic options. It could thus be predicted that presenting abolition as a constitutional issue about the rights of every Londoner to control the running of the city promised to convert Conservative voters to opposition to the proposed reforms. This was vital if the Government was to be dissuaded from its proposed reform. The advertising was thus to perform the bold task of *changing the grounds of the debate* and of establishing new grounds on which opponents of the Government's policy could win.

3.  All of this was dependent on a vision of *how the advertising could work* in a political marketplace where the public is daily bombarded with the views of political commentators and politicians. Clearly, the commerical media value of this would be many times the media budget for any advertising. And so the advertising campaign was *designed to excite, influence and work in conjunction with other media*. The advertising would have to win other media, and also politicians, over to its point of view if its influence was not to be swamped.

Thus the campaign was intended to function as a catalyst, setting in motion a series of influences which would surround the Government and convince it that to continue to pursue its proposed reform was increasingly unwise. Conservative Party activists would become alarmed, Conservative MPs and Lords would express their concern, and all of this would put pressure on the Government. This may be represented diagrammatically:

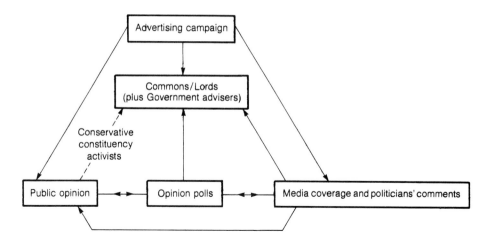

Figure 1. *Model of how the advertising could work*

It was a bold plan; arguably nothing like it had ever been attempted before. But would it work?

## CRITERIA FOR MEASURING THE ADVERTISING'S EFFECTIVENESS

The fact that advertising was designed to excite, influence, and work in conjunction with other media and the utterances of politicians themselves makes it difficult to identify its effects in isolation. Advertising effectiveness can nevertheless be demonstrated against a number of criteria, namely:

— By demonstrating that the advertising was seen by the public, the media, and the politicians.
— By demonstrating that a change in public opinion, which was reflected in opinion polls, and a related change in press coverage of the issue, can be explained only by the advertising. (To this end, extensive use is made of the MORI tracking study, conducted periodically among a representative sample of adult Londoners, and which measured awareness of the advertising and attitudes to abolition.)
— By demonstrating that the political decision makers believed that the proposed legislation had become unpopular, and that this was linked to the advertising. The understandable unwillingness of the Government and its Parliamentary supporters to be drawn on these issues force us to rely on the views of those close to, or with expert knowledge of, the political decision makers.

The Government's ulitmate decision to press ahead with the abolition of the GLC elections, and later the abolition of the GLC itself, in the face of massive opposition from the public and 'expert' opinion, was of course its choice. At the end of the day the Government runs the country, not advertising. However, the anti 'Paving' campaign appears to have done everything that could reasonably have been expected from it, and more.

## THE EFFECTS OF ADVERTISING: VISIBILITY

The salience of the advertising campaign among the public, the media and the politicians is unquestionable. The campaign started in early March, with poster locations throughout London and two press bursts during the month. Posters ran continuously until the end of June. By the beginning of April 1984, 52 per cent of adult Londoners claimed to be aware of the advertising without any visual prompting. By May this had risen to 63 per cent. Prompted awareness of the specific creative executions, copies of which are in the Appendix, was equally positive, as Table 1 reveals.

TABLE 1:  PROMPTED AWARENESS OF SPECIFIC
EXECUTIONS

|  | April (817) % | May (1048) % | July (1032) % |
|---|---|---|---|
| *(Have you seen this advertisement?)* | | | |
| 'From Now' | 26 | 40 | 36 |
| 'Kind of Place' | 23 | 40 | 42 |
| 'Petition' | 19 | 28 | 27 |
| 'Dustbin' | n/a | 25 | 31 |
| (Other) | – | – | 28 |

Source: MORI Tracking Study 1984

With such high awareness of the campaign among the general public, it followed that among political commentators and politicians, to whom the advertising was particularly heavily targeted through media-buying policy, awareness must have been almost universal. All the available evidence supports this notion of saturation coverage and universal awareness[5]. Advertisements like 'What kind of place is it that takes away your right to vote and leaves you with no say?' and 'Dustbin' thus became familiar reminders of the democratic issue. The press not only commented on the advertising but quickly came to treat it as an issue in its own right[6].

If the Government has its way there won't be any GLC elections to vote in next year. **SAY NO TO NO SAY.**

Politicians were also clearly aware of the advertising. Not only was it commented upon in the House but reports of this were carried in the press[7], and Government ministers spontaneously mentioned the advertising in public interviews[8]. In April Patrick Jenkin, Secretary of State for the Environment and the Government minister charged with seeing the 'Paving' and abolition legislation through Parliament, announced that the Government was considering the introduction of legislation to prevent local authorities spending ratepayers money on advertising 'for political purposes'. 'We have never seen a campaign of this sort before', he exclaimed[9].

## THE EFFECTS OF ADVERTISING: THE MECHANISM OF CHANGING PUBLIC OPINION

It can clearly be demonstrated that there was a marked change in public attitudes to the abolition of the GLC and of the GLC elections within the period in question, and that this can be directly linked to the advertising. Londoners' opposition to the abolition of the GLC and of the elections to it grew markedly between January and the beginning of April 1984, as Table 2 demonstrates.

In the period from January until the beginning of April, when the MORI fieldwork was conducted, the press had devoted relatively little attention to the GLC issue. Such coverage as there was had not as yet, and on balance, become critical of the Government's proposed reforms, as Table 3 indicates. One month of the anti 'Paving Bill' advertising had been the only strong influence warning of the anti-democratic consequences of the proposed legislation and it must be largely credited with having achieved these significant shifts of opinion, particularly in relation to the cancellation of the elections. Support for this contention is to be found in the MORI survey among the majority of the country's TV and national press political editors. Despite the natural inclination, among such a sample, to minimise the effects of advertising, 71 per cent claimed that the advertising campaign had played a significant role in increasing public opposition to the 'Paving Bill'.

It was vital that the advertising should stimulate and influence media coverage of the issue. It was essential that the advertising confirmed the core issue of democratic rights for journa-

TABLE 2:   APPROVAL AND DISAPPROVAL OF THE GOVERNMENTS
PLANS TO:

|  | Jan (420) % | April (817) % | May (1048) % |
|---|---|---|---|
| 1. *Abolish the GLC elections* | | | |
| approve | 16 | 14 | 13 |
| disapprove | 55 | 70 | 69 |
| no opinion/don't know | 29 | 16 | 17 |
| 2. *Abolish the GLC* | | | |
| approve | 19 | 18 | 17 |
| disapprove | 50 | 62 | 64 |
| no opinion/don't know | 30 | 20 | 18 |

Source: MORI Tracking Study

lists and political commentators, and persuaded them that the public was motivated by it – in particular by means of opinion polls. Thus press and television coverage would become critical of the proposed legislation; this would both unnerve the Government and further strengthen public opposition to the reform. There is clear evidence that all of this actually occurred.

Regrettably, detailed content analysis of television coverage is in practice impossible. However, such an analysis of the national press and London's own *Evening Standard* newspaper reveals that press coverage of the plans to abolish the GLC and its elections increased markedly from the beginning of April 1984. From that date the press coverage also became, on balance, markedly more critical of the Government's proposed reform and performance on the issue. Table 3 demonstrates this. It is based on an analysis of national newspapers, and measures coverage of the GLC issue using tabloid page sizes as the standard unit of measurement.

TABLE 3:   ANALYSIS OF PRESS COVERAGE OF GLC

| (*Note*: Units of measurement are full tabloid page size equivalents) | Jan | Feb | Mar | Apr | May | June |
|---|---|---|---|---|---|---|
| *Abolition issue* | | | | | | |
| critical of legislation | 3 | 6 | 8 | 18 | 22 | 28 |
| neutral | 4 | 2 | 4 | 6 | 6 | 4 |
| supportive of legislation | 4 | 5 | 6 | 2 | 4 | 3 |
| *Coverage of other aspects of GLC (traffic planning, women's committee, minority groups, etc.* | | | | | | |
| supportive of GLC | 2 | 2 | 4 | 1 | 8 | 4 |
| neutral | 3 | 3 | 4 | 2 | 9 | 1 |
| critical of GLC | 2 | 2 | 2 | 2 | 6 | 12 |
| *Coverage of Ken Livingstone as individual personality* | | | | | | |
| pro | 2 | 2 | 2 | 3 | 12 | 6 |
| neutral | 1 | 1 | 1 | 2 | – | – |
| anti | 3 | 3 | 3 | 1 | 2 | 2 |

The last week of March was key to this change, and the role of London's *Evening Standard* and its publication of a public opinion poll revealing increasing public opposition to the Government's proposed reforms appears to have had a seminal influence[10]. Henceforward, and from April to June, the publication of further opinion polls revealing ever stronger public opposition to the Government's proposed reforms attracted immediate and widespread press coverage that was highly damaging to the Government's case[11]. It seems likely that this regular flow of opinion poll information consolidated and intensified opposition to the proposed legislation among both public and politicians, and within the press.

Interesting support for the view that it was the advertising which initially motivated both the public, and then the media, by persuading them that democratic rights lay at the core of abolition, and that once converted the media simply reinforced this perception, is to be found in a MORI survey among most of the country's leading television and national newspaper political editors[12]. This evidence confirms that it was the advertising which converted press and television to the view that abolition was an important public issue and that 'democratic rights' lay at its core.

It has proved impossible to ascertain what influence the much-publicised movement of public opinion may have had on the critics of the proposed legislation within the Conservative party and in the House of Lords. Clearly, it can only have been an encouragement. Detailed content analysis of the press reveals that the parliamentary rebellions of senior Conservatives such as Heath, Pym, Rippon and Gilmour, and rebellions in the Lords at various stages of the Paving Bill's progress, each excited immediate and major splurges of publicity that were highly damaging to the Government's case[13].

Thus it can reasonably be claimed that from the beginning of April increases in, and consolidation of, opposition to the proposed legislation is founded on several interconnected factors – namely the nature of the press (and TV) coverage, the vociferousness and stature of the eminent critics of the legislation, the advertising, and the effect of the published opinion polls. It has also been shown that it can only have been the advertising which first stimulated public opinion, the opinion polls, and press and television coverage in an anti 'Paving Bill' direction, and so triggered the whole mechanism of opposition.

While politicians and the quality press talked of abolition almost exclusively in terms of democratic principle, qualitative information and detailed content analysis of the press reveal that first the public, and later the tabloid or popular press, also saw the issue in broader, emotional, and human terms. There was a growing feeling, even among Conservatives, that the Government was abusing its power, behaving dictatorially and selfishly, and arrogantly attempting to eliminate an organisation merely because of its political colour. The advertising was praised for capturing and projecting this feeling in March 1984[14]. Its wit and use of popular views about the remoteness, insensitivity and unaccountability of central Government seem to have helped position the GLC as being 'of the people'. In such circumstances the British public empathised with the underdog – there was growing emotional sympathy with Ken Livingstone, who was increasingly positioned as the defender of democracy and Londoners' rights.

The advertisement 'If you want me out you should have the right to vote me out', featuring Ken Livingstone, seems to have played on, and helped foster, these sentiments. Certainly it seems that advertising must have played a major role in creating these new and more positive feelings towards the GLC and its human face, Ken Livingstone[15]. Again, the press seems to have followed, rather than championed, this change of public mood – although in responding to it, it confirmed and consolidated Livingstone's new status[16]. In the coming months, the

# "IF YOU WANT ME OUT YOU SHOULD HAVE THE RIGHT TO VOTE ME OUT."

Everyone's entitled to their view. The British constitution says you express it through the ballot box.

That's the law.

Unfortunately the Government doesn't like the law as it stands in relation to the GLC.

Today the first bill relating to the abolition of the GLC gets its second reading in the House.

It's devised to wipe out next year's GLC elections. Whether you're Labour, Tory, Liberal or SDP, you'll have no say.

Not since the last World War has your statutory right to vote been withdrawn in this way.

And it's a cynical dismissal of public opinion.

In a recent MORI poll 61% of Londoners of all political persuasions said no.

Only 22%, by the way, said yes.

In every straw poll, overwhelming public opinion has said no to abolition.

On 26th March Tom King the Conservative Secretary for Employment outlined in the House the elementary rights of people to register their vote without interference.

That was in relation to the Trade Union movement.

This Government steadfastly refuses to apply the same principles to the rights of 7 million Londoners.

You may hold the view of course,

that they were voted into power democratically and have the right to do as they wish.

But, nowhere in the Tory manifesto was there a mention of abolishing your right to vote in local elections.

Ask yourself why the Government is intent on doing away with the GLC in the first place.

There has not been a single proposition motivated by the desire to improve London.

What you might have heard have been outbursts.

"Red Ken spending our money on weirdos again."

(For the record less than one

per cent of GLC expenditure is allocated to all minorities.)

Don't let bigoted arguments of this kind blind you to the real issue.

This country's centuries old democratic tradition is at stake.

Local Government is one of the checks and balances which safeguard us against the abuse of central Government power.

And it would be an abuse of power for any Government to abolish a democratic institution such as a local authority, simply because it did not like the incumbent administration.

**SAY NO TO NO SAY.**

press sometimes seemed surprised at the degree of popularity with which it now credited him, and the extent of its own volte-face.

> Only last year the plan (Abolition) seemed accepted as a popular and justified modernisation of local Government.... Yet today abolition is regarded on almost all sides as a gratuitous personal attack on a noble democratic institution. The GLC's left-wing leader, Mr Ken Livingstone, whose more lunatic activities and expenditures so delighted the Tories at the last General Election has emerged as the apostle of electoral freedom, despite having never led any party to victory at any poll. His financial irresponsibility, IRA sympathies and ratepayer support for gay co-operatives are forgotten as he covers London with posters calling on the citizenry to defend their vote.
>
> *The Economist*, 19 May 1984

In conclusion, it has been demonstrated that a marked change in public attitudes to the abolition of the GLC and its elections can be attributed to the advertising. It has also been demonstrated that the advertising – in part through the mechanism of public opinion polls – influenced media coverage of the issue which, in turn, seems to have consolidated and intensified opposition to the Government's proposed legislation[17]. The advertising triggered this opposition by convincing the public, the media, and perhaps many politicians, that the issue was one of democratic principle. It also stimulated emotional sympathy with the GLC 'underdog' in what it portrayed as its unequal and hence unfair fight with central Government.

Such principle and feeling was capable of transcending party political loyalties and converting Conservative voters to opposition to the proposed reform, as the MORI Tracking Study confirmed.

TABLE 4: ATTITUDES OF CONSERVATIVE VOTERS TO GLC ABOLITION

|  | January % | May % |
|---|---|---|
| Disapprove | 26 | 34 |
| Approve | 42 | 44 |
| Neither/nor | | |
| Don't know | 32 | 21 |

## THE EFFECTS OF ADVERTISING: IMPACT ON THE DECISION MAKERS

Beyond all reasonable doubt the advertising campaign and the other media coverage which it influenced had the effect of undermining Conservative Party and Government confidence in the legislation, and created the climate in which the Bill was defeated by the Lords on 28 June 1984.

Attempts to question Conservative MPs and members of the House of Lords on the impact of the anti-abolition campaign on their own attitudes and behaviour have proved abortive. Non-co-operation was the predominant reaction. Clearly there are vested interests which work against admissions of being influenced by outside 'propaganda', and also party political considerations that might also taint any responses. Given these problems, the best opportunity to ascertain MPs' opinions in a vaguely unguarded way – namely through MORI's annual omnibus to a representative cross-section of members of Parliament – yielded a remarkable result. Over one hundred MPs were sampled in June 1984 and asked whether they considered abolition of the GLC and metropolitan county councils a vote winner or vote loser. Opposition party members unanimously claimed that it was a vote loser: 43 per cent of the representative sample of Conservative MPs claimed it was a vote loser and only 42 per cent claimed it was a vote winner.

There is considerable circumstantial evidence to indicate that the advertising, and the opposition to the proposed legislation which it helped stimulate, produced a lack of confidence in the proposed legislation among Conservatives in Parliament, so creating the circumstances in which the Paving Bill was defeated and amended. It is only reasonable to assume that Parliamentarians were more than aware of the increasingly critical press coverage of the issue and the numerous published opinion polls revealing ever stronger opposition to abolition which appeared between March and June 1984. In addition MPs must have been aware of the declining percentage of Londoners who, according to published opinion polls, declared an intention to vote Conservative in either a General Election or a GLC one, and who contrasted with relative stability in voting intentions elsewhere in the country[18].

We cannot know what 'behind the scenes' pressures were placed on the Government by Conservative Party members concerned by the Government's course. However, concerns about the threat to Conservative Party fortunes in the capital may explain the efforts of leading London Conservatives to counter the GLC's propaganda, and their public criticism of the Government for not doing so[19].

In the circumstances we must rely on the opinions of those with expert knowledge of the politicians. The country's television and national newspaper editors were in no doubt that the advertising had directly persuaded the political decision makers that abolition was an unpopular reform[20].

But perhaps the final words should belong to Patrick Jenkin. On being ousted from the Cabinet in 1985, he claimed that Cabinet colleagues had failed to support him over local Government reforms because they had recognised the growing unpopularity of the proposed measures.

## CONCLUSION

Despite the difficulties of establishing causal relationships, there is clear evidence that the advertising was widely seen, shifted public opinion, influenced media coverage of the Paving Bill and thus created the climate in which the Government's original proposals were overturned by Parliament so that the GLC achieved a stay of execution. In the longer term, the campaign may be judged to have helped stimulate a renewed public and opposition party commitment to the restoration of democratically-elected metropolitan authorities.

Demonstrating the cost-effectiveness of the campaign in terms of conventional commercial profit is clearly impossible. In the political market-place, public and party attitudes may be regarded as the bottom line – and no exact financial value can be placed on these. Perhaps the closest we can come to demonstrating the campaign's 'value for money' is in the calculation that the commercial value of the positive media coverage of the issue which the advertising appeared to stimulate was many times the advertising budget.

The anti 'Paving Bill' advertising, and the anti-abolition campaign, of which it formed a part, have been profoundly significant. The widely acknowledged effectiveness of the campaign has undoubtedly given further impetus to the fast-growing corporate advertising sector. More importantly, the campaign has actually extended perceptions of the power and influence of advertising itself – in particular in its ability to influence other media. In addition, trade unions and other bodies, not traditionally associated with the skills of marketing and advertising, show increasing interest in such activities. Advertising and market research must rise to the occasion and demonstrate the skills that are required. In particular there is a need to advance access to, and hence content analysis of, television news and current affairs programmes.

## APPENDIX: REFERENCES AND NOTES

1. The MORI tracking study of a representative sample of all adult Londoners revealed that half of them (56 per cent) spontaneously mentioned abolition when asked of Government plans concerning the GLC. On prompting, awareness of the plan rose to four-fifths (81 per cent). Qualitative research indicated that these figures were in a sense highly misleading: for even among those aware of the issue it was of very low interest. The GLC, like other Government bodies, was felt to be remote, its functions were not understood, and its fortunes were thus a matter of popular indifference.

When prompted, 50 per cent opposed abolition and 19 per cent supported it. People rationalised these responses on a wide variety of grounds as the following figures indicate.

REASONS FOR ATTITUDE TO ABOLITION

| | Attitude to abolition | |
| --- | --- | --- |
| | Approve %| Disapprove % |
| The GLC do a good job | 3 | 29 |
| Save money/stop waste of money | 50 | 1 |
| Fares would go up | – | 23 |
| Services would deteriorate | 1 | 10 |
| Ought to keep local government authority/autonomy | 1 | 1 |
| Need an overall body for London | – | 10 |
| Why change it/OK as it is | 1 | 9 |
| Because of the leader/politics | 21 | 1 |
| Don't know | 3 | 5 |

Source: MORI January 1984

Qualitative research helped to explain why opinion reflected party-political loyalties. Those who disapproved of abolition often simply disliked change or were motivated by Labour party loyalties. Concern that services, and in particular public transport, would deteriorate were common among the latter. Those who approved of abolition were often Conservative party voters who believed it would save money by ending the profligate expenditure of 'Red Ken' on dubious minorities.

2. Academic support for the fact that the media made Ken Livingstone one of the most vilified people in public life is to be found in C. T. Husbands, 'Attitudes to Local Government in London' *London Journal* II, (1), 1985. The most recent quantitative confirmation of the widespread public ignorance of the GLC's responsibilities and activities was to be found in Harris Research Centre, *Survey of Public Opinion in London* (June 1983).

3. The intention was that the Government would then be widely seen to have lost the popular, and hence moral, argument for its policy. For it to have then persisted on its original course would thus threaten to undermine its popularity and authority, and prejudice its future electoral fortunes. It would also have promised to excite rebellion within the party. The threat of such a scenario might induce the Government to drop or radically amend its schemes.

4. The qualitative research conducted in January 1984 revealed that respondents had largely forgotten that the GLC Council was democratically elected by all Londoners every four years but, when reminded of this, and that the legis-

lation thus meant the loss of their vote and hence control over how London was governed, they objected vehemently. This perception seemed to transform attitudes to the issue: suddenly the Government was felt to be sacrificing the democratic rights of the citizen through its desire to abolish one GLC administration out of political spite. In this context, its policy immediately became less acceptable and objections became quite emotional and intense.

5. For example, the MORI survey among the majority of the country's TV and national press political editors reveal 100 per cent awareness of the campaign.

6. The cost and ethics of the campaign became the subject of numerous articles, many of which were lengthy and boasted vaguely sensationalist headlines (for example, *The Daily Telegraph*, 24 March 1984 and 16 April 1984; *The Times*, 4 June 1984; *Evening Standard*, 21 June 1984; *Daily Mail*, 21 June 1984; and *Daily Express*, 21 June 1984).

   Some of these sought out and published the comments of the GLC's advertising managers. When the *Daily Mail* obtained an advertising strategy document it made a 'scoop' of the story (*Daily Mail*, 23 March 1984).

   Readers letters on the subject of the advertising were published (for example, *The Times*, 21 April 1984; and *Daily Star*, 24 April 1984).

   Indeed the campaign seems to have stimulated interest in the broader issue of political advertising in general, a subject on which eminent advertising personalities expressed their views in the press (for example, Winston Fletcher in *The Times*, 20 June 1984).

7. *Hansard*; and for examples and reports of this in the press see *The Times*, 5 and 10 April 1984. MPs letters on the subject of the advertising were published in the press, for example the letter of Richard Tracy (Conservative MP) in *The Daily Telegraph*, 10 April 1984.

8. For example, interview with William Waldegrave, the Environment Minister, in the *Evening Standard*'s 'Great Debate', *Evening Standard*, 22 March 1984.

9. *Financial Times*, 19 April 1984. Other papers carried the story, for example *The Times*, 19 April 1984.

10. On 22 March, London's *Evening Standard* newspaper began a series of articles under the banner of 'The Great Debate' to 'bring home to Londoners the momentous issues involved' in abolition. The initial article paid tribute to the vigour of the anti 'Paving Bill' advertising. On 26 March it published a MORI opinion poll, commissioned by the paper, which revealed that public opposition to abolition of the GLC had grown to 61 per cent of adult Londoners while only 22 per cent approved of the Government's plans. Other papers were quick to report the survey results (for example *The Times*, 27 March 1984; and *The Guardian*, 27 March 1984) and from that point onwards coverage of the abolition issue in the national press became distinctly more critical of the Government's position. On 27 March both the *Evening Standard* and *The Guardian* paid tribute to the 'masterly' and 'skilled' advertising campaign of the GLC which was credited with having achieved 'substantial shifts' in public opinion. Other journals were quick to link the results of this poll to the advertising (for example, *The Economist*, 7 April 1984). On 30 March the *Evening Standard* concluded the 'Great Debate' by saying that 'This House Supports the Retention of the GLC'.

11. For example, the April MORI poll commissioned by the GLC was published by the *Evening Standard*, 16 April 1984. The paper claimed that the 62 per cent who opposed abolition was 'not necessarily a direct result of the massive advertising campaign to keep the GLC'.

    A MORI poll, commissioned by the GLC, of voters' opinions in Finchley and Greenwich which revealed that 66 per cent of the Prime Minister's Finchley constituents opposed abolition was reported in *The Economist*, 14 April 1984.

    An Audience Selection poll which found that 54 per cent opposed abolition of the GLC and only 15 per cent favoured it, was reported in the *Financial Times*, 16 May 1984 and in *The Guardian*, 16 May 1984.

    The May MORI poll, commissioned by the GLC and which found that 69 per cent of Londoners opposed the cancellation of the GLC elections and that 64 per cent opposed abolition, was reported in *The Daily Telegraph*, 8 June 1984 and *The Guardian*, 8 June 1984.

    A Harris poll, commissioned by 'The London Programme', and which indicated that Ken Livingstone would win a by-election with an increased majority, was reported in *The Times*, 22 June 1984.

12. The survey was conducted by MORI in June 1986. Twenty-four interviews were achieved, a sample which represented 80 per cent of all leading political editors and journalists working for television and the press. In the context of the fact that such a sample of 'experts' must have a natural inclination to deny that they were influenced by advertising and to minimise its effects in comparison with the power of their own media, the results are remarkable. Of those interviewed, 71 per cent claimed that the advertising had been influential in persuading the media to see abolition of the GLC as an important public issue. Even more remarkable was the fact that 67 per cent of the sample claimed that political journalists and commentators had not initially seen the issue as one of democracy versus central government control, and that 50 per cent of the sample claimed that they had come to see the issue in this light as a result of the advertising campaign.

13. The parliamentary rebellions that won such adverse publicity for the Government's proposals may be listed as follows:

— In early April there were press reports of the opposition of the Tory Reform Group and of the intention of various senior conservatives (notably Heath and Pym) to oppose the legislation.
— On 11 April, Heath led 19 other Conservative rebels who voted against the 'Paving Bill' on its second reading.
— On 10 and 11 May, Heath led two revolts during the Bill's committee stage on the floor of the Commons.
— On 23 and 24 May, there was chaos during the third reading of the Bill as a result of the 'filibustering' of the SDP Liberal Alliance.
— Press speculation in early June that the Lords would inflict injury on the Bill came to fruition when, on 11 June, there was a Government majority of only 20, despite extensive and controversial whipping, on an amendment condemning the Bill as a dangerous precedent.
— On 28 June the Bill sustained its most notable setback – the Lords passed an amendment preventing the Government from cancelling the GLC elections until the main Bill abolishing the Council had received the Royal Assent, and voted down the 'interim provisions' whereby the GLC would have been controlled, from May 1985 until early 1986, by councillors nominated by central Government.

14. Qualitative research conducted in March 1984 revealed this feeling that the Government was abusing its power, and abandoning all sense of fair play. Qualitative research conducted on a regular basis throughout the period revealed that such feelings grew stronger in the following three months. Central Government was taking something away from London against the wishes of the majority of its citizens and, even among those who otherwise favoured abolition, this was felt to be wrong.

Although the MORI tracking study is of limited relevance here, the available quantitative data is at least consistent with the claims, and indicated that the relevant shift in recorded opinion had, for the most part, already taken place by the end of March. By 2 April the number of Londoners claiming that the proposal to abolish the GLC had made them think less of the Government had risen from 43 per cent (January) to 54 per cent: by July the figure had risen to 57 per cent. The April figures also revealed that, of those who had seen the advertising, 68 per cent disagreed that the Government was trying to abolish the GLC in the interests of Londoners and 62 per cent agreed that it was really trying to abolish the GLC to silence a political opponent: among those who claimed not to have seen the advertising the scores were 59 per cent and 47 per cent respectively.

Thus in March there were extremely positive reactions to the Ken Livingstone execution, even among Conservative opponents of the GLC, during its qualitative pre-testing: two months before such an execution would have been unthinkable.

15. No influence, other than the advertising and the opinion polls which it influenced, can explain the conversion. In March the press had still not begun to treat Livingstone favourably. Nor had it publicised any activity of Livingstone which was likely to court public favour. Support for this comes from the MORI survey of the country's national newspapers and TV political editors (for details of survey see footnote 12): 92 per cent of those interviewed believed that the advertising had been effective in causing the public to sympathise with the GLC.

16. Detailed content analysis of the press reveals that the change in coverage of Livingstone can be dated with surprising precision. In mid-March the flow of critical press articles came to a stop. The timing coincides with the appearance of the advertising campaign, and the first burst of press executions. There then followed a period when Livingstone received little, although on balance more favourable, coverage. Then, in May, his new status was recognised. The event which first gained him extensive favourable coverage was the opening of the Thames Barrier at which his mother, Ethel, an avowed monarchist, met the Queen. Virtually every national newspaper devoted extensive coverage to the story. 'Red Ken' had become 'Our Ken': the publication of a book on his life and interviews with his mother provided the press with much human interest material on the man with a long history of reptilian pets.

The press still found an outlet for its criticism of the GLC's left-wing policies. In May and June there was much more extensive, and on balance more critical, coverage of items such as the GLC women's committee, the Talgarth Road traffic experiment and the GLC's attempts to pressurise Zola Budd into an anti-apartheid statement. However, this was now visibly separated from the issue of abolition and the champion of Londoners' democratic rights, 'Citizen Ken'.

17. Further evidence of the compound and interrelated impact of media coverage, opinion polls, and the advertising in stimulating opposition to abolition of the GLC and its elections is to be found in a MORI survey conducted in July 1984 which compared the views of Londoners to those of residents within the other metropolitan County Councils that were also to be abolished by the legislation. Of Londoners, 80 per cent were aware of the plans to abolish the

GLC whereas only 47 per cent of those interviewed in the other Metropolitan authorities were aware of the intended fate of their own councils. Among those aware of the abolition threat, opposition was much more intense in London: 50 per cent of Londoners 'strongly disapproved' of abolition of the GLC whereas only 32 per cent of those in the other areas 'strongly disapproved' of the plans to abolish their own authorities.

18. These trends are authoritatively documented in C. Husbands, op. cit.

19. In June John Wheeler, London's senior Conservative MP publicly attacked the Government for its failure to counter the GLC's 'effective "save us" fight', and to outlaw its advertising campaign (*Evening Standard*, 27 June 1984). The same week Lady Porter, Conservative Leader of Westminster City Council, admitted to the effectiveness of the GLC's advertising campaign when she claimed that Londoners had been 'conned' by it at the launching of an organisation of Tory politicians and businessmen called 'Efficiency in Local Government' which aimed to counter the GLC's propaganda. (*Financial Times*, 19 April 1984).

20. For details of the survey see footnote 12. The results were again quite remarkable. In resonse to the question of what had persuaded the political decision makers that abolition was an unpopular reform, 75 per cent of those sampled in the MORI survey claimed it was the advertising. This score was exceeded only by the 83 per cent who mentioned the opinion polls. Amazingly the editors gave the media comment about the issue a score of only 67 per cent.

# 9

# Promoting the Privatisation of British Telecom

## INTRODUCTION

This is a case history about the advertising of a product which had no price, was not on sale, which could not be recommended and which could not even be mentioned in TV advertising. Worse, there was no precedent for such a campaign and, unlike any other advertising campaign, it had only one chance to succeed. Failure could not even be contemplated.

Advertising the flotation of British Telecom was a unique problem.

## BACKGROUND

In October 1979 Sir Keith Joseph pledged the Government to the policy of returning nation-alised industries to the private sector. Between the autumn of 1979 and the summer of 1984, 14 nationalised companies had been returned wholly or in part to the private sector. The flotation of British Telecom was to be the fifteenth, and largest – indeed the largest share flotation ever, anywhere in the world.

In order to groom British Telecom for privatisation, the Government had appointed a new Board of Directors, most of whom had business experience outside the public sector. The new Board and the Government proceeded to restructure British Telecom on a commercial trading basis and invested heavily in capital projects to enable the company to provide the most modern and high tech services. By the summer of 1983 this task had largely been completed and it became apparent that the possibility of a public flotation could become a reality. This paper sets out to demonstrate the effectiveness of advertising in re-shaping the corporate image of British Telecom, and how advertising was subsequently used successfully to educate and motivate over 2 million people to apply for shares at the time of the company's flotation in November 1984.

## RE-SHAPING THE CORPORATE IMAGE

Although the company had been restructured to meet the needs of the commercial world, it was clear that the public held consistent and particular views about British Telecom (Table 1).

Dorland recognised that the public face of British Telecom would have to change before it

TABLE 1:   THE IMAGE OF BRITISH TELECOM AMONG THE GENERAL PUBLIC

|  | September 1983 |
|---|---|
| Use the most up-to-date technology | 102 |
| Very profitable | 105 |
| Provide a good service | 106 |
| Charge too much | 102 |
| Spend a lot on R & D | 104 |
| Are doing a lot to become more efficient | 93 |
| Essential to Britain's success | 100 |
| Polite and helpful when you deal with them | 94 |
| Spend a lot improving their service | 100 |
| Owned by the Government | 120 |
| Like their advertising | 119 |
| Respond quickly to the needs of business | 106 |
| Give good value for money | 100 |
| Waste a lot of money | 90 |
| Slow to respond when you need help | 123 |
| Provide non-profit-making services to the community | 82 |

(February 1983 = 100)

Source: MORI

became a desirable privatisation property, and proposed a corporate advertising campaign designed to show the true face of British Telecom. This campaign, known as 'The Power Behind the Button', was conceived by Dorland seven months before we even knew that there would be a major flotation campaign and that we would handle it.

The corporate campaign was timed to begin in November 1983. However, a series of anti-privatisation advertisements placed by the British Telecommunications Unions Committee necessitated a series of press advertisements by British Telecom to counter the points made. The anti-privatisation campaign played on the fears of excessive pricing, removal of public telephone boxes in rural areas, the loss of emergency services and special facilities for the disabled.

We countered this anti-privatisation campaign by very factual, unemotional press advertising designed to allay people's fears. The main corporate campaign used television with national newspaper support. The campaign began with an overview of British Telecom's activities, designed to show how British Telecom helps in banking, airfreight, education, social services, etc. We covered maintenance of the emergency services and public telephones in rural areas. The campaign then moved towards specific areas of high technology. These commercials featured data transmission via laser light lines, System X, National Networks and services to the financial community. All in all, it was a campaign designed to show that British Telecom was not just about telephones but also about the high speed, high tech aspects of life.

Our interpretation of research showed that by June only one image still required reinforcement. We needed to relate the technology of Telecom to the everyday lives of ordinary people. For this we were presented with a golden opportunity in the Olympic Games.

Every night, via satellite, British Telecom was beaming the Games across the world from Los Angeles. We reinforced this demonstration by explaining that it was British Telecom who enabled them to be seen on TV as they happened. By August 1984 we had seen the attitude shifts shown in Table 2.

TABLE 2:   THE IMAGE OF BRITISH TELECOM AMONG THE GENERAL PUBLIC

|  | September 1983 | August 1984 |
|---|---|---|
| Use the most up-to-date technology | 102 | 142 |
| Very profitable | 105 | 102 |
| Provide a good service | 106 | 114 |
| Charge too much | 102 | 91 |
| Spend a lot on R & D | 104 | 146 |
| Are doing a lot to become efficient | 93 | 136 |
| Essential to Britain's success | 100 | 130 |
| Polite and helpful when you deal with them | 94 | 110 |
| Spend a lot improving their service | 100 | 139 |
| Owned by the Government | 120 | 150 |
| Like their advertising | 119 | 188 |
| Respond quickly to the needs of business | 106 | 135 |
| Give good value for money | 100 | 125 |
| Waste a lot of money | 90 | 85 |
| Slow to respond when you need help | 123 | 92 |
| Provide non-profit-making services to the community | 82 | 91 |

(February 1983 = 100)

Source: MORI

## THE PREPARATION OF THE FLOTATION CAMPAIGN

Although Dorland is British Telecom's agency for corporate advertising, we were not involved in the planning of the flotation campaign until it became apparent to the Government and Kleinwort Benson that a major agency would be required to provide the creative and media services for the magnitude of the flotation envisaged. Therefore, in April 1984, the Department of Trade and Industry, together with Kleinwort Benson, invited Dorland to submit proposals for the run-up to the flotation of British Telecom.

### Organisation and Structure

The organisational structure of those involved with the flotation was complex. Briefly, the Government – in the guise of the Department of Trade and Industry – uses a merchant bank, Kleinwort Benson, to sell the company, British Telecom. Figure 1 shows the relationship of the Government with its various advisers, and their various advisers.

The complexity of this structure cannot be over-emphasised. Among all the people who constituted the Marketing Committee that steered the flotation advertising, there were few who had any experience of large-scale consumer advertising.

Figure 1. *British Telecom flotation marketing committee: structure for approval of advertising*

## Legal Constraints

The Advertising Code of Practice specifically prohibits the selling of shares. There must be no hint of hype of the company being sold. Political advertising is also not acceptable, and this was felt by many to be a 'political' campaign.

## Timing

In order to provide time to educate a largely uninitiated potential market we at first looked for a long campaign period. Those members of the public who were unfamiliar with shares and share ownership would need longer to assimilate the information about the offer, whereas those who were already interested in investments would start from a higher knowledge base. It was of real concern to us that opinion in certain Government departments favoured a very short campaign of only a few weeks, until we were eventually able to convince them of the necessity for a longer campaign.

## Existing Shareholders

Table 3 from Target Group Index (T.G.I.) research showed that in 1983 we were largely a nation of savers, not investors. According to T.G.I., there were 2.5 million shareholders among the general public. (There were a number of conflicting pieces of research in this field but our planning base was T.G.I.)

It was clear to Dorland that the market for British Telecom shares could only partly be satisfied by existing, active shareholders plus some of those who had savings with Building Societies, National Savings, Unit Trusts and Life Assurance Companies.

It was convincing the Marketing Committee of this fact, and the consequent need to advertise to a target audience of virtually everyone, that required the greatest persuasion by the agency and was to prove *a most significant decision*. The 'safe' route of advertising to the existing holders of equities would not, in our opinion, have resulted in sufficient applications;

TABLE 3: THE UK SAVINGS AND INVESTMENT MARKET

| April 1983–March 1984 | Adults aged 15 + '000s | % of all adults |
|---|---|---|
| Own stocks and shares | 2 544 | 6 |
| Have savings in building societies | 23 586 | 54 |
| Have deposit or savings account in a bank | 15 062 | 34 |
| Have a life assurance policy | 19 268 | 44 |

Source: Target Group Index B.M.R.B.

would not have created the interest necessary to convert the City's negative view and would not have satisfied the 'wider share ownership' aims of the Government.

Although it seems strange, with the benefit of hindsight, the period April to July 1984 was actually one of great uncertainty for the Flotation Marketing Committee. No flotation of this size had ever taken place before, and in some previous cases the Government's privatisation policy had led to charges of a 'quick buck for the City' or an incompetent pricing policy. Some flotations had resulted in a very weak aftermarket, something which would have been politically damaging for the Government had the same thing occurred with British Telecom.

The Government's concept of wider share ownership, of which British Telecom was a cornerstone, had taken something of a knock with two high-profile flotations for British Aerospace and Jaguar. Four months after the British Aerospace flotation only 17 per cent of the original shareholders remained, and Jaguar's shareholder register had shrunk by 60 per cent in only a month. In order to satisfy the concept of wider share ownership, we had to win over new shareholders and retain them.

Fleet Street, too, had the jitters about the British Telecom flotation. For example, the *Sunday Times* ran a headline warning 'City fears a B.T. disaster'.

## CREATIVE STRATEGY

### *Developing the Target Audience*

The potential market for ownership of British Telecom shares by the public was very wide. It covered all socio-economic groups, all age groups and both sexes. This flotation was to be for everyone.

It would need to be for everyone on the practical basis of obtaining enough subscribers to the share offer. And it would need to be a mass target audience to satisfy the political objective of wider share ownership. There is no doubt that this flotation would have failed had it been aimed only at the institutions and the professional and financial men of the City of London.

Initially, our proposals caused some dismay because they deliberately ignored the City in the advertising. We believed that the City had made up its mind that the flotation would not be a success and that advertising would not change that professionally considered view. But we believed that the City would be influenced indirectly by an emotional campaign aimed at the general public. The City is only interested in a share that has 'a market' and our advertising would create the interest which makes a market. As the campaign proceeded the City became more optimistic. By November, some journalists were recommending British Telecom shares, even before the price had been announced.

### The 'One Chance' Factor

The flotation of a company is a once-only opportunity. On a certain day a prospectus becomes available. A few days later the offer closes. Unlike selling ordinary consumer goods and services there is no time to see how successful your offer has been and to adjust the marketing accordingly. It is a 'do or die' piece of timing. Therefore we had to build flexibility into the creative approach and undertake the necessary research on a continuous basis to ensure that we hit the bull's-eye in November.

### Creating a Sense of National Event

The target audience for advertising was to be the first-time investor. Because of the restrictions imposed both by law and by the Advertising Code of Practice, we were unable to 'sell' the shares on their merit. We were in fact restricted to talking about the prospectus, and even that did not exist at this time. Therefore we sought to draw people emotionally into the concept of the sale of British Telecom as a historic, national event – a golden opportunity for the small investor.

However, research had shown us that ordinary people needed to feel that they were not alone in expressing their interest for British Telecom. So we set about providing them with the opportunity to join in an event which would become a talking point in offices, pubs and shops throughout the country. We wanted people to enthuse each other, and gain reassurance from their peer groups that their interest was justified. The more of a talking point that we could make British Telecom, the easier it would be to dispense specific information about the offer via editorial and other media which were unfettered by the legal restrictions that beset the advertising.

### Advertising Objectives

The campaign was divided into three phases: Alert, Maintenance and Action.
   The Alert phase was designed to:

1.  Create a high saliency for the flotation.
2.  Communicate that the offer applied to everyone, not just big City investors.
3.  Elicit response.
4.  Stimulate indirectly the appeal of the flotation to the City.

   The Maintenance phase sought to:

1.  Impart specific information about the offer.
2.  Allow people to identify with the offer by responding to people similar to themselves.
3.  Elicit response.

The Action phase, immediately prior to the publication of the prospectus, had three objectives:

1. To ensure that people had their money ready (some deposit accounts require a period of notice).
2. To highlight the eight-day application period. It was crucial that this was understood by the general public. This is the 'one chance' factor.
3. To instil a sense of urgency.

## CREATIVE DEVELOPMENT AND EXECUTION

### The Alert Phase

We had to create a desire for what could not be described because of legal restrictions.

We hit on a creative treatment for television which satisfied the need for authority and the sense of national event. It succeeded because it quoted from the Telecommunications Act itself. We deliberately made this non-political by using phrases such as '*Parliament* made it possible for the people of the United Kingdom to own British Telecom shares'. The level of debate was raised above the clamour of party politics. This privatisation was now the will of Parliament.

In the press we opened with two full-page advertisements (see page 140) featuring ordinary members of the public who had expressed an interest in buying British Telecom shares. The copy was crafted and honed so that it not only satisfied the lawyers but also sounded good.

*All* advertising carried a means of response; either a coupon or a telephone number. Even the posters carried a telephone number. When you phoned 0 272 272 272 you were answered personally, not by an answering machine.

Those who responded were sent a pack of information about British Telecom as a company and share ownership in general, and of course in that mailing piece it was possible to say far more about the prospects for British Telecom than would be possible in advertising.

The Alert phase press continued with individual members of the public – the garage owner, the housewife, the truck driver, the supermarket owner, the roof tiler, the farmer and so on (see page 141). In each press advertisement there was a nuance of copy change to fit the picture. For example, in the picture of the farmer with the headline 'If you can drive a tractor you can share in British Telecom's future', the opening words of the copy read 'Do you own something in the country? Have you ever thought of owning something in the City?' With both press and television the emphasis was on 'sharing British Telecom's future'.

The Alert phase advertising was qualitatively researched both in its development stages and in its final form. As a result some parts of the copy were clarified, and the value of running the composite advertisements before the individual advertisements in the press was confirmed. The composite advertisements gave reassurance that the offer was open to everyone.

### The Maintenance Phase

Having talked at people very hard for four weeks, the campaign changed gear and allowed people, in effect, to talk to us.

We wanted to show people being involved in the campaign. But the law prevents anyone

# Now everyone can share in British Telecom's future.

Soon you will have the chance to be an owner of a company that plays a large part in our everyday lives.

An Act of Parliament has made it possible for each one of us to buy British Telecom shares.

For everyone it is an historic opportunity to share in the fortunes of one of Britain's leading companies. The offer will be designed particularly to attract the small investor buying only a modest number of shares.

Applying for the shares will be easy. You will be able to use a simple form in the British Telecom prospectus which will be widely available in November. Or any bank or financial adviser can help you.

You may invest thousands, or even millions. The minimum, however, is about £250, of which less than half has to be paid immediately. The rest will be payable in two instalments over about 15 months.

As a personal shareholder from the start, you will enjoy additional benefits if you keep your shares. You can choose a bonus of free shares, which you will receive after three years. Alternatively, if you are an individual telephone subscriber, you may choose instead to receive (according to the amount you have invested) one or more discount

vouchers, worth £18 each, which can be used in part payment of your telephone bills.

You will appreciate that the market value of any share can go down as well as up. But you may be sure that you will be sharing in the fortunes of a leading company in a vital and growing sector of the world economy.

If you want to know more about owning shares in British Telecom, send off the coupon to P.O. Box 1, Bristol BS99 1BT, or telephone (24 hour service) 0 272 272 272.

Please send me details about British Telecom and share ownership.

Mr/Mrs/Miss ...........................................

Address ...........................................

Postcode ...........................................

ISSUED BY KLEINWORT, BENSON LIMITED ON BEHALF OF H.M. GOVERNMENT.

Launch press advertisement

from giving opinions about companies which are to be floated on the stockmarket. And so all the television advertising for this period was designed to make people ask the sort of questions that the public as a whole was asking.

We had a series of vox-pop advertisments with ordinary people from all around the country asking questions that they thought they were relevant, and these took the mystery away from buying shares. These people had been selected through street interviews and telephone

# If you can drive a tractor, you can share in British Telecom's future.

Do you own something in the country? Have you ever thought of owning something in the City?

The sale of British Telecom shares this November is an historic opportunity for more people than ever before to take a part in share ownership. It will be the largest new share issue in the history of the City and as many people as possible will be invited to share in the fortunes of this major British company.

You can apply direct by using a simple form which will be part of British Telecom's prospectus – widely available in November. Or any bank can help you.

Although how much you apply for is up to you, the minimum is only about £250. Less than half has to be paid immediately, the rest in two instalments over about 15 months.

As an ordinary shareholder, you will, of course, receive any dividends the company may declare.

As a personal shareholder from the start, if you keep your shares for three years, you will enjoy the additional benefit of a bonus of free shares.

You will appreciate that the market value of any share can go down as well as up. But you may be sure that you will be sharing in the fortunes of a leading company in a vital and growing sector of the world economy.

If you want to know more about owning shares in British Telecom, send off the coupon to P.O. Box 1, Bristol BS99 1BT, or telephone (24 hour service), 0 272 272 272.

Please send me details about British Telecom and share ownership.

Mr/Mrs/Miss ........................................................
Address ........................................................
........................................................
........................................................
Postcode ........................................................

ISSUED BY KLEINWORT, BENSON LIMITED ON BEHALF OF H.M. GOVERNMENT.

'Alert phase' press advertisement

research as being people with savings of approximately £1 000. Many of the people on television were also used in press advertisements (see opposite).

The national press advertisements concentrated on giving such facts as we were able to impart about the benefits for founder shareholders and the mechanics of applying for shares. In fact, throughout this period, there were only two stories to tell – although for those unused to the financial world both the stories were somewhat complicated and needed to be explained clearly and simply.

There were two benefits available for founder shareholders. At the time of buying shares in November, individuals could opt for either the voucher scheme which (depending on how many shares you purchased) issued telephone bill discount vouchers, or the alternative scheme which was free bonus shares, if you kept your original holding for three years.

We created a number of advertisements to explain these offers. Through research we learnt that showing a table of the number of vouchers received for the amount of money invested was understood and found to be helpful. We worded the copy differently for different publications, allowing a much looser, less 'financial' style in the popular press compared with the copy styles in the quality press.

Specific advertisements were created to fit specific publications. For example, the first spread of the first issue of *Working Woman* showed two girls with the headline 'The working woman's guide to owning British Telecom shares'. The Sunday supplements featured the headline 'The Sunday morning guide to owning British Telecom Shares'.

As the Maintenance phase progressed, research showed two communication gaps which needed to be filled. The first was that some people still did not fully understand what a prospectus was. The second mystery was the short period during which you could apply for shares. TV commercials addressing both these points supplanted the vox-pop commercials for the last three weeks of the Maintenance phase, and press advertisements supported them.

All the advertising was pre-tested and adjusted as we went along. We used group discussions to supplement the quantified work that was being carried out and advertising was able to be adjusted at very short notice. Advertisements were produced to enable qualitative work to be carried out on Monday nights. The debriefs took place on Wednesday mornings and revised advertisements were in the press by the weekend. Only in this way could we keep ahead of the 'one chance' factor.

*The Action Phase*

This final phase took place ten days before the issuing of the prospectus. It was the call to action. The television execution was simple and direct.

In the press, again picking up the gaps in knowledge which the research had shown, we ran two press advertisements. The first showed the minimum investment that was required and the second one talked about the eight-day application period.

## MEDIA STRATEGY

No budget had been set for the flotation advertising and the first job of the media department was therefore to develop an outline plan in order to arrive at a budget. The significant decision to aim at 'everyone' had two important media consequences: first, it would be a long campaign – about fourteen weeks – and second, it had to be flexible enough so that the weight

# Buying British Telecom shares.
# Suppose I answer this ad today; what happens next and when?

"I haven't really got the faintest idea how I'd actually physically go about acquiring a share."

PETER SIMPSON

"Where is it possible to get the information for British Telecom shares?"

GEORGE HIGGS

If you've never bought shares before, your first reaction, once you start, could be one of surprise.

Because it's a whole lot easier than you might think.

In principle, buying shares is just like anything else. You hand over the money; the owner hands over the goods.

But before you do anything else, you examine what's on offer.

**First, the information pack.**

We have put together an information pack, specially for this sale.

It gives you a lot of background data about British Telecom – the networks, the satellites, the optical fibres and so on. All the 'power behind the button'.

You get the latest Stock Exchange booklet about buying, selling and owning shares. There are two main returns that can come from this: dividend income, and growth in the value of the shares, although neither can ever be guaranteed.

You also get a question-and-answer leaflet that tells you about personal founder shareholder benefits – cheaper telephone bills for up to three years, or a free bonus share issue for those who keep their shares.

**In November, a prospectus.**

A simple document will be published, written in plain English. Where an information pack gives you outlines, this

document will set out what is on offer and includes an application form. It will tell you more about the latest figures and activities of the business and includes a forecast of profit and dividend.

It will tell you what the shares cost, and how you pay for them.

Suppose you invest £1,000. You would pay £400 when you apply in November, £300 in summer 1985, and the remaining £300 in early 1986.

**No obligation, no commitment.**

Replying to this ad means you are ordering your information pack and booking your prospectus. Nothing more.

**Ring 0 272 272 272 any time** of the day or night.

**Or return the coupon to** P.O. Box 1, Bristol BS99 1BT.

**Find out more about sharing British Telecom's future.**
Please send me details about British Telecom and share ownership.

MR/MRS/MISS
ADDRESS                    BLOCK CAPITALS

POSTCODE

ISSUED BY KLEINWORT, BENSON LIMITED ON BEHALF OF H.M. GOVERNMENT.

'Maintenance phase' press advertisement

and direction of the advertising could be adjusted throughout the campaign to respond to the continuous research.

Because advertising was to be in three phases it meant that each phase needed to be considered as virtually a campaign in its own right, achieving high levels of coverage and frequency to ensure that the message of each phase was successfully communicated. The

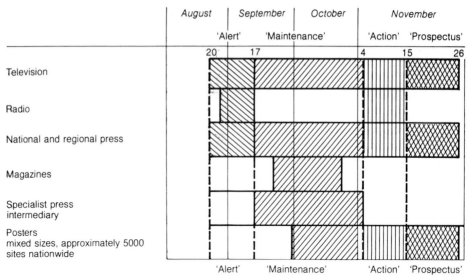

Figure 2. *Media plan*

media plan, therefore, while reaching all adults, also had sufficient flexibility to ensure that each target group would be exposed to sufficient weight of advertising concomitant with their understanding of the flotation within each phase.

It was central to the campaign's success that the creative and media people worked very closely together to carry out the plans and to react swiftly to the opportunities which arose, and also to respond to the changes dictated by the continuous research programme. The danger of having a long and intense campaign was that the public would become bored and the campaign dull. It was therefore decided to use a wide variety of media types, not in order to reach different people, but rather to reach the same people in many different ways – and in so doing to keep the campaign fresh.

We also used a variety of different media because of the particular benefits which each one was able to give. Television undoubtedly did the job of creating and maintaining the excitement about the campaign during the Alert phase, and of allowing people to identify strongly with the vox-pop commercials during the Maintenance phase. However, it was the various branches of the press which allowed us to address specific parts of our 'everyone' target group with messages more directly applicable to each one, and also to vary the tone of the advertising according to the environment in which it appeared. Various specialist press media were used to reach the important, but small, group of financial advisers, bank managers, solicitors and so on, who would need to be well informed about flotation in order to advise their customers and clients. Posters were used throughout the campaign to communicate the simple 'it's for everyone' message that was the theme of the whole campaign.

The publicity that the campaign received before it had even run caused two serious media problems: first, many media owners thought that they automatically had some 'right' to be included on the schedule, and second was the belief that the budget was several times bigger than it really was – which created obvious negotiation problems. These problems were exacerbated by the fact that we were not allowed, at any stage, to reveal the budget. Since a 'share of budget' is very often the basis for negotiating, particularly with television companies, this was a serious problem.

## QUANTITATIVE RESEARCH

The campaign was subject to a series of quantified research measurements undertaken by MORI specifically to monitor the overall effectiveness of the marketing campaign and the propensity of the public to invest.

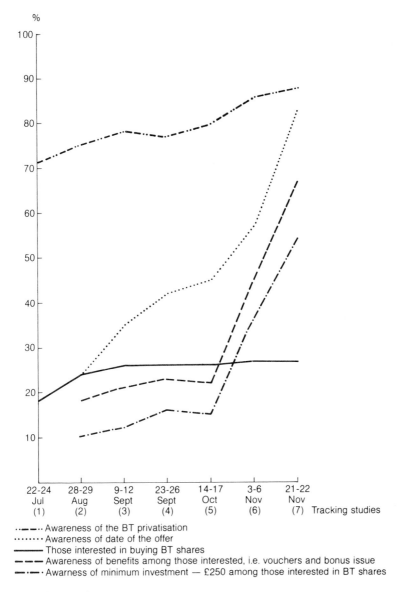

Figure 3. *Campaign tracking*

Figure 3 demonstrates the need for an extended campaign. It was not until some seven weeks after the campaign had started that awareness levels started to rise dramatically on the key campaign points:

1. Awareness of the date of the offer.
2. Awareness of the minimum investment (£250).
3. Awareness of the special benefits.

Once the level of interest had been raised to 26 per cent, that figure remained static for the remainder of the campaign. The Alert phase task of stimulating interest had achieved its target after four weeks, while the Maintenance phase of advertising successfully communicated, to those interested, the key facts that they wanted to know in order to come to a decision.

Advertising had a particular role to fulfil in enabling people to gain information. This of course, was done in two ways. The first was by gleaning information from the advertisement itself and the second was in responding to the advertisement, and gaining information from the information pack.

## POST PROSPECTUS TELEVISION

With the publication of the prospectus the television requirements changed. We wanted people to *act now*. The final television commercials reflected the urgency that was necessary, rounding off the whole campaign by using much of the earlier material, reprised and re-edited but coupled with a faster music track.

## RESULTS

Figure 4 opposite shows the build up of responses from telephone calls and coupons. In all, 1.3 million people responded.

The public applied for more than five times the number of shares allocated. In all, 1 373 706 people applied for 800 shares each or fewer. Altogether, 2 141 647 applicants were allocated shares of which 2 127 were institutions. By May 1985 only 450 000 people had sold their shares, confirming the MORI research that indicated that most investors were in it for the long term (The 1986 T.G.I. figure moved from 2.5 million to 5.3 million shareholders.)

Fleet Street had changed its tune by November. Gone were the gloom and doom stories. On 18 November, *The Observer* described it as 'A National Event, a brilliant piece of Social Engineering'. And *The Sun* described it as 'A Brilliant Success'.

The campaign has spread the ownership of shares more widely. However, it does not appear to have changed savers into investors overnight. It is more as though we had created a new class of share – 'the popular share' – the Government privatisation share, perceived by the public as a share with a fair amount of safety but a small element of risk.

This first 'popular share' is a share which is bought, sold or held for reasons other than the usual financial reasons that drive the share market. The private British Telecom shareholder will have been motivated by emotion in the first place, and is probably retaining his share because of apathy rather than for any other reason.

This is an important new element in the share market. This attitude was reflected by our target market in that they showed in research that they were not interested in the price of the

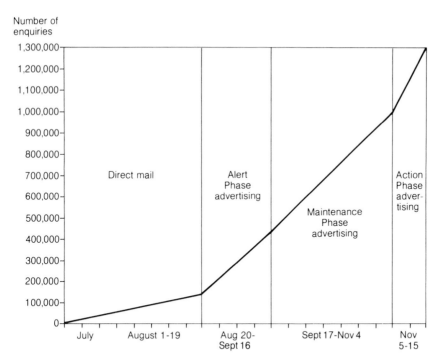

Figure 4. *Offer campaign response level*

share, only the amount of money they needed to get into the game. It is this factor more than any other that stamped the British Telecom share as a different product from any that had gone before it.

# 10

# Chip Pan Fire Prevention 1976–84

## INTRODUCTION

In 1981 there were 21 deaths and 1372 injuries caused by 15000 chip pan fires. The key question was whether advertising could do anything to reduce this catalogue of personal tragedy, or whether accidents were unavoidable.

This paper sets out to demonstrate that advertising can, and did, affect the number of accidents and thus make a valuable social contribution.

### *Background*

The number of deaths and injuries caused by chip pan fires has been mentioned already; however, the scale of the problem is wider than human cost alone.

Chip pan fires are the biggest cause (31 per cent) of domestic fires and result in over £8 million of property damage, and this is only the tip of the iceberg, since the vast majority (95 per cent) of chip pan fires are unreported. Furthermore, chip pan fires represent a cost to the taxpayer in terms of emergency services such as the Fire Brigade, the National Health Service, and the Police.

Against this background of waste and human anguish, the Home Office (HO) and the Central Office of Information (COI) asked the agency to put forward advertising recommendations 'to reduce the death, injury and damage caused by chip pan fires'.

## THINKING BEHIND THE ADVERTISING STRATEGY

A reduction in casualties and damage could be achieved *either* by trying to prevent accidents happening in the first place *or* by educating the public about how to contain a fire efficiently and safely so that it does not get out of control because the wrong actions are taken (eg putting water onto it or moving the pan outdoors). Both these routes would achieve the advertising objective: the 'prevention' strategy, by reducing the number of chip pan fires, and the 'containment' strategy, by minimising the injuries and damage caused, albeit without reducing the number of accidents.

Initially we examined the prevention option. The main causes of chip pan fires are

148

*overfilling*, so that oil overflows onto the hotplate or ring when the chips are put in, and *inattendance*, when the oil can reach a flashpoint and self-ignite.

However, there seemed to be two obstacles to encouraging preventive action. The first concerned the nature of accidents. Although deep-frying is extremely common (more than 80 per cent of housewives deep-fry at least monthly), most people have not experienced a chip pan fire.

In fact it is estimated that only about 15 per cent of households have had such a fire, and we assumed that, in general, people do *not* overfill their pans or leave them unattended. Thus an accident can be defined as being an aberration from normal behaviour probably caused by misjudgement or distraction. We were doubtful, initially, whether advertising could stop someone from making such a misjudgement or being distracted in the domestic environment that may have contributed to it, eg being in a hurry to prepare a meal, forgetting to check the level of oil, being called away from the kitchen to answer the door or settle a crying baby.

The second problem concerned people's unwillingness to believe that accidents might happen to them personally. Our own exploratory qualitative research indicated that people recognised that a chip pan was such an obvious hazard from the point of view of burns and scalding, as well as fire, that they claimed to take extreme care anyway. This, allied to the fact that most people have not experienced a chip pan fire, encouraged the belief that accidents happen to 'other' people who are more 'careless' or 'stupid'.

In considering these twin problems – the momentary, aberrational nature of accidents and the unwillingness to take the risk of a fire personally – we concluded that the prevention route did not appear to be particularly promising. On the other hand, we felt that the containment route was more fruitful. Initial qualitative research indicated that there was ignorance about what to do in the event of a fire and uncertainty about whether, at the moment of danger, the individual would do the 'right' thing, or simply panic. Thus we concluded that the role of advertising should be to inform people about the correct containment procedure and instil confidence in its effectiveness.

However, in reflecting on this proposed strategy, it occurred to us that demonstrating how to cope with a chip pan fire was a possible way to address the prevention issue. Above all, we felt that it could *personalise* the problem in such a way that advice about how to prevent accidents was more likely to be heeded. We believed this for two reasons. First, we felt that showing someone tackling a chip pan fire would raise doubts in the viewers' minds about whether *they* could do this in such an eventuality. By raising this doubt about *their* ability to cope, we felt that advice about how to prevent a fire occurring in the first place would be welcomed. We felt that showing the containment procedure would encourage viewers to want to take more notice of preventive advice in order to avoid the greater of two evils.

The second potential benefit of this strategy lay in the tone voice in which the advertising could address the target audience. Rather than saying, 'Don't do this because it might cause an accident' – advice which might be rejected or ignored for the reasons outlined earlier – we wanted the advertising to say, 'Well, it's happened – unluckily – but here's what to do'. The possibility ot the advertising being accusatory, and therefore being rejected, could be replaced by advice which was unmistakably reasonable, helpful and positive.

In effect, we hypothesised that, by turning the problem on its head, we could maximise the potential benefit of the advertising.

Instead of saying:

'Don't overfill your chip pan or leave it unattended, because you may cause a fire and possibly injure youself.'

we wanted to say:

'Here's what to do if you're unlucky enough to have a chip pan fire; putting it out isn't easy, so why not remember why it happens in the first place.'

The advertising model which we postulated can be represented diagrammatically (see Figure 1).

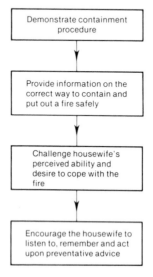

Figure 1. *Advertising Model*

## CAMPAIGN DETAILS

TV was the natural choice for both media and creative reasons: it reaches the wide audience of 'all housewives' and it was the logical choice to show the containment procedure with the most dramatic impact. The campaign line encapsulated the strategy:

FIRE: IF YOU DON'T LET IT START, YOU WON'T HAVE TO STOP IT

Two 60-second commercials – 'Inattendance' and 'Overfilling' – were produced, and these have been used since 1976, although in 1982 they were edited to 40 seconds, (see pages 151 and 152 for storyboard examples). Both showed the initial cause of the fire and then the actions required to put it out:

— turn off the heat;
— cover the pan with a damp cloth;
— leave the pan to cool down.

The dramatic effect of the commercials was heightened by combining real-time with slow-motion sequences.

# INATTENDANCE

If you go out of
the kitchen

and leave your
pan of cooking
fat or oil with
the heat on

it's going to
get very hot.

When it gets
hot enough

it'll catch fire.

When you notice it

the first thing

you'll have
to do

is turn off the
heat. The second
thing you'll

have to do is get a
tea towel, run it under
the tap and wring it out
until it's just damp.

The third thing you'll
have to do is place it
over the area of the fire.
And the fourth thing is
to leave it alone until
it is completely cooled
down.

Of course, if you don't
leave your pan unattended
in the first place you
won't have to do any of this.

# OVERFILLING

If you fill your chip pan more than half full of cooking fat or oil

it will bubble over when you add the chips.

When it touches the heat it will naturally catch light.

Having started a fire you should set about putting it out.

The first thing you should do if you can reach the knob safely is turn off the heat.

The second thing you'll have to do

is get a towel, run it under the tap,

and wring it out until it's just damp.

The third thing you'll have to do is place it over the area of the fire

and if you haven't already done it, turn off the heat. The fourth thing is

leave the pan alone for half an hour or so . . . until it's completely cooled down.

Of course, if you don't overfill your chip pan in the first place, you won't have to do any of this.

| 1976 | Yorkshire |
|------|-----------|
|      | Granada |
| 1977 | Granada (reminder) |
| 1979 | Central |
| 1982 | Harlech |
|      | Tyne-Tees |
| 1983 | TVS |
|      | Harlech (reminder) |
|      | Tyne-Tees (reminder) |
| 1984 | London |

The campaign has appeared on a regional basis in ten areas since 1976, and Table 1 shows the chronology of the advertising. The advertising has always appeared in the period January–March/April and at a national equivalent expenditure level of about £1 million. (Reminder campaigns were about half this level.)

## CAMPAIGN RESULTS

### Sources

The primary source for evaluating the campaign has been the Fire Statistics (derived from the reports made by fire brigades on every fire to which they are called), which are available for the six campaigns between 1976 and 1982, (data for 1983–84 not yet being available). The Fire Statistics have been analysed by the HO and the COI, and these behavioural data have been supplemented by two quantitative consumer surveys in 1976 and 1983. The rationale for the methodology and the results of combining statistical behavioural data with consumer attitudes and claimed behaviour have been written about by N Phillips.[1]

### The Results

There are a number of benefits in regional advertising: the ready availability of control areas, the opportunity to experiment with different media and media weights and, with particular reference to this case history, the opportunity to see whether the advertising is working in different areas over time.

The overall results of the campaigns evaluated between 1976 and 1982 are shown in Table 2 and show 'net' declines of between 7 per cent and 25 per cent over a twelve-month period.

There is clear evidence that the advertising has been successful in reducing the number of chip pan fires. The most disappointing result is in the Central area (the Midlands). This is an area with one of the lowest incidences of reported chip pan fires per thousand households in the UK. We cannot explain why this is the case, but it implies that it is likely to be more difficult to produce an effect from a lower base.

Further analysis of the data adds credence to the causal effect of the advertising. As we would anticipate, the advertising is having its maximum effect during and immediately after the campaign.

TABLE 2:    YEAR–ON–YEAR PERCENTAGE CHANGE IN REPORTED CHIP PAN FIRES

|  |  | advertised area | control area | 'net' change |
|---|---|---|---|---|
| 1976 | Yorkshire | − 20 | + 1 | − 21 |
|  | Granada | − 24 | + 1 | − 25 |
| 1977 | Granada* | − 32 | 0 | − 32 |
| 1979 | Central | − 2 | + 5 | − 7 |
| 1982 | Harlech | − 19 | − 2 | − 17 |
|  | Tyne-Tees |  |  |  |

\* Six months only
Source: HO and COI

Figure 2 shows the pattern of actual fires against forecast in the 1976 campaigns and indicates that from about August the effect of the advertising was diminishing before the reminder burst in the Granada area re-depressed the number of fires.

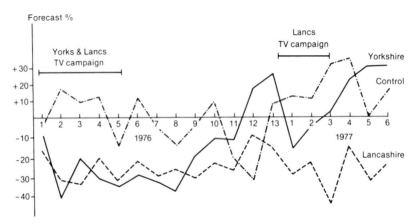

Figure 2 . *Change in the number of calls to fat pan fires relative to the forecast number*
*Source:* Home Office

TABLE 3:    YEAR–ON–YEAR CHANGE IN CHIP PAN FIRES 1982

|  | during campaign | next 25 weeks | next 15 weeks |
|---|---|---|---|
| Harlech | − 27 | − 20 | − 8 |
| Tyne-Tees | − 33 | − 17 | − 15 |
| control | − 6 | − 2 | + 1 |

Source: COI

A similar pattern over time was observed in the 1982 areas (see Table 3). Further credence is added to the advertising effect if 'pure' and overlap areas are analysed separately. We would anticipate that the effect would be less in overlap areas because of reduced advertising impact (due to dual or triple ITV tuning). This proved to be the case, as shown in Table 4.

TABLE 4:    COMPARISONS OF YEAR–ON–YEAR CHANGES IN CHIP PAN FIRES IN 1982

|  | during campaign | next 25 weeks | next 15 weeks | total 52 weeks |
|---|---|---|---|---|
| 'pure' areas | − 30 | − 18 | − 12 | − 19 |
| overlap areas | − 14 | − 14 | + 2 | − 9 |

Source: COI

Not only has the advertising produced an effect, but it has generally been cost-effective, because a 12 per cent drop in fires represents an estimated saving of £1 million in property damage alone, excluding the benefits of reducing injuries and deaths and savings to the emergency services.

Moreover, these results have been achieved with increasing cost-efficiency. The Yorkshire campaign had 2 800 housewife TVRs (circa £2 million +) and used the original 60-second commercials; by 1982 the advertising weight had been reduced by over half and 40-second commercials were being used. This represents a saving of over 70 per cent.

In summary, therefore, we believe there is a prima-facie case for the effectiveness of the advertising: different regions over a six-year period have all responded positively. The number of chip pan fires has been reduced, and this decrease translates directly into reductions in casualties and property damage.

The hypothesis that the advertising is effective is supported by further analysis of the data. The pattern of reduction over time and the differences between 'pure' and overlap areas confirm a common-sense view of how the advertising is likely to work: with greatest effect during the campaign and in pure, non-overlap areas.

In addition, it has been possible to improve the efficiency of the campaign by reducing the weight of advertising and the lengths of the commercials with no apparent loss of impact.

## ADVERTISING AWARENESS AND RECALL

Our confidence that these decreases were a function of the advertising is heightened by the high levels of awareness recorded. Spontaneous awareness of chip pan fire advertising increased sharply after just one burst and was sustained at very high levels thereafter (Table 5).

TABLE 5:    SPONTANEOUS AWARENESS OF CHIP PAN FIRE ADVERTIS-
ING 1976

|  | pre-campaign % | after first burst % | post-campaign % |
|---|---|---|---|
| Yorkshire | 62 | 90 | 96 |
| Lancashire | 47 | 85 | 90 |
| control | 53 | N/A | 57 |

Source: RSL

The pre-campaign levels were caused by and correlate with levels of exposure to COI fire fillers (screened at the discretion of the ITV contractors) in 1974–75. They were not shown during the campaign, and recall and prompted awareness measures show that the paid-for advertising was what was remembered. Similarly, high levels of advertising awareness were achieved in 1983, with no evidence of a decline even four weeks after the TV advertising had stopped.

The impact of the advertising is further confirmed by the way the advertising appears to increase the awareness of chip pan fires as a potential kitchen hazard (Table 6).

TABLE 6:   SPONTANEOUS FIRST MENTION OF CHIP PAN
FIRES AS A DANGER IN THE KITCHEN

|  | Pre–advertising % | Post–campaign % |
|---|---|---|
| Yorkshire | 12 | 28 |
| Granada | 18 | 33 |
| control | 10 | 17 |

Source: RSL 1976

Indeed, we are sufficiently confident of the impact and memorability of the advertising to be considering further media experimentation in the future to increase media flexibility and cost-efficiency and also, it is hoped, to reduce or minimise the 'decay' effect noted earlier.

## HOW THE ADVERTISING WORKS

In theory, understanding how this campaign works does not matter: the objective of reducing chip pan fires appears to have been achieved. However, understanding can help to improve our confidence that the advertising was effective.

It is tempting to conclude from the fact that reported chip pan fires decreased that advertising prevented fires occurring in the first place. However, it is possible to explain the decrease by the containment theory: more people knew how to cope with and put out a chip pan fire as a result of the advertising, and therefore did not *need* to contact the fire brigade.

We cannot determine with certainty whether prevention or containment was the more significant, since we would need to know whether unreported fires increased or stayed the same; these have never been monitored because of the large samples sizes required. However, we believe, on the available evidence, that a combination of prevention and containment was responsible for the decrease in the number of reported fires.

There seems to be no doubt that the advertising increased knowledge of the correct containment procedure, as Table 7 shows. Furthermore, housewives' confidence that this technique would work increased to 75 per cent and, equally importantly, incorrect (and dangerous) practices declined.

However, we do not think that increased knowledge of the containment procedure *is* the sole reason for the decrease in the number of reported chip pan fires. Had it been, then we

TABLE 7:    OBSERVED REACTIONS OF RESPONDENTS TACKLING A CHIP PAN FIRE

|  | Yorkshire | | Granada | | control | |
|---|---|---|---|---|---|---|
|  | pre % | post % | pre % | post % | pre % | post % |
| turn off heat | 68 | 84 | 57 | 80 | 75 | 70 |
| cover with damp cloth | 53 | 74 | 39 | 75 | 40 | 52 |
| leave to cool down | 42 | 62 | 22 | 47 | 41 | 33 |
| open doors/windows | 5 | 24 | 5 | 20 | 7 | 3 |

Source: RSL

would expect that those fires to which the fire brigade *was* called would be more serious than before. But this did not happen: the brigades did not have to fight a higher proportion of fires, injuries were no more common or severe, and the nature and level of damage caused by fires that were reported did not increase.

Also, we believe that the decay effect observed earlier is more likely to be caused by people forgetting prevention advice than by their forgetting the 'new' information about the correct containment procedure.

Furthermore, we think that the twin 'effect' of advertising may explain the relatively disappointing results in the Central area. We do not know precisely why there should be such a low incidence of reported chip pan fires. Survey data suggest that their knowledge of the 'damp cloth' technique appears to be no better than in other areas (before advertising), so we assume that 'Midlanders' are more careful and have fewer fires. If this is the case, then the prevention advice is less relevant and the observed effect may be only a reflection of the containment component.

In summary, neither containment nor prevention alone seems to explain the reduction in chip pan fires; as a result, we believe that both were important.

## CONCLUSION

The purpose of this paper was to demonstrate the effectiveness of advertising in reducing the deaths, injuries and damage caused by chip pan fires. We believe there is clear evidence that advertising achieved this objective in six monitored campaigns between 1976 and 1982.

We believe that a causal relationship has been established between advertising and the reduced number of chip pan fires and that proof of this effect is enhanced by the way in which advertising works over time, or, more accurately, by the way the advertising effect decays over time.

The creative strategy of using the containment procedure not only to inform but also to encourage preventive behaviour produced highly visible advertising and appears to have helped achieve greater public awareness of both containment and preventive practices.

Furthermore, we believe the advertising has been not only effective but progressively more efficient. The campaign now costs two-thirds less in real terms than in 1976.

This advertising campaign has had a measurable and worthwhile effect on society: savings in damage to property have generally covered the cost of the advertising and there have been additional savings in loss of life, injuries and fire brigade expenditure.

## REFERENCES

1.   Phillips, N., 'Measuring attitudes and behaviour – practical implications for advertising', *Admap*, March 1979.

# 11

# Advertising's Part in the Regeneration of London Docklands

## INTRODUCTION

The brief given to Gold Greenlees Trott when appointed by the London Docklands Development Corporation (LDDC) at the end of 1981 was very simple: 'Show us how advertising can be used to help regenerate London Docklands.' What we hope to do in this paper is to demonstrate how bold, impactful advertising can contribute to the solution of daunting social and industrial problems.

We will leave you, we hope, with our conviction that advertising is an integral part of the successful regeneration of London Docklands. This belief is shared by Nigel Broackes, who was, until recently, the Chairman of the LDDC. He wrote in the second paragraph of his 1982-83 Chairman's Statement:

> In this first full year, the London Docklands Development Corporation (LDDC) has seen the crossing of the first, the psychological, threshold. The next few months will transform the development scene as well. After so many years in which attention is focused on other regions and the new and expanding towns, the emphasis really is shifting back to the potential of the capital's inner city. Advertising for investment, long banned for London, is now allowed and three major campaigns - with black London crows as stars - have undoubtedly helped create the necessary general climate of interest in the area. Those who follow this up rarely fail to be impressed by the range of construction activity in hand throughout the eight square miles.

## BACKGROUND

The final closure of London's docks in the period 1968-81, when most commercial sea traffic moved to Tilbury, was the last chapter in the steady decay of the riverside from Tower Bridge to the Woolwich Ferry.

In an attempt to stem the decline the local councils (Tower Hamlets, Newham and Southwark) and the Greater London Council established the Dockland Joint Committee in 1974. Its brief was to attract new business to the area. Unfortunately, it had neither the resources nor a wide enough remit and was largely unsuccessful. The Dockland Joint Committee was disbanded upon the formation of the London Docklands Development Corporation in 1981.

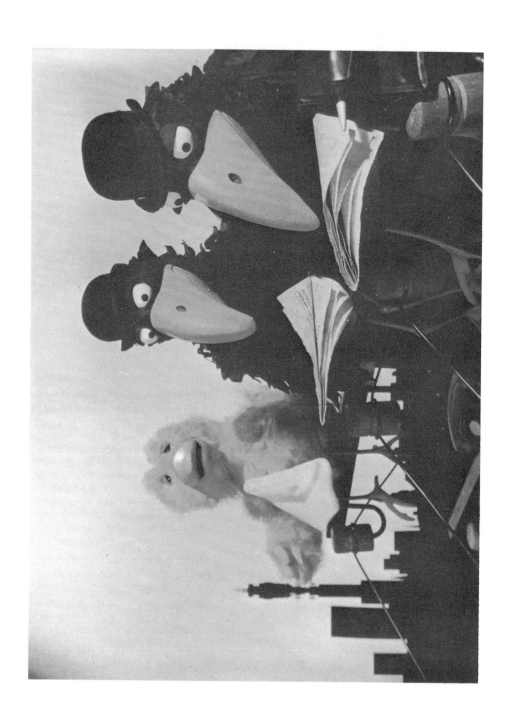

The LDDC's brief is to regenerate eight square miles of Newham, Southwark and Tower Hamlets through the encouragement of industry, commerce, housing and social provisions, including better public transport and general urban infrastructure.

Although it has a wide range of social and environmental responsibilities its principal focus is on economic development, for without industry and employment the community would continue to stagnate.

The major marketing tool which the LDDC has to encourage economic development is the Isle of Dogs Enterprise Zone. The March 1980 Budget set up a number of these zones (which we have listed in Table 1), and gave them a wide range of benefits, particularly 100 per cent capital allowances, and a ten-year rates holiday, to encourage industrial and commercial activity in otherwise depressed areas of the country.

TABLE 1:    FIRST GENERATION OF ENTERPRISE ZONES

| Enterprise Zones | Area (ha) | Date of coming into operation |
|---|---|---|
| 1.  Salford | 174 | 12/8/81 |
| 2.  Trafford | 178 | 12/8/81 |
| 3.  Swansea | 298 | 11/6/81 |
| 4.  Wakefield | 57 | 31/7/81 |
| 5.  Clydebank | 231 | 3/8/81 |
| 6.  Dudley | 219 | 10/7/81 |
| 7.  Hartlepool | 109 | 23/10/81 |
| 8.  Corby | 113 | 22/6/81 |
| 9.  Newcastle | 89 | 25/8/81 |
| 10.  Team Valley }<br>11.  Gateshead } | 365 | 25/8/81 |
| 12.  Speke | 136 | 25/8/81 |
| 13.  Isle of Dogs (LDDC) | 195 | 26/4/82 |
| 14.  Belfast Inner City }<br>15.  Belfast North Foreshore } | 208 | 21/10/81 |

Source: Zone Authority

The important thing to note about the Isle of Dogs Enterprise Zone is that it was set up in April 1982, six to nine months after the others. Although the Isle of Dogs is only a relatively small part of the Docklands area, the LDDC have concentrated resources on it as a 'vanguard' for the rest of the area. The major effect we will seek to demonstrate in this paper is how advertising has encouraged new businesses to move to the Isle of Dogs.

## THE PRODUCT

At the time of designation the Isle of Dogs had 105 firms, employing between them 641 people, mainly in transport and distribution, light engineering and construction. The area has several important buildings, notably in the West India Docks, but much of the enterprise zone consisted of vacant land, vacant water and vacant, almost derelict buildings.

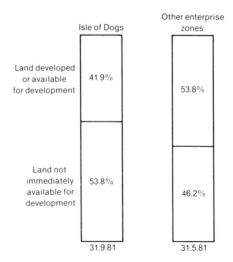

Figure 1. *Usable land*

*Source:* Yearly Economic and Land Development Survey (YEALDS)

Figure 1 compares the proportion of usable land in the Isle of Dogs with other enterprise zones. In 1981 roughly 58 per cent of the Isle of Dogs was unusable, compared with an average of 46 per cent for other areas. This land required major clearance and site preparation before development could take place.

The Isle of Dogs was not connected to mains electricity, and the provision of modern services was essential. Above all, access to the Isle of Dogs was extremely difficult. There were no major roads to or from the area, and no public transport.

## STRATEGY DEVELOPMENT

We have outlined the objectives of the LDDC. The key target groups to motivate to encourage investment, development and new businesses are businessmen in general, and investors, developers and potential business relocaters (in-movers) in particular. We have called these groups the 'main actors':

— investors
— developers
— in-movers

We used research to try and understand the concerns of these groups, their knowledge and opinion of London Docklands and the LDDC, and what influences their investment decisions.

We also interviewed other potentially influential people, such as local and central government, and the local community.

— 30 in-depth interviews with key decision-makers in the City, in finance and property;
— 70 telephone interviews with business people;
— informal discussion with the LDDC and with government;
— 4 group discussions with the local community.

### Influences in Decision-making

Figure 2 illustrates the interrelation of the main actors. We found that the decision whether or not to invest in the Docklands rested on a number of factors, both rational and emotional.

MAIN ACTORS

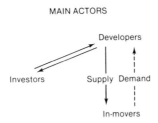

Figure 2. Decision-making amongst main actors

In-movers, unless they were large enough to be their own developers, could not move into the Docklands unless there were premises (developments) for them to move into.

Developers could not develop unless there was an infrastructure and developable land. They would not develop, nor would investors invest, unless they *perceived* that there would be demand (and hence reasonable occupancy at profitable rent levels) for their developments.

Thus confidence that the Docklands would be a success was all-important, and the confidence of the main actors was affected by their perceptions of the opinions of the other groups. Figure 3 attempts to model these influences.

Just as the main actors' perceptions of the attitudes of central and local government to the future of Docklands, conveyed partly by the media, could affect their investment decisions, so the attitudes of government and the media were shaped by their perceptions of the progress that Docklands was making – a vicious circle!

Not only did Docklands have to be successful, it had to be seen to be successful, and in the absence of any perceived progress on the ground in the early days of the LDDC, we concluded that confident, aggressive advertising was one of the few ways that this vicious circle could be broken.

### Attitudes to Docklands

Against this background it was reassuring to find that most groups we spoke to expressed a strong emotional desire to see the successful regeneration of Docklands. Many saw it as a tragedy that such a large and important part of London, so close to the City, had been allowed to decay for so long, and, as you might expect, the local community were particularly keen to see new industry, new jobs and new amenities in the area.

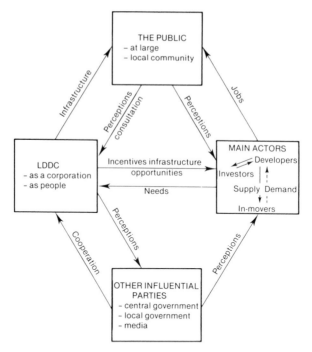

Figure 3. *Model of influences on decision making*

However, although developers and investors saw the potential of the location, they were very cynical and disillusioned about its prospects after the series of false starts. (One merchant banker told us that he was devoting his time to something with more short-term potential – the Channel Tunnel!)

Central and local government felt that this time they had created the right climate for the regeneration of the area, but emphasised the magnitude of the task, and the importance of the LDDC as a catalyst for development.

### Attitudes to the LDDC

Awareness of the LDDC among government and most City investors was quite high. Among developers and potential in-movers it was low. (A survey which the LDDC conducted amongst AB London businessman showed it to be 30 per cent in March 1982.)

The local authorities of Newham, Tower Hamlets and Southwark, which are all Labour-controlled, took a certain amount of exception to this free enterprise cuckoo in their midst. (Southwark still refuses to have any working contact with the LDDC.)

Not surprisingly, surrounded by indifference ('the phone never rings'), cynicism ('Oh here we go again'), and downright hostility, and with such a large responsibility to bear, morale among LDDC employees was not very high.

### Barriers to Purchase

Our principal objectives were to persuade private capital to invest in Docklands and relocators to move into the area.

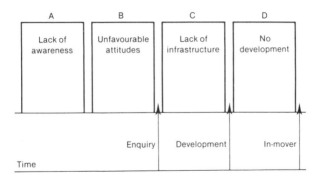

Figure 4. *Barriers to purchase*

We characterised the problems in fulfilling these objectives in terms of barriers to purchase:

— *lack of awareness*; obviously if one has never heard of Docklands or the LDDC, then one cannot relocate there, we have already seen that awareness of the LDDC was low among London businessmen.
— *unfavourable attitudes*; if one knows about Docklands, but holds the sort of attitudes that we uncovered in our exploratory research then one is unlikely to consider relocating there.
— *lack of infrastructure*; the lack of infrastructure would severely inhibit development in the early days of the LDDC.
— *no development*; without development there would be no firms moving to the area.

The first two of these, the ones which Nigel Broackes referred to earlier as the psychological barriers to the development of Docklands, we felt able to tackle with advertising.

As Figure 5 demonstrates, we reasoned that raising awareness and changing attitudes would lead to enquiries; if the LDDC concentrated on improving the infrastructure this

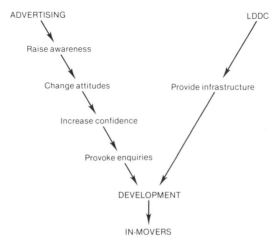

Figure 5. *The development process*

in turn would lead to development, and if there was development then there would be in-movers.

*Roles for Advertising*

Figure 6 attempts to summarise the roles for advertising. The explicit role of our advertising for Docklands was to raise awareness of the LDDC, communicate the benefits of the enterprise zone, to generate enquiries, and hence to funnel investment into the Isle

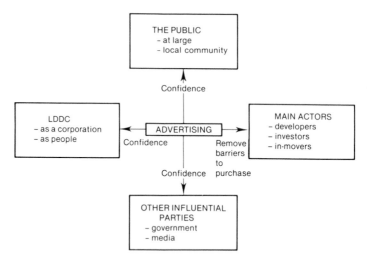

Figure 6. *A summary of the roles for advertising*

of Dogs. The implicit role was to demonstrate to all interested and influential parties, through the style and scale of the advertising, that the LDDC meant business, and that this time Docklands would be regenerated.

## THE ADVERTISING STRATEGY

We are evaluating in this paper the launch phase of the LDDC campaign, which covers a period from June 1982 to July 1983. By the end of this launch phase we planned to have removed the psychological barriers to the development of Docklands.

We conceived the advertising in three stages which correspond to our barriers to purchase model. Stage one (June–July 1982) was designed to create impact, to raise awareness of the LDDC, and to instil the feeling that this time something really was going to happen in Docklands. In stage two (February–March 1983) we began to communicate the specific benefits of the area, particularly the Isle of Dogs Enterprise Zone, with a view to generating enquiries. Stage three (June 1983) concentrated on the development opportunities in Docklands. In particular, we were keen to communicate that things *were* happening, and that this was not, therefore, another false start in the regeneration of the area.

*Media Strategy*

As Figure 7 shows, the majority of businessmen move less than 30 miles when relocating. Most property developers, the national media, the City and local community are based in London; therefore we concentrated our media in London.

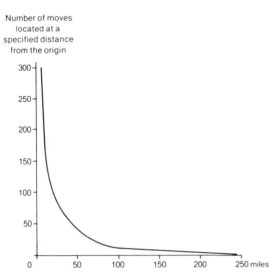

Figure 7. *Distance of move associated with all openings with an origin, 1966-75*

*Source:* Department of Industry

The first burst of advertising was deliberately designed to be a multi-media extravaganza. We wanted everyone to know that something special was happening in Docklands. TV was used as the lead medium (we took the centre break in News At Ten every weekday for four weeks). The quality press was also used to increase coverage against businessmen, and give some national exposure, local radio and 48 sheet posters increased frequency of exposure and conveyed certain tactical messages.

In the second and third bursts we used TV alone in order to maximise cover of our

TABLE 2:    MEDIA PLANS, LDDC LAUNCH CAMPAIGN

| | 1982 | | | | | | | 1983 | | | | | |
| | Jun | Jul | Aug | Sep | Oct | Nov | Dec | Jan | Feb | Mar | Apr | May | Jun | Jul |
|---|---|---|---|---|---|---|---|---|---|---|---|---|---|---|
| TV (London) | £250 000 | | | | | | | | £300 000 | | | £100 000 | | |
| | 500 men TVRs | | | | | | | | 500 men TVRs | | | 200 men TVRs | | |
| national press | £245 000 | | | | | | | | | | | | | |
| outdoor | £65 000 | | | | | | | | | | | | | |
| radio | £65 000 | | | | | | | | | | | | | |
| total | £625 000 | | | | | | | | £300 000 | | | £100 000 | | |

diverse target market. We have since started to use 48 sheet and supersite posters for frequent copy rotation and tight geographical targetting, and colour press to illustrate more detailed success stories for Docklands.

The total budget for the first three bursts was £1025000 (see Table 2 for breakdown by media).

## Creative Strategy

To achieve the objectives we had set for the campaign, the creative work had to embody a number of features.

1. It had to position the LDDC as a development area, so that potential in-movers and developers would consider it alongside the longer established 'greenfield' sites such as Milton Keynes.
2. It had to contain powerful, logical arguments, not glib advertising slogans, to appeal to our businessmen target groups.
3. It had to be bold, confident, aggressive and single-minded.

Docklands major benefit as a location was its proximity to London. This had emerged clearly from our exploratory research. Its importance is underlined by the fact that even our rival development areas (as one of our early press advertisements demonstrated – see page 169) stress how close *they* were to London.

The line we developed, which is common to all the creative work, is:

'Why move to the middle of nowhere, when you can move to the middle of London.'

This communicates both the rational benefits of Docklands, ie its location and the fact that it is a development area, and the emotional reinforcements of the LDDC's confidence and determination.

The fact that we were talking about our capital city, and indeed that London had been losing businesses and employment to some of these greenfield areas, gave us the right, we felt, to adopt this tone of voice.

The first commercial featured a group of crows having a meeting on Nelson's Column, and discussing how long it had taken them to get there. Crows were used as a one-off joke ('as the crow flies') but proved to be so memorable and popular in post-testing that they were retained as a creative vehicle for subsequent TV advertising.

## STRUCTURE AND METHODS OF EVALUATION

The analysis we have made of the roles of advertising, and in particular the barriers to purchase, will form the basis of our evaluation of the success of the advertising. We will concentrate on evaluating the advertising against the rather narrow objective of economic regeneration on the Isle of Dogs, as this was the LDDC's principal focus over the advertising period.

The nature of this analysis, and the fact that we had three stages of advertising (and the nature of language) lead one naturally to think of the activities as sequential. Of course this is not the case; all the dimensions that we will be discussing would have been

The advertisement reads: "What's the point of moving out if you've got to keep coming back?" — CENTRAL LANCASHIRE, PETERBOROUGH, WALES, MILTON KEYNES. "WHY MOVE TO THE MIDDLE OF NOWHERE, WHEN YOU CAN MOVE TO THE MIDDLE OF LONDON?"

changing throughout the campaign period as we have shown in Figure 8. For the sake of clarity, however, we will continue with the analysis as if the activities were neatly sequential.

The methods of evaluation are as follows:

— pre-advertising awareness check, AB businessmen, London area – NOP;
— tracking study – London businessmen, local residents – SRA;
— YEALDS – monitor of all enterprise zones;
— qualitative study by University College London, reasons for moving to Docklands.

*Awareness and Attitudes*

The first two barriers in our model of development and advertising effect are lack of awareness and unfavourable attitudes.

Table 3 shows spontaneous awareness of the LDDC and prompted awareness of the advertising among London businessmen before and after the first burst of Crows

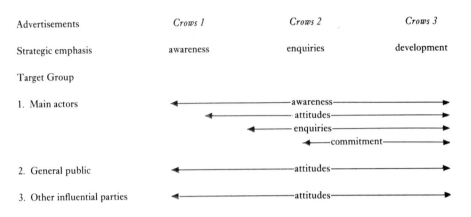

Figure 8    *Effects of advertising over time*

TABLE 3:    AWARENESS OF THE LDDC AMONG LONDON BUSINESSMEN

|  | March 1982 | July 1982 |
|---|---|---|
| Spontaneous awareness of the LDDC | 30% | 50% |
| Prompted advertising awareness of the LDDC | 38% | 70% |

Sources: NOP
         SRA

advertising. This increased by 20 percentage points to 50 per cent, and prompted awareness after the first burst was 99 per cent.

The pre-advertising recall figure at 38 per cent is surprisingly high considering that the LDDC had done no advertising themselves prior to Crows 1. However the 'Dockland Joint Committee' had run a TV campaign (featuring Cliff Michelmore) and this may have confused respondents. In any case, as Table 3 shows, prompted awareness of LDDC advertising almost doubled following our first burst of Crows advertising.

TABLE 4:    SPONTANEOUS AWARENESS OF DEVELOP
            MENT AGENCIES/CORPORATIONS AMONG
            LONDON BUSINESSMEN

|  | July 1982 |
|---|---|
|  | % |
| LDDC | 50 |
| Welsh DA | 41 |
| Milton Keynes DC | 20 |
| Scottish DA | 13 |
| Merseyside | 13 |

Source: SRA

Table 4 shows spontaneous awareness of the LDDC compared with other development areas; after just one burst of advertising it was already the best known development area among London businessmen. This is despite the longer advertising history of, and concentration on London as a prime market by, other development corporations.

Figures 9 and 10 show how awareness of the LDDC and its advertising continued to

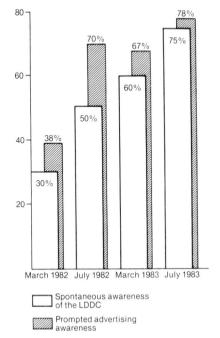

Figure 9. *Awareness of the LDDC amongst London businessmen*
*Sources:* NOP, SRA

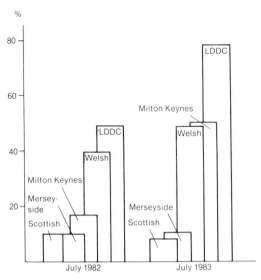

Figure 10. *Spontaneous awareness of development areas amongst London businessmen*
*Source:* SRA

grow over the campaign period, in line with our objectives, and at the expense of rival development areas.

TABLE 5:     BUSINESSMEN'S ATTITUDES TO THE LDDC

|  | July 1982 % |
|---|---|
| is committed to success | 81 |
| will succeed | 54 |
| has attracted business | 44 |
| has created more housing | 35 |
| has created more recreation | 29 |
| won't succeed | 4 |

Source: SRA

Table 5 shows the attitudes of London businessmen to the LDDC after the first burst. Their estimate of the LDDC's commitment to success and the fact that over half of them now thought it would be a success is impressive. Particularly when you think that many of them had never heard of the LDDC before we started advertising, and that our exploratory research (admittedly qualitative) showed such a high level of cynicism about the whole enterprise.

It seemed that we had swept away many people's psychological barriers to investing in Docklands in just one burst!

## Enquiries

Following the success of the first burst in building awareness and changing attitudes about Docklands we concentrated the second burst on communicating the specific benefits

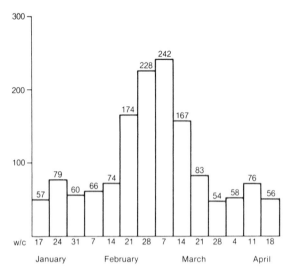

Figure 11. *Number of enquiries received by the LDDC by week, Jan-Apr 1983*
*Source:* LDDC

of Docklands, particularly the tax and rates benefits of the Isle of Dogs. The principal objective was to turn interest into enquiries. Figure 11 shows the enquiries generated during the second Crows burst in February–March 1983.

The average number of enquiries per week before the advertising began was 67. This trebled to an average of 203 a week during the campaign, and then fell back to 65 a week afterwards.

In all, the second burst of the campaign generated 811 enquiries from firms for information about the Isle of Dogs or Docklands generally during the burst itself.

During the total campaign period of a year the LDDC received over 4 000 enquiries (when we started advertising there were only 105 firms in the Isle of Dogs in total!). This gave the LDDC a list of potential in-movers and developers which they followed up through personal contact and direct mail. The size and type of the enquiries also helped them plan the development of Docklands more systematically.

## *Commitment*

Once the psychological barriers have been crossed and the prospect has made an enquiry, the final hurdle is the product itself.

The developer needs land to develop; the businessman needs developments to move into. As we have already described, much of the land in the Isle of Dogs was actually unusable.

In the period 31st September to 31st May, the LDDC invested £12.3 million in land reclamation, site clearance and site preparation, and in the provision of services. This amount was far in excess of any other enterprise zone (eg Salford £3.3 million, Swansea £4.9 million, Clydebank £5.9 million, and Corby £4.7 million), but was an essential step in the regeneration of the area. The results are shown in Figure 12.

In 1981 roughly 58 per cent of the Isle of Dogs was 'not available for development' compared with 46 per cent in other areas. Two years later the LDDC had reduced the amount of unusable land by 31 per cent to 69.21 hectares, ie to 40 per cent of the total, which compares with a drop of 25 per cent in the other areas.

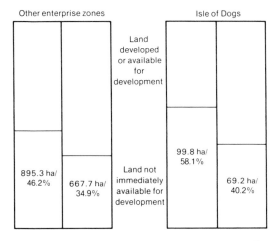

Figure 12. *Proportion of usable land*
*Source:* YEALDS

Having prepared the land for development, the LDDC needed to attract private investment from the City, not least because they had spent all their own money on fundamental site preparation!

One of their early development successes was in housing, and we decided to feature this in our third Crows film to illustrate the development opportunities in the area.

TABLE 6:    ATTITUDES TO LDDC IN THE CITY

|  | March 1983 | July 1983 |
|---|---|---|
|  | % | % |
| has attracted new business to the area | 41 | 55 |
| has created more housing | 44 | 45 |
| has created more recreational facilities | 29 | 31 |

Source: SRA

As Table 6 shows, the proportion of the City respondents in our tracking study who agreed with a number of statements about how the LDDC was progressing increased markedly over the period of the third burst, particularly on the issue of attracting businesses to the area. Reassuringly, the local residents, who are on the ground, and therefore ought to know, agreed with them (see Table 7).

TABLE 7:    ATTITUDES TO THE LDDC AMONG LOCAL RESIDENTS

|  | March 1983 % | July 1983 % |
|---|---|---|
| has attracted new business to the area | 37 | 54 |
| has created more housing | 35 | 45 |
| has created more recreational facilities | 26 | 32 |

Source: SRA

The creation and maintenance of this bandwagon effect is the key strategy behind subsequent advertising campaigns for the LDDC and, as Figure 13 shows, private investment has poured into the Isle of Dogs.

Figure 13 shows the total investment in site development by type of investor over the period 1 June 1981 to May 1983 in the top nine enterprise zones (all those in which more than £5 million has been invested).

YEALDS defines three types of investors: private developers, private producers who are developing the land for their own use, and others, mainly public authorities.

The outstanding enterprise zone in terms of site development over this period was Corby. An exceptionally large proportion of this investment was from large firms building premises for their own use eg, RS Components, Euramax Aluminium, Associated British Foods and A.C. Nielsen.

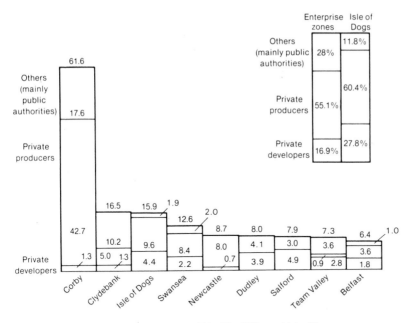

Period: June 1981 to May 1983 except Isle of Dogs
(start September 1981) and Belfast (start October 1981)

Figure 13. *Total investment in site development by type of investor (£m)*
*Source:* YEALDS

In terms of private producers the Isle of Dogs was second only to Corby in the magnitude of their incoming investment, and second only to Salford in terms of private developers – and this despite the fact that the Isle of Dogs was set up more than six months after these areas. In fact, in line with their objectives, 88.2 per cent of investment in the Isle of Dogs was from private investors, compared with an average of 72 per cent for other areas.

If we are correct in our analysis of how development in the Docklands area will occur, then given that we have now removed the psychological barriers to purchase, generated enquiries, provided an infrastructure, and begun to develop land, we should now see growth in the number of in-movers to the area.

TABLE 8:   IN-MOVING FIRMS BY ENTERPRISE ZONE (TOP EIGHT)

|  | 1st Jun 1981 –31st May 1982 | 1st Jun 1982 –31st May 1982 | 1st Jun 1982 –31st Dec 1983 | total |
|---|---|---|---|---|
| Clydebank | 62 | 82 | 37 | 181 |
| Isle of Dogs | 10 | 67 | 52 | 129 |
| Swansea | 39 | 42 | 20 | 101 |
| Corby | 21 | 42 | 27 | 90 |
| Dudley | 20 | 44 | 21 | 85 |
| Salford | 11 | 35 | 38 | 84 |
| Belfast Inner City | 15 | 36 | 14 | 65 |
| Trafford | 21 | 33 | 7 | 61 |
| total for all 13 enterprise zones | 251 | 474 | 299 | 1 024 |

Source: YEALDS

Table 8 shows the number of new firms that started in the top eight enterprise zones over the period 1st June 1981 to 31st December 1983. Over that period the Isle of Dogs has attracted more firms than any other enterprise zone except Clydebank. In fact as time has gone on, and in line with our analysis, the LDDC has been increasingly successful in attracting firms to the area.

Figure 14 shows the number of firms attracted to the area in successive periods for the top three enterprise zones. The Isle of Dogs began slowly – not surprisingly, given its

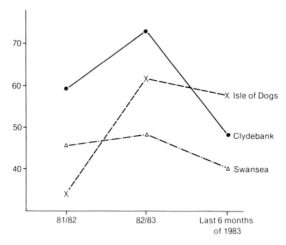

Figure 14. *Number of incoming firms (top 3)*

late start. In the 1981–82 period, before we started advertising, it only captured 10 of the 251 firms which moved into enterprise zones (a 4.0 per cent share of the market). In 1982–83, during our first burst of Crows advertising it improved very rapidly, taking 14.1 per cent of the market. In the last six months of 1983, following our third burst of advertising and the development activity we have described, the Isle of Dogs gained more incoming firms than *any other* enterprise zone, capturing 17.4 per cent of the market.

The 129 new firms that have moved into the Isle of Dogs over these two years have more than doubled the number of enterprises and jobs in the area.

## CONCLUSIONS

### *Has the Advertising Worked?*

Our analysis was that if we used advertising to raise awareness of the LDDC, to change attitudes towards the LDDC and to generate enquiries for the LDDC, and if the LDDC could improve the infrastructure of the Docklands area, particularly in the Isle of Dogs, then we would attract investment and new firms to the area.

We have raised awareness, we have improved confidence in the LDDC and we have generated enquiries. The LDDC have invested huge sums in improving the land, and we have attracted private capital, new firms and new jobs. The LDDC is now indisputably one of the top development areas in the country.

However, even though our analysis appears to have been correct, this in itself does not necessarily demonstrate a causal link between our advertising and a bulldozer starting work in the Isle of Dogs. To demonstrate such a link we need to find out from people locating to the Isle of Dogs why they moved there.

The University College of London carried out a study into the reasons why companies locate to the London Docklands Enterprise Zone in June 1984. They interviewed 62 firms who had moved into three major developments in the Isle of Dogs since 1982, using a semi-structured questionnaire.

They found that awareness of Docklands advertising was very high (88 per cent), and that over 70 per cent of the sample recognised the crows campaign correctly and identified it with Docklands.

When asked why they had considered moving to the Isle of Dogs the majority (58 per cent) said that they already knew the area, but of the rest, over 80 per cent said that they had made their first enquiry as a direct result of the advertising (ie 35 per cent of the total interviewed – see Table 9).

TABLE 9:   STIMULI FOR EXPLORING SITES IN THE ENTER-
          PRISE ZONE

|                              | number | %   |
| ---------------------------- | ------ | --- |
| total                        | 62     | 100 |
| aquaintance with area        | 20     | 32  |
| local search                 | 6      | 10  |
| contacts in area             | 10     | 16  |
| total with local knowledge   | 36     | 58  |
| advertising/publicity        | 22     | 35  |
| other                        | 5      | 8   |

Source: University College of London June 1984

The UCL report goes on to conclude that as well as generating enquiries the LDDC has two further, related functions.

> First it counteracts negative images of the Isle of Dogs/East End which are held by company personnel, their customers and competitors. Second it fulfils a psychological function in reducing perceptions of risk. A high visibility campaign reinforces executives' decisions to locate in the area, and supports the gamble that the area has potential.

This survey demonstrates conclusively the direct (or explicit) role that our advertising has played in the regeneration of Docklands. Their analysis of how the advertising has worked is totally in line with the model that we have devised and confirms the indirect (or implicit) roles for advertising which we have described. Finally, it highlights an important by-product of the advertising which is that it reinforces the decisions of in-movers once they have moved.

# 12

# Golden Wonder: A Potted Success Story

## INTRODUCTION

Golden Wonder's success with Pots has realised a volume sales increase of 31 per cent and a rise in profits of 136 per cent from 1982 to 1985. The only altered variable in the marketing mix was the advertising, and this paper will demonstrate the ways in which better thought out and executed advertising worked.

Certain aspects of the story have a broader significance.

1.  In 1982, although Golden Wonder had brand leadership and a growing brand share, the market was declining at 30 per cent per annum. Many would apply the classic solution of withdrawing support and 'milking' the brand. Golden Wonder took the alternative view, and committed themselves to further support.
2.  The new advertising sought to usurp all the best existing values of the field for Golden Wonder and to amplify these contextually with heightened emotional rewards and benefits. The advertising succeeded in building brand preference for Golden Wonder and, more importantly, in reintroducing growth to the market.
3.  The consumer behaviour 'mechanism' underlying the growth was fundamental to strategic intent. It involved increasing the frequency of use of existing users, and accepting some further declines in penetration.
4.  The advertising effect is remarkable for its longevity, a finding entirely consistent with the advertising's role of building the Pots eating habit.

Golden Wonder now owns a buoyant market. It provides immeasurably heightened potential for future profits and is one where the price of a successful competitive intrusion is far higher than it was prior to the new advertising's introduction.

## BUSINESS BACKGROUND

During 1980–85 Golden Wonder Limited was part of Imperial Foods, a division of the Imperial Group, which was taken over by Hanson Trust in May 1986.

Golden Wonder's business and reputation are founded on its major crisp brand and the bagged snacks, Wotsits and Ringos.

178

Instant hot snacks are dehydrated snack meals in pots, which are prepared by adding boiling water and are ready to eat from the pot in four to five minutes. The product consists of a base of noodles, rice or potato with dehydrated vegetables, soya pieces or meat and a flavoured sauce. Packaging consists of a plastic pot and a foil lid.

Golden Wonder were the first company in the UK market, launching Pot Noodle into a Lancashire test market in October 1977. Pot Noodle met with considerable success, and it was rolled out into half the country in November 1978. It then went national in November 1979 when supplies could meet demand.

1980 was a year of intense activity for this embryonic market. Three key competitors launched nationally in the first six months:

| | |
|---|---|
| Batchelors | Snackpot |
| Knorr | Knoodles |
| KP | Quicklunch |

Golden Wonder launched a second range, Pot Rice, into test in Lancashire in June, and this brand was supported nationally in February 1981.

By 1980 a huge market had been created where none had existed in 1976. It comprised 115 million individual pots, a market worth £42m at retail selling prices then. Advertising support was heavy in 1980 and 1981, with all brands using television:

TABLE 1:   ADVERTISING EXPENDITURE 1980/81

| | (£000 at card rates) | |
|---|---|---|
| | 1980 | 1981 |
| Pot Noodle | 1480 | 1248 |
| Pot Rice | 246 | 976 |
| Snackpot | 999 | 379 |
| Quicklunch | 1050 | 954 |
| Knoodles | 858 | – |

Source: MEAL

In February 1982 Golden Wonder launched a further innovative potato-based range of three products in Lancashire. These were branded as Pot Casserole. However, by 1982, severe problems were becoming evident for both the market and this important new source of profits for Golden Wonder.

## THE PROBLEM

### Business

The market had peaked in early 1981. The retail audit (MGS/NMRA) showed that volume consumer purchases in the twelve months to April 1982 had fallen to 70 per cent of the level achieved in the preceding year. Golden Wonder Pot sales were, however, broadly stable. The total Golden Wonder brand share, consolidating Pot Noodle, Pot Rice and Pot Casserole, had risen from 43 per cent in 1980 to 65 per cent in March/April 1982.

The problem facing Golden Wonder related to the projected steep rate of market decline. A programme of product testing conducted by Schlackmans Research had demonstrated that Golden Wonder had a superior product in terms of its combination of price, product size, recipes and eating enjoyment. But competitors would fight to protect their hold on this market for as long as possible.

With these three competitors now sharing only 35 per cent of the market, none of them had a financial basis for advertising in 1982. The absolute weight of advertising had clearly contributed to the market's spectacular growth. With only Golden Wonder advertising in 1982 and beyond, support levels could never again match those at the market's peak.

A further new problem for Golden Wonder in 1982 was that of price competition aligned to dealing from rival brands seeking to maintain share and recoup their investment. This put pressure on Golden Wonder's margins, and profits from Pots had fallen by 33 per cent year over year in 1981/82.

### The Consumer

1. *Buying Patterns* Special analysis of AGB's Personal Purchases Index had revealed that:

— Cumulative penetration built rapidly to 23 per cent of all individuals aged 13 to 64 over two and a half years, but saturation was reached by mid 1981.
— There was a low level of repeat purchasing. For many buyers the products failed to meet expectations.
— A 'fatigue' effect was evident from depth of trial analyses. A steady 5 to 10 per cent dropout from the market was apparent over bi-monthly periods from early 1981, even among people who had repeat purchased relatively frequently. There was a steady loss of buyers, and repeat buyers were decreasing their weight of purchase.

2. *Consumer Attitudes* Qualitative research showed that the products were very much seen and used as fillers or hot snacks between meals, not as meal substitutes. This was in direct contradiction to the usage occasion portrayed in several of the early commercials. Individual brand images were not developed; consumer preferences were as much flavour- or recipe-based as brand-based.

Almost by definition Pots were recognised as artificial and lacking in goodness. At the same time they fulfilled a useful function and were acceptable for what they were. Even loyal frequent consumers were often unwilling to admit openly to liking them because of the negative associations of artificiality and convenience. Consumer commitment to the product category and the Golden Wonder brand appeared essentially private and somewhat precarious.

### The Trade

The erratic market performance and subsequent decline had led to disenchantment and scepticism among the trade. The chief executives of two of Britain's biggest and most influential multiple food retailers publicly spoke out against the product category, criticising it for being representative of developments that were in neither the manufacturers' nor consumers' interests. A clear danger existed that the 90 per cent plus levels of grocery distribution achieved, along with the quality of display, would collapse and accelerate further market decline.

In June 1982 Golden Wonder consolidated their advertising account by moving the Pot Noodle, Pot Rice and Pot Casserole brands into the agency which already handled their crisp and snack brands. New marketing and advertising strategies were developed. This paper will demonstrate the success that these adventurous strategies had in reversing the apparently inevitable decline of this market.

## MARKETING STRATEGY

The new marketing strategy was based on two platforms:

— To own the market with a brand share in excess of 90 per cent as quicky as possible.
— To create a new momentum for the market which would reintroduce volume growth.

This momentum would require more closely matching the full rewards of the products to consumer needs. It would thus be based on brand values beyond speed and convenience. The critical elements involved were:

1. *Building a Brand Personality in a Commodity market* Golden Wonder had to aim to create a distinctive brand personality in what was essentially a commodity market of 'those pot things'. The brand names' interchangeability and the similarity of advertising styles had tended to contribute to confusion in the establishment of brand identities. There was little to connect Pot Noodles, or Pot Rice and Pot Casserole together that separated them from Snackpot or Quicklunch.

2. *Developing Stronger Coporate Branding* Although Pot Noodle was virtually a generic description, Golden Wonder was little known and comparatively poorly rated as a manufacturer in this market. Pot Noodle was the anchorpoint for Golden Wonder's instant hot snacks, and its reputation was deservedly high.

Overall, Golden Wonder branding was required to unite an expanding range – Pot Noodle, Pot Rice and Pot Casserole – and to link an increasingly disparate collection of recipes.

3. *Identification of Key Product Rewards* Golden Wonder needed to appropriate for itself the best values of the market, and establish a character that implied a superiority of eating experience and rewards. The products themselves were undeniably controversial, and Golden Wonder's range shared their generic characteristics and weaknesses. Even among users there was a certain amount of 'aiming off', and expectations were not high.

The new positioning for Golden Wonder Pots had to be unique and stem directly from the nature of the products and the key product rewards. These were identified as:

1. *Immediate Gratification* The emphasis has to be on immediate satisfaction rather than convenient preparation. Hunger would be the trigger: enjoyment and satisfaction would correlate

positively with the degree of hunger felt. Pots had to be presented as honest filling snacks, not an inferior meal. They would be all the more satisfying because, unlike sandwiches, they are hot.

2.   *Taste Sensation*  People had to be encouraged to think more in terms of the flavours being stimulating. Eaters had after all described the taste experience as 'tangy', 'spicy', 'highly flavoured', 'rich', and 'not routine'.

3.   *Indulgence*  Eating the product had to be fun. The sheer enjoyment of eating had to be far more important than the speed of making it.

## ADVERTISING STRATEGY

### Roles for Advertising

The roles defined for Golden Wonder advertising were those which advertising can fulfil better than any other element in the marketing mix.

1.   To remind people about Golden Wonder Pot Snacks and encourage them to eat them more often.
2.   To re-excite people.
3.   To appropriate for Golden Wonder all the best values of this market, and imply superiority of taste, satisfaction and rewards.
4.   To bring to life the brand values that are not immediately obvious over and above convenience, and to make Golden Wonder famous by developing a brand personality which would unify Pot Noodle, Pot Rice and Pot Casserole.

### Target Group

It was fundamental to the strategy to concentrate on existing users rather than seeking fresh ones. More specifically, the vast majority of triallists comprised Golden Wonder buyers. The majority were Pot Noodle users, heavier purchasers, satisfied triers with generally favourable attitudes towards the brand and particular recipes – and people rather experimental in their tastes.

Demographically, the target group was chiefly women, who accounted for 72 per cent of instant hot snack buyers. They were younger – aged under 35 – and biased strongly towards the working (C2/D) class.

Men could not be ignored because they represented 42 per cent of adults who buy *or* eat the product, and because their approval would be important. Neither could children, particularly teenagers, both in their roles as eaters and as a 'communications-conscious' pressure group.

Essentially the advertising was preaching to the converted. They were already supporters. Their enthusiasm needed arousing. It was not necessary to spend too much valuable advertising time educating people. They already knew how to make the product, they already knew of its convenience, and they already knew the sorts of occasions for which it was best suited. Instead, the focus could be more on the rewards and enjoyment of the products, and on building a distinctive brand personality.

*Target Responses*

Cor, I'm hungry enough to fancy one right now!

Golden Wonder's Pot Snacks are always the best – lots more satisfaction, lots more flavour, lots more enjoyment.

## A POTTED CREATIVE RATIONALE

Eating Pot Noodle had to become more of a unique experience. Wouldn't it be nice, then, if watching a commercial for Pot Noodle were as singular and enjoyable an experience as tucking into a pot of them? A pot of Pot Noodle, or Pot Rice, or Pot Casserole, is full of rewards; pots of taste, pots of warmth, pots of satisfaction – even pots of fun. But all these rewards come in one quick, convenient, instant package. In a word, they're potted.

That represented the basis for the 'potted' advertising. By never using a sentence when just one word would do (like 'hungry') and by never playing a whole scene when one shot would suffice (like the local yokel saying 'Wur'), 'Potted' commercials gave room to show people working up just the sort of hunger that Pot Noodle, Pot Rice and Pot Casserole satisfy. The result: advertising as instant, enjoyable and unique as the brand it's there to sell.

Two potted commercials were developed: 'Camping' for Pot Noodle and Pot Rice and 'Builders' to roll out Pot Casserole. (Subsequently both of these commercials were modified to be range commercials.) A third commercial in the series, 'Snowman', replaced 'Camping' in the mix for the winter of 1984.

## MEDIA STRATEGY AND BUDGET

Five key decisions had to be made before media plans could be finalised. These involved the budget level, media choice, allocation by region, allocation over time and allocation by product.

1. *Budget Level* Recommendations to test different weights of advertising regionally, and within each advertising budget, sales and profit relationships were not made because the market was already so different region by region that the proper evaluation of such tests was rendered impossible. A first fiscal year expenditure of £700 000, consistent with continued profit protection, but deployed in harmony with other strategic considerations was all that could be afforded.

2. *Media Choice* Television was used as the sole medium. It has the coverage and the frequency required. It has the ability to dramatise both the need for, and the rewards of, the brand in a distinctive way.

3. *Regional Breakdown* The brand had a highly skewed profile of sales on a regional basis. A comparison of the audit data with other data sources indicated that London was a surprisingly poor area for products of this sort. An analysis of MGS data showed (Table 2):

THE NEW 30-SECOND
POT NOODLE AND POT RICE COMMERCIAL

# A 30-SECOND COMMERCIAL
# INTRODUCING THE NEW POT CASSEROLE RANGE

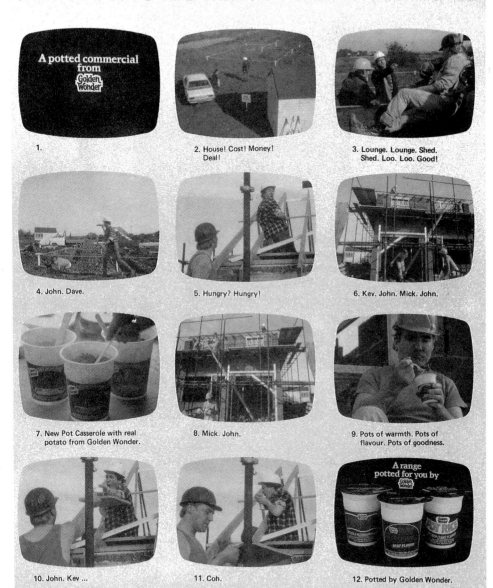

1.

2. House! Cost! Money! Deal!

3. Lounge. Lounge. Shed. Shed. Loo. Loo. Good!

4. John. Dave.

5. Hungry? Hungry!

6. Kev. John. Mick. John.

7. New Pot Casserole with real potato from Golden Wonder.

8. Mick. John.

9. Pots of warmth. Pots of flavour. Pots of goodness.

10. John. Kev ...

11. Coh.

12. Potted by Golden Wonder.

TABLE 2:   REGIONAL SALES PROFILE 12 M/E JUNE 1983

| Area | % Population | % Sales | Index of Consumption |
|------|-------------|---------|----------------------|
| London | 22.8 | 16.5 | 72 |
| Southern | 6.9 | 7.8 | 113 |
| Wales/West SW | 10.3 | 13.5 | 131 |
| Midlands/East England | 21.3 | 19.7 | 93 |
| Lancs | 13.3 | 19.5 | 147 |
| Yorks | 10.4 | 9.7 | 93 |
| North East | 5.0 | 4.4 | 88 |
| Scotland/Border | 10.1 | 8.9 | 88 |

Source: MGS/NMRA

These indices were used in conjunction with airtime costs as a basis for allocating advertising weight on a regional basis. (Consumer penetration data from TGI and AGB were entirely consistent with this audit date.)

4.   *Allocation Over Time*   In the reminder role designated for it, it was judged essential that the advertising should be in front of the consumer for as long as possible. This led to a proposed drip pattern of advertising. However, the new campaign had initially to be introduced at a heavier weight.

In the case of a weak sales area with a relatively low budget such as London, a constant presence was clearly not possible. In this instance it was felt more important to have an effective introduction to the campaign and to the new product range.

The Pots market has been seasonal showing a consistent pattern of + 14 per cent over the norm in January/February and − 11 per cent in June/July/August. The decision was taken to concentrate advertising into the November–April period.

5.   *Allocation by Product Type*   Any advertisement for any variety or flavour had to be an advertisement for all Golden Wonder Pots. However, the launch of a significant new range, as with the national roll-out of Pot Casserole with a separate commercial within the campaign, had to generate trial in a relatively short period. The Pot Casserole roll-out was planned on the basis of a level of 400 TVRs in four weeks in new areas.

After the winter 82/83 roll-out of Pot Casserole, the media strategy for each year involved continuous weights of 70 TVRs per week in each region for as long as the advertising weight deployed lasted. Each year the regional allocation was reviewed and adjusted in line with sales

TABLE 3:   TELEVISION ADVERTISING

| | Network housewife ratings | | | | |
|---|---|---|---|---|---|
| Year: | 1981 | 1982 | 1983 | 1984 | 1985 |
| Golden Wonder | | | | | |
| Original campaign | 2038 | 206 | – | – | – |
| New campaign | | 404 | 690 | 1300 | 1230 |
| Total | 2038 | 610 | 690 | 1300 | 1230 |
| Competitive | 2233 | – | 65 | – | – |

Source: BARB

and consumer penetration changes. When 'Snowman' was introduced into the mix it ran only at times of cold weather.

The total level of television advertising over the period can be seen in Table 3.

## SALES RESULTS

The effect of the new campaign was to provide a dramatic turnabout in consumers' purchasing of Pots. Golden Wonder's sales rose marginally in 1983, before shooting ahead in 1984 and 1985. More importantly, total market sales turned into a growth pattern in 1984 and 1985, reversing the steep decline of the earlier two years.

TABLE 4:  CONSUMER SALES CHANGE

| | Annual % volume change | | | |
|---|---|---|---|---|
| Year: | 1982 | 1983 | 1984 | 1985 |
| Golden Wonder Pots | − 4 | + 1 | + 16 | + 12 |
| Total market | − 24 | − 12 | + 7 | + 8 |

Source: MGS/NMRA

The factors underlying the renewed growth of Golden Wonder Pots were:

1. *Brand Share* Figure 1 shows the Golden Wonder brand share on a consistent upward trend to a level approaching 80 per cent, prior to the new campaign's introduction. Over the first winter season of the advertising, Golden Wonder's share advanced further to 90 per cent as planned. Subsequently, in the face of the one remaining competitor, Quicklunch, it advanced to 97 per cent.

Knoodles and Snackpot remained on the market until mid 1983 and mid 1984 respectively, when progressive de-listing forced their withdrawal. The effect of this was further decreases in display space for the category, an important yet unquantified depressing variable for a product bought for fairly immediate consumption. Once the Golden Wonder brand share had reached 90 per cent, the growth pattern achieved could be fuelled only by market growth, and this is indeed what happened.

2. *Market Growth* Golden Wonder moved into major year-on-year sales increases in the winter season of 1983/84 having held steady over the first winter, largely as a result of brand share gains (Figure 2).

The comparable picture for the total market (Figure 3) shows a progressive slowing of the level of decline from the start of the advertising until, in February and March 1984, growth was finally re-introduced to the whole market – for the first time in three years. This growth pattern was then maintained for virtually the whole of the next two-year period.

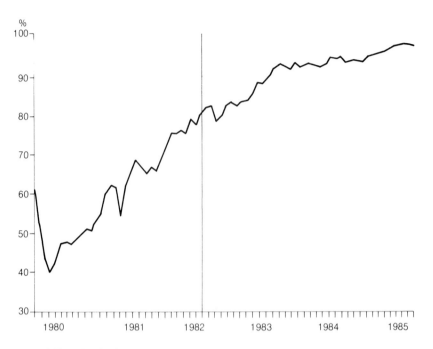

Figure 1. *Golden Wonder volume brand share*
*Source:* MGS/NMRA

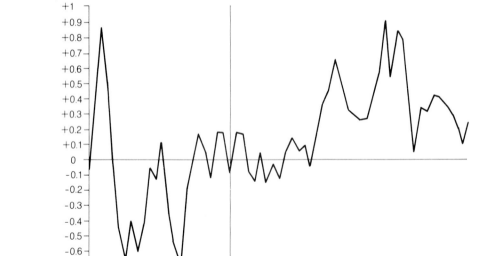

Figure 2. *Year on year changes in Golden Wonder*
*Source:* MGS/NMRA

Volume (thousands of Pots)

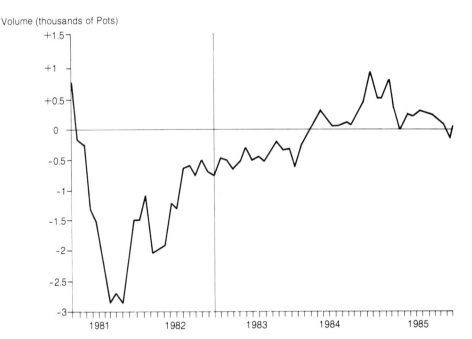

Figure 3. *Year on year changes in total market*
*Source:* MGS/NMRA

## CONSUMER BEHAVIOUR

Underlying this turnabout in consumer sales was a dramatic change in consumer purchasing patterns. The number of people purchasing Pots slipped further, but the average weight of purchase (and thus the frequency of eating, since Pots are bought for immediate consumption) increased.

A special analysis of sales growth, based on the AGB Personal Purchases Panel, compared the 44 weeks ending in March 1984 with the comparable period for 1985. The base for this survey is a nationally representative sample of 8 000 individuals aged 13 to 79.

TABLE 5: CONSUMER PURCHASING CHANGES

|  | Period 1<br>44 weeks ending<br>3/3/84 | Period 2<br>44 weeks ending<br>3/3/85 |
|---|---|---|
| Purchase penetration | 6.8% | 6.1% |
| Average weight of purchase in period | 6.9 | 10.9 |

Source: AGB/PPI

These buyers of Pots were further broken down into three groups: buyers in both periods ('Repeat'), buyers in the first period who had not bought in the second ('Lapsed'), and buyers in the second period who had not bought in the first ('New').

TABLE 6:   CONSUMER PURCHASING CHANGES

|  | Period 1<br>44 weeks ending<br>3/3/84 | Period 2<br>44 weeks ending<br>3/3/85 |
|---|---|---|
| 'Repeat' buyers |  |  |
| Purchase penetration | 3.3% | 3.3% |
| Average weight | 12.9 | 15.8 |
| 'Lapsed' buyers |  |  |
| Purchase penetration | 3.5% |  |
| Average weight | 3.1 |  |
| 'New' buyers |  |  |
| Purchase penetration |  | 2.8% |
| Average weight |  | 5.2 |

Source: AGB/PPI

This analysis demonstrated that the sales growth had come from precisely the change in consumer behaviour posited in the advertising strategy. Existing users were consuming more Pots. *Even those heavier buying long-term users had significantly increased their weight of consumption.* Moreover, people leaving the market were being replaced by heavier-buying newcomers.

The gains of 25 per cent in consumer purchases, which can be derived from the comparison, exceed the 16 per cent recorded on the retail audit (Table 4). They are, in fact, closer to the ex-factory growth level recorded since new un-audited distribution channels, such as convenience stores, late night corner shops and canteens, were opened up in 1983/84.

The sceptic could, of course, attribute all this to the natural development of the market over time. A small loyal hard core of regular users had emerged. They had tried the brands and flavours of interest to them, and settled on their repertoires. Competition had been largely eliminated, so there was less brand confusion and experimentation leading to below par product experiences driving people from the market. The issue is whether Golden Wonder Pots were, in these circumstances, their own advocates and source of growth, or whether the new advertising made a contribution to the sales growth evident from the date of its introduction.

The dramatic reversal of the trend and its timing for not only the Golden Wonder brand but also the whole market would indicate that a new force far beyond the product itself was operative. And it would seem that force was the new advertising – but that needs to be demonstrated.

## DID THE ADVERTISING AFFECT SALES?

Firstly, there were no changes to the Golden Wonder Pots range. The launch of Pot Casserole was completed in February 1983, and the same 11 products still comprised the range at the end of 1985. There have been no perceptible changes to recipes, product quality or pack graphics. Distribution has remained stable, though quality of distribution in terms of siting and facings may not be as good as it was at the market's peak in 1981. There have been no major consumer promotions for Golden Wonder Pots – merely a single four for the price of three flavour trial generating offer targeted at the independent trade. As Figure 4 shows, the real price paid for Golden Wonder Pots has varied over time, but the price low coincided with the sales low in early 1982 and the current price is just 1p below the 1980 and 1983 peak levels. Indeed the real price of Golden Wonder Pots was exactly the same at the end of 1985 as it had been at the campaign's introduction in November 1983. Thus no variable other than advertising could have effected the turnaround in Pots sales.

Figure 4. *Golden Wonder Pots real price (deflated by RPI Food; December 1985 = 100)*
*Source:* MGS/NMRA: Government statistics

Secondly, we have the findings of extensive econometric analysis. JWT built a model of brand sales, using MGS/NMRA four-weekly data for the 76 periods from March 1980 to December 1985. The independent variable in this model is consumer sales of Golden Wonder Pots in total. Explanatory variables are:

— Television advertising for the period: Golden Wonder and competitive.
— Price changes relative to the preceding period.
— Relative temperature in that period.
— Sales in the previous period.

The model comprises two sequential models that provide a close fit to the observed data. The $R^2$ for the period, prior to the new advertising in November 1982 (1980–8), is moderate at 0.53, but for 1983–85 $R^2$ is 0.85. The market model is summarised in Table 7, and its fit with actual consumer purchases shown in Figure 5.

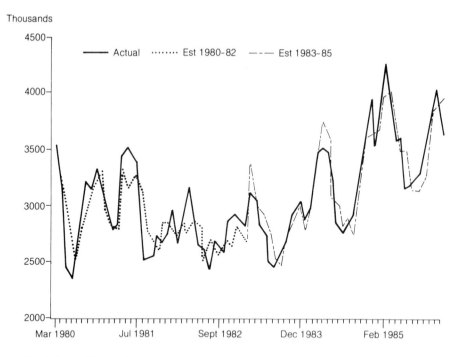

Figure 5. *Market model, actual and estimated volume sales*

TABLE 7: THE MARKET MODEL

*Multiple regression of MGS/NMRA data March 1980 to December 1981*
*Dependent variable Y = Consumer sales of Golden Wonder Pots (000 units)*

| Equation | | B Co-efficients | |
|---|---|---|---|
| | | 1980–82 | 1983–85 |
| Y = A | Constant | 1342.00 | 908.00 |
| + B₁X₁ | Golden Wonder advertising in current period (TVRs) | 0.32 | 1.07 |
| + B₂X₂ | Competitive advertising in current period (TVRs) | 0.25 | – |
| + B₃X₃ | Lagged dependent variable – sales in previous period | 0.54 | 0.81 |
| + B₄X₄ | Price change in current period from previous | – 103 36.40 | – 391 65.10 |
| + B₅X₅ | Relative temperature | – 82.43 | – 330.00 |
| | Corrected R² | 0.53 | 0.85 |

We can draw the following conclusions:

1. *Price* Real price was not statistically significant in explaining sales variation but price change was. The effect of a 1p price increase in any period being a drop of 3.7 per cent of the average four-weekly volume in 1980–82, and a drop of 9.9 per cent of average four-weekly volume in 1983–1985. The difference is related to the changed competitive environment, as in the later period Golden Wonder's price elasticity represents that of the whole market, without competitive pricing considerations.

2. *Temperature* Temperature variability was derived by comparing the mean daily temperature for each month with the long-term average temperature for that month (obtained from the Monthly Digest of Statistics). This gives an indication, with quantifiable expression, for periods of unusual weather conditions. There is an inverse relationship between sales and relative temperature. Sales increased by 10 per cent of the monthly average in months which were cold enough to represent half the usual monthly temperature (i.e. December 1981, January/February 1985).

3. *Seasonality* Seasonality is a factor in the market but is highly correlated with the timing of advertising. No separate variable for seasonality has been incorporated in the model.

4. *Advertising* Over the period when there was competitive advertising, that competitive advertising made a contribution to Golden Wonder sales only marginally less than Golden Wonder's own advertising. This explanatory variable did not exist for the 1983–85 component of the model as there was no competitive advertising.

This is a market which is highly responsive to advertising. Television advertising is by far and away the most important variable in explaining sales variations for both Golden Wonder and the total market. The advertising in this model contributes in two ways, the immediate and the 'longer-term' effects. The new campaign for Pots was far more effective than the earlier ones on both of these counts.

The 'immediate' (within period) advertising effect of the new campaign is just over 100 000 Pots for 100 TVRs, over three times the level pertaining for 1980–82 TV advertising. Additionally, the longer-term effect of the advertising – as represented by the carry-over sales from period to period – has risen from 54 per cent in 1980–82 to 81 per cent in 1983–85.

With a period to period carry-over effect of 81 per cent of sales, the total sales gain attributable to the advertising is 5.3 times that of the 'immediate' effect – a total of over half a million extra Pots sold for each 100 TVRs delivered by the new campaign. This compares with a mere 70 000 additional Pots for each 100 TVRs of the old advertising. A seven-fold increase in the level of sales attributable to advertising was the measure of the new campaign's effectiveness compared with previous Golden Wonder advertising.

On this basis, the advertising over 1983–85 has contributed just over twenty million Pots to Golden Wonder sales cumulatively – the difference between a continued decline of 2 per cent per annum and the healthy growth achieved.

Clearly the 'Potted' advertising campaign has made a huge positive contribution to the turn-around in sales of Golden Wonder Pots. It has revitalised and reinjected growth into the product category, which is now effectively owned by Golden Wonder. It has achieved this by intensifying the consumption of remaining product field users. On this basis we would accept the high level of advertising 'carry-over' or long-term effect. Product consumption is clearly *stimulated by* the advertising, but product enjoyment is enhanced by the extrinsic or emotional values conveyed. Thus the advertising works in conjunction with product consumption to create greater rewards or more 'total utility' from a Golden Wonder Pot; the consumer gets more enjoyment and the frequency of consumption intensifies. The long-term effect of the advertising clearly embraces this increased commitment to Pots. Based as it is on advertising experience feeding into heightened rewards from continuing product consumption, it is entirely credible that an advertising exposure can 'work' for over a year.

## HOW DID THE ADVERTISING WORK?

The advertising was directly responsible for generating increased consumption which, while hugely significant in commercial terms, was not at a level which consumers themselves were sufficiently conscious of to be able to recount in face-to-face interviews. Therefore, the way the advertising worked has to be broached indirectly by demonstrating how each element of the advertising strategy was met.

### Impact

A continuous Millward Brown tracking study run through 1983–84 indicated that among Pots users the advertising achieved high levels of advertising awareness and recall with good communication. The commercials scored highly for memorability and entertainment from their introduction, though people naturally were less prepared to credit them directly as a stimulus for consumption.

TABLE 8:   ATTITUDES TO POTS TV COMMERCIALS

| *Base: all housewives who have ever bought Pots recalling the advertising* *(1/11/82 to 21/8/83)* | | |
|---|---|---|
| % saying (ad) was: | 'Camping' | 'Builders' |
|  | 98 | 195 |
|  | 100% | 100% |
|  | % | % |
| It's the sort of commercial that sticks in your mind | 39 | 48 |
| It's entertaining | 39 | 40 |
| It tells you about the products | 26 | 32 |
| It makes you want to eat the products | 18 | 12 |
| It's a bit silly | 11 | 20 |
| It's a bit confusing and hard to follow | 6 | 3 |
| It's a bit boring | 1 | 2 |

Source: Millward Brown

The advertising definitely had impact and was entertaining for its target group.

### Communication

Since the new campaign was developed in 1982, six qualitative research projects among Pots eaters or buyers have been conducted by Schlackmans. These have explored both animatics of the commercials and the finished commercials themselves. What has emerged from this is clear evidence that Pots advertising has met all of the strategic objectives set, whilst having a unique creative approach ideally fitted to Golden Wonder Pots.

A 1985 report states:

'Builders' is a favourite. It was almost always spontaneously referred to by all the groups and was recognised and remembered when shown. It appeared to have all the necessary elements because it communicated all the product benefits, whilst providing entertainment value at the same time.

In summary it conveys that the product was a snack which was quick, filling, substantial and suitable to fill grown men. Further, it conveyed an enjoyment factor and tastiness through the verbal consumer noises made during the commercial.

(Schlackman)

Or, in a consumer's own words:

> That gives it all. The people don't have to speak. It's giving us warmth, goodness and quickness and nobody has to say anything about it, they're just all jumping about and eating it.

'Camping' and 'Snowman' were identifiably commercials from the same campaign but were favoured more by housewives than by men or teenagers, because of the family values. As planned from its introduction to the mix, 'Snowman' conveyed energy-giving, warming and 'good for you' qualities, less evident in 'Builders' or 'Camping'. To quote two more respondents.

> It's just a typical thing that could happen. If you were out playing in the snow you could get cold, and want to come in and warm yourself and fill yourself up for a while.

> That tells you everything. Its goodness, it's warm, it's filling.

All three Pots films have conveyed Golden Wonder Pots as 'a snack'; hot, substantial, and moreover nourishing snacks eaten in the context of the creation of energy, warmth and hunger satisfaction. They have achieved this with the basic category identifiers of 'quick and convenient' underpinning all other responses.

*User Imagery*

The Golden Wonder Pot user is now typically a young (under 35) Northern adult working-class man or woman. A major quantified study conducted in November 1985 among heavy Pots users (eaters in the last two months who represent 80 per cent of the total market) indicated that their image of Pots eaters was young, relatively classless but, furthermore, one of energetic, fun-loving people getting the most out of life. A selection of the key dimensions from the study is set out below. Trends are not available, but the wide social acceptability of

TABLE 9.  THE USER IMAGERY OF GOLDEN WONDER POTS

| *Percentage of eaters in the last two months of Golden Wonder Pots saying they were likely/unlikely to be eaten by:* | | |
|---|---|---|
| | Likely | Unlikely |
| 428 = 100% | % | % |
| Teenagers | 99 | – |
| Young adults | 98 | 1 |
| Working-class people | 90 | 2 |
| People who work in offices | 88 | 7 |
| People with modern ideas | 86 | 4 |
| Fun-loving people | 79 | 2 |
| People who enjoy the outdoors | 79 | 9 |
| People who live in the 'fast lane' | 77 | 10 |
| People who work outdoors | 76 | 13 |
| Adventurous people | 73 | 10 |
| People who lead a quiet life | 47 | 19 |
| People who are houseproud | 45 | 24 |
| Middle-aged people | 45 | 35 |
| People who are set in their ways | 16 | 66 |
| Business executives | 18 | 69 |

Source: Schlackman: November 1985

Pots among current users is clear. No sense of alienation, guilt or self-doubt is evident.

All of this evidence indicates that the new campaign has met its objective of re-exciting eaters and bringing to life those values that are not immediately obvious over speed and convenience, and that this has been central to the advertising's success.


## ADVERTISING'S DEVELOPING CONTRIBUTION TO INCREASED SALES

Clearly the advertising did not have the success in its first 1982/83 season that it enjoyed over subsequent winters. Factors contributing to this are:

1.  Relatively steep price rises over the autumn and winter of the campaign's introduction to finance advertising and protect profits.
2.  Better media deployment as our understanding of the campaign has developed. Over and above the campaign's growing presence, familiarity and established style, the deployment of the TV budget has been better able to concentrate the TV presence on areas of higher user density and to use singlemindedly the drip deployment of TVRs to maximise the brand's presence over time.
3.  The third commercial 'Snowman' introduced a 'cold weather' element to the pool of commercials and consolidated the developing effectiveness of the campaign.

Irrespective of advertising weight deployed, sales increases were achieved in all ITV areas in *both* 1984 and 1985. Those sales increases were spread pro rata across the range, and the sales profile of Pot Noodle, Pot Rice and Pot Casserole remains the same in 1985 as it was in 1983.


## COMMERCIAL SUCCESS

The commercial value of the advertising is clear from the trend in real profits (net of all overheads and expenditure) accruing to Golden Wonder from Pot Noodle, Pot Rice and Pot Casserole:

TABLE 10:   GOLDEN WONDER POTS: REAL PROFITS

Net profits deflated by RPI: Index 1981/82 = 100
GOLDEN WONDER FISCAL YEAR (NOVEMBER–OCTOBER):

| | |
|---|---|
| 1980/81 | 150 |
| 1981/82 | 100 |
| 1982/83 | 177 |
| 1983/84 | 179 |
| 1984/85 | 236 |

Source: Golden Wonder

The new campaign paid for itself from its introduction, and raised profits by 75 per cent in 82/83. As sales have forged ahead, Golden Wonder are now reaping record profits from a brand which appeared to be in unarrestable decline prior to the introduction of new advertising.

## CONCLUSIONS

To summarise the arguments:

1.  Since the introduction of the new advertising strategy and executions, consumer pur-
    chases have moved into a growth phase. Over the campaign's first winter, Golden Wonder
    Pots increased their brand share of a market whose rate of decline had been arrested. In
    its second winter, the advertising was responsible for reintroducing growth to the total
    market, a pattern maintained to date.
2.  This was achieved by increasing the frequency of eating Golden Wonder Pots among
    people using the product field prior to the introduction of the new advertising, rather
    than by penetration gains. The advertising has worked in the way envisaged in the
    strategy.
3.  Econometric analysis has established a particularly strong relationship between the new
    television campaign and increased consumer purchases. An immediate short-term effect
    and a longer-term lagged effect of advertising are discernible. Combining these two
    effects for both the early pre- 1983 Golden Wonder advertising and the new campaign,
    and comparing the results, indicates that the new advertising is seven times as effective as
    the 1980–82 advertising.
4.  Over the period 1983–85, over 20 million incremental Pots sales can be attributed to the
    new campaign. This figure exceeds the cumulative gains made over the three years,
    suggesting that Golden Wonder sales would have continued to decline at around 2 per
    cent per annum without the new advertising.
5.  The longer-term effects of the advertising are particularly important. The total sales gain
    attributable to the advertising is 5.3 times the short-term (within period) effect. This is,
    we believe, because of the progressive development of the relationship between product
    consumption and the added, primarily emotional, rewards communicated by the adver-
    tising. The advertising has worked to increase people's total enjoyment of the product
    and, as a result, to intensify their consumption, and to build the Pots eating habit over a
    long period.
6.  The advertising has met its objective of having good impact in order to re-awaken and re-
    excite people about Pots. It has built a classless image founded on modernity and fun,
    and created a sense of excitement around Golden Wonder Pots. Satisfaction of a real
    hunger has been central to all communications.
7.  The 'real' annual profits accruing to Golden Wonder from Pots has more than doubled
    over the three years of the new campaign. 'Pots of warmth, Pots of goodness, Pots of
    satisfaction' was the message. Pots of extra sales and Pots of extra profits were the
    results. This is a 'Potted' success story for Golden Wonder which, we believe, is directly
    and demonstrably attributable to its change of advertising.

# 13

# Benylin: Effective Use of Advertising to Increase Sales and Market Share

INTRODUCTION

This case history recounts the success of a television campaign for the cough treatment Benylin during the period April 1985 to May 1986. The campaign was a notable success for a product which had never advertised direct to the consumer before; over a year in which competitive volume fell by 3 per cent, Benylin volume grew by 11 per cent.

Benylin had been brand leader for many years. This case history shows how an unexpected development in a stable market (the introduction of a National Health Service Limited List) allowed the brand leader, by an aggressive response through advertising, to reinforce its position in the market. In the September 1985/April 1986 season Benylin achieved a market share of 24.6 per cent volume, 34.7 per cent sterling.

The case history falls into two parts, firstly an account of the circumstances which prompted Benylin to advertise on television, and secondly an analysis of the advertising campaign.

## PART 1: HOW BENYLIN WAS PROMPTED TO ADVERTISE ON TELEVISION

### Product Background

Benylin Expectorant, for the treatment of coughs, was introduced in 1949 as a prescription-only product and became available 'over-the-counter' in 1973. It remained, however, a 'P' product – meaning that the general public could only buy Benylin from a retail chemist with a qualified pharmacist on the premises or, of course, through prescription from the doctor.

The effective formula of Benylin, enhanced by its prescription and pharmacy-only status, led to the consumer perceiving Benylin as a serious medicine for coughs, with a reputation un-rivalled by brands available on general sale.

Additions to the Benylin range have been made over the years to provide a spectrum of pre-sentations to treat all types of cough. The presentations currently being marketed by Warner-Lambert Health Care are Benylin Expectorant, Benylin Paediatric (specially formulated for children), Benylin Mentholated Linctus and Benylin Fortified Linctus (see page 199).

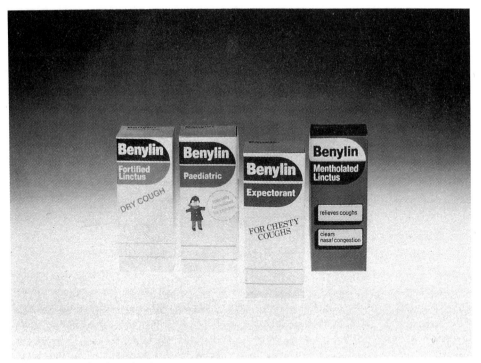

The four presentations of Benylin cough medicine

## The Limited List

In November 1984 the Government announced that it intended to save £100m on the National Health Service drug bill in the coming fiscal year. The method chosen to achieve this saving was by restricting the products a doctor could prescribe on the National Health Service in seven therapeutic areas. The areas were cough and cold remedies; analgesics; antacids; vitamin supplements; tranquillisers and sedatives; laxatives; and tonics. Doctors were left with a list of basic, mostly generic, products to prescribe in these categories.

After some consultation with the British Medical Association and other interested parties, the Limited List came into effect on 1 April 1985, and from that date Benylin and every other branded cough medicine was no longer available to be prescribed on the National Health Service.

*The effect of the Limited List on Benylin* The effect on the profile of Benylin sales was drastic. Table 1 shows the share of Benylin business generated by prescriptions in the four-year period from December 1982 to December 1986.

In 1984 20 million prescriptions had been written for coughs and related conditions, and Benylin had a 20 per cent share of that market. These 4 million prescriptions represented 52 per cent of Benylin sterling sales.

TABLE 1:  BENYLIN – PRESCRIPTION/OTC SPLIT 1983–1986 (STERLING)

|  | 1983 | 1984 | *Year ending November* 1985* | 1986 |
|---|---|---|---|---|
| % Prescription | 49 | 52 | 12 | 0 |
| % OTC | 51 | 48 | 88 | 100 |

\* Limited List introduced 1 April 1985
Source: Warner-Lambert Health Care

The prime objective of the advertising campaign was to replace the sales that the 4 million prescriptions had generated. However, in addition to the loss of the prescription volume a number of other potential problems, which the delisting of Benylin might have caused, were identified.

### The Potential Problems

1.  The value of the doctors' prescriptions as an introduction to Benylin, and the medical credibility of the product so gained, would no longer be available.
2.  The opportunity to reinforce the pharmacists' recommending behaviour by the through-put of Benylin prescriptions, and consequent stocking in the pharmacy, would cease.
3.  The delisting of Benylin might have undermined the perception of Benylin as an effective and serious medicine.
4.  Benylin, as market leader, could suffer from attack by others in the market during the period of instability caused by the Limited List.
5.  New products could take advantage of the unsettled market to command a dangerous entry share.

*The Opportunities* The delisting of Benylin also gave rise to a number of opportunities – the most important of which was that Benylin could be advertised to the public above-the-line for the first time. Until 1 April 1985, Benylin had only been advertised direct to the doctor and the pharmacist, with consumer advertising restricted to point-of-sale material in the pharmacy. This was a tradition encouraged by the Association of the British Pharmaceutical Industry and The Pharmaceutical Society with semi-ethical brands such as Benylin – doctors and pharmacists object to the advertising of medicines to the public as it may prejudice their professional skills by encouraging patients and customers to demand unsuitable medicines.

The freedom to advertise provided two major opportunities for Benylin:

1.  The advertising could reassure current Benylin users of the efficacy of their chosen brand.
2.  Benylin could now compete openly not only against all the other delisted 'P' cough products, but also against the General Sales List (GSL) products available in drugstores and supermarkets.

### Selection of Benylin Products for the Advertising Test

Four formulations of Benylin are available, three for adults and one for children. Prior to the introduction of the Limited List, non-prescribed volume in each formulation was:

|  |  | *% of Benylin total volume* |
|---|---|---|
| For adults: | Benylin Expectorant | 73.5 |
|  | Benylin Fortified | 12.0 |
|  | Benylin Mentholated | 2.5 |
|  |  | 88.0 |
| For children: | Benylin Paediatric | 12.0 |
|  |  | 100.0 |

The possibility of single advertisements covering the complete range was rejected from the start: such advertising was felt to be potentially confusing, and irrelevant to individual consumer needs. It was therefore decided that Benylin Expectorant should be the formulation supported, given its pre-eminent importance. However, it was also felt that Benylin Paediatric was a formulation which had particular potential, and provided it could be supported without risk of confusion *vis-à-vis* Benylin Expectorant, it could repay advertising investment.

### Creative Strategy

It was agreed that the advertising produced for the Expectorant and Paediatric formulations of the brand should be distinctively different, in order to avoid possible future confusion. Almost 90 per cent of Benylin volume went through adult formulations: the advertising introduction of the Paediatric formulation might have detracted from the perceived strength/efficacy of the adult products and, equally, this perception of strength/efficacy might have made a Paediatric positioning unacceptable to the consumer. Equally, the highly competitive nature of the market made clear branding of key importance. Since both formulations were heavily branded as Benylin, it was necessary that advertising for both should act in a strongly complementary manner.

Against this background, the advertising created for each formulation concentrated on the following features and benefits:

*Benylin Expectorant*

1. Benylin had amassed a user-base of millions of cough sufferers since its introduction – it was tried and trusted.
2. Benylin had been proven effective in clinical trials – it worked better than other available cough preparations (see opposite).
3. Benylin was a serious medicine – it was only obtainable from the pharmacist (removal of Benylin from the list of National Health Service-prescribable products did not alter the brand's retail distribution).

*Benylin Paediatric*

1. Benylin's proven formulation for adult coughs had been specifically adapted to make it equally as effective for children.
2. Benylin's paediatric formulation was both effective for, and acceptable to, children.
3. Benylin's soothing efficacy provided relief from the child's symptoms enabling both child and parents to obtain sufficient sleep, thus speeding recovery (see page 203).

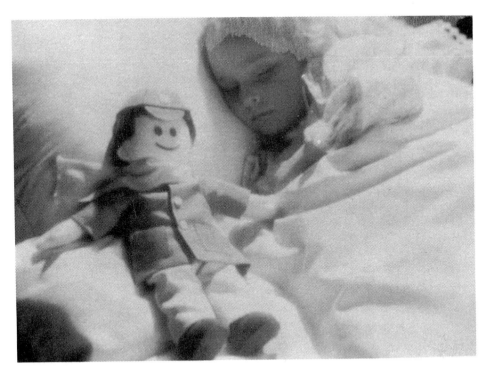

Benylin Paediatric TV commercial

### Selection of Advertising Medium/Test Markets

It was believed that television would be the most effective medium available for the consumer advertising launch of Benylin. Television's ability to influence consumer purchase in the OTC pharmaceutical market had been clearly demonstrated by Warner-Lambert's own experience (via brands such as Sinutab, Veganin, Listerine, etc.), and it was confidently expected that it would be the medium of first choice for the 1985/86 season (September 1985–April 1986). However, it was also accepted that TV advertising in support of a national brand would require a substantial capital investment, and that *evidence* of the effectiveness of the medium would be required to justify that investment.

It was therefore agreed that a test of the medium should be conducted as early as possible, i.e. from 1 April 1985, the date when the National Health Service Limited List came into effect and when the brand was free to advertise. Two commercials were shot, both 30 seconds, one for Benylin Expectorant and one for Benylin Paediatric, to the creative strategy outlined above.

An additional factor supporting the choice of television was its ability to run effective regional campaigns at substantial test-market discounts. After considerable negotiations with TV contractors two test campaigns were organised, one for Benylin Expectorant in London, the other for Benylin Paediatric in Yorkshire, both running for six weeks from 1 April to mid-May 1985. The weight of advertising achieved in both campaigns was considerable, amounting to a total of 686 housewife TVRs in London and 739 housewife TVRs in Yorkshire.

## PART 2: AN ANALYSIS OF THE ADVERTISING CAMPAIGN

*Results of Test Campaign*

The results achieved in both London and Yorkshire were very encouraging. Over the four-month period March to June 1985, Nielsen reported a volume growth of 36 per cent for Benylin year-on-year, compared to a growth of 5 per cent for the rest of the market. In these two areas, Benylin's total share of the market grew by 21 per cent, a rate of increase 58 per cent higher than in the rest of the country.

The test campaigns demonstrated that even during a period of the year when consumer use of cough preparations was in seasonal decline (Figure 1), the advertising developed for the brand generated very substantial volume growth. In addition, qualitative research (group discussions) also produced very encouraging results. The commercial for Benylin Expectorant was judged to:

1. Reassure the existing Benylin user of the effectiveness of Benylin.
2. Encourage trial among non-users.
3. Direct the consumer towards the pharmacy, Benylin's only retail outlet.

The commercial for Benylin Paediatric was effective in:

1. Communicating the soothing and reassuring nature of the formulation.
2. Demonstrating Benylin Paediatric's effectiveness on, and suitability for, children.
3. Demonstrating that the formulation worked fast.
4. Reinforcing the perception that Benylin Paediatric was a tried and trusted formulation.

The quantitative and qualitative data generated by the test campaigns therefore demonstrated very positive indications that the advertising strategy was highly effective. On the basis of this data, Warner-Lambert Health Care and Newlands Knight and Round took the decision to go national with this advertising in the 1985/86 season.

*National 1985/1986 Season: Campaign Plan*

The market for cough preparations is seasonal, though the precise timing of the peaks and troughs varies from year to year. The pattern of consumption for 1984/1985 and 1985/1986 is shown in Figure 1. In planning Benylin's first national campaign, it was felt strongly that as continuous a presence in advertising as possible was highly desirable, over the whole September/March period. It was argued that potential consumers not suffering from a cough at the time of exposure to advertising for a cough preparation, were unlikely to register that exposure. On the other hand, potential consumers actually suffering from coughs and exposed to relevant advertising at the same time, were likely to respond unusually strongly.

Figure 1 shows that the incidence of coughs, and therefore the use of cough preparations, in fact occurs throughout the year, but with a fairly extended major season, beginning in September and running through to March/April. Continuity of advertising over the major seven- to eight-month period was therefore highly desirable, but very expensive. In order to maximise the period that could be effectively covered, a radical solution was adopted. A 10-second commercial for Benylin Expectorant was developed, which communicated the two key elements of the successful 30-second commercial:

1. Benylin is the No. 1 name for coughs because of its proven effectiveness.
2. Benylin is only available at pharmacies.

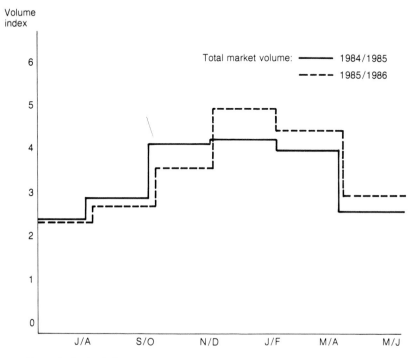

Figure 1. *Cough, cold and influenza remedies – seasonality*
*Source:* Nielsen

After this 10-second commercial was developed, it became a key factor in enabling Benylin to achieve its desired strategy of an extended period of advertising. Fully 50 per cent of the total weight of advertising planned and achieved in the 1985/1986 campaign was delivered by this 10-second execution.

The basic national campaign run over the 1985/1986 season therefore used two commercials, one 30-second and one 10-second, both for Benylin Expectorant, rotating 50:50 by weight (H/W TVRs). Using this timelength combination, seven two-week bursts of advertising were run over seven months from September 1985 to March 1986. Some 1000 H/W TVRs were achieved (100–150 per two-week burst). Alongside this national pattern, two regional variations were included.

The first regional variation was for Benylin Paediatric. The Yorkshire test, using the Benylin Paediatric commercial solus, had produced encouraging volume growth in both the paediatric and adult formulations. There was still a concern, however, that running the Paediatric and Expectorant commercials together could cause confusion. It was therefore decided to limit the possible risk, and to run a mix of Paediatric and Expectorant advertising in two areas only: Yorkshire and Midlands. Approximately 20 per cent of Benylin advertising in these two areas was in support of the Benylin Paediatric formulation.

The second variation from the national plan was an advertising pressure test. The results from the April/May tests were strongly positive, and the future success of the Benylin brand was critical to Warner-Lambert's overall position in the UK market. It was therefore agreed that an aggressive test of the brand's potential was appropriate, and a double-weight advertising test was therefore included. Extensive negotiations with TV contractors were again undertaken, and a very satisfactory arrangement was concluded with Tyne Tees Television Limited.

In the event, Benylin advertising appeared throughout the UK from September 1985 to March 1986. In excess of £750 000 was spent on airtime, and the pattern of advertising delivered was as follows:

TABLE 2: BASIC CAMPAIGN PLAN 1985/86 SEASON

| H/W TVRs | Sep | Oct | Nov | Dec | Jan | Feb | Mar | TOTAL |
|---|---|---|---|---|---|---|---|---|
| *N. East Pressure Test* | | | | | | | | |
| No. of Weeks | 2 | 4 | 4 | 5 | 3 | 2 | 2 | 22 |
| Expectorant TVRs – 30-second | 100 | 175 | 250 | 250 | 75 | 75 | 75 | 1000 |
| – 10-second | 100 | 175 | 250 | 250 | 75 | 75 | 75 | 1000 |
| | 200 | 350 | 500 | 500 | 150 | 150 | 150 | 2000 |
| *Rest of UK\** | | | | | | | | |
| No. of Weeks | 2 | 2 | 2 | 2 | 2 | 2 | 2 | 14 |
| Expectorant TVRs – 30-second | 75 | 50 | 75 | 75 | 75 | 75 | 75 | 500 |
| – 10-second | 75 | 50 | 75 | 75 | 75 | 75 | 75 | 500 |
| | 150 | 100 | 150 | 150 | 150 | 150 | 150 | 1000 |

\* In Yorks and Midlands, ratings include Benylin Paediatric (30's)

Note: Under 'Rest of UK', certain minor regional variations were included in the plan.

### 1985/1986 Campaign Results

The results from Benylin's first national TV campaign fully endorsed the positive readings established in the test markets.

Analysis of the Nielsen data on a partially indexed basis for the eight-month season September to April shows the following comparisons between 1984/1985 and 1985/1986:

TABLE 3: ANALYSIS OF NIELSEN DATA

| | Sep–Apr 84/85 | Sep–Apr 85/86 | Change |
|---|---|---|---|
| *Volume (National)* | | | |
| Total market excluding Benylin | 100 | 97 | − 3% |
| Benylin | 100 | 111 | +11% |
| Benylin share | 24.9% | 27.6% | +11% |
| *Sterling (National)* | | | |
| Total market excluding Benylin | 100 | 101 | + 1% |
| Benylin | 100 | 123 | +23% |
| Benylin share | 30.3% | 34.7% | +16% |

Excluding Benylin, total consumption of OTC cough preparations actually fell by 3 per cent in the 1985/1986 season, a surprising result in view of the expectation that, after the introduction of the Limited List, OTC purchase would rise significantly. While this did not happen for the rest of the market, it did happen for Benylin.

National volume for the brand rose by 11 per cent, in stark contrast to the rest-of-market fall of 3 per cent, and volume share rose from 24.9 per cent to 27.6 per cent. More dramatically, Benylin's brand strength allows it to command a significant premium on price: the sterling OTC value of the brand at RSP grew by a stunning 23 per cent, while the rest of the market remained virtually static.

Two further conclusions were drawn from the 1985/1986 results. First, the result of the North East pressure test was dramatically encouraging, as demonstrated below.

TABLE 4: RESULT OF THE NORTH EAST PRESSURE TEST

| | Sep–Apr 84/85 | Sep–Apr 85/86 | Change |
|---|---|---|---|
| *Volume (North East)* | | | |
| Total market excluding Benylin | 100 | 92 | – 8% |
| Benylin | 100 | 120 | + 20% |
| Benylin share | 27.6% | 33.1% | |

Source: Nielsen

Compared to the national growth rate of 11 per cent achieved by the campaign, the double-weight test in the North East doubled the rate of growth.

Second, detailed analysis of the Nielsen data for Yorkshire and Midlands provided reassuring evidence that the Paediatric execution was in no way damaging to the overall results achieved by Benylin. Additional group discussions were also undertaken, in May 1986, in which both the Expectorant and Paediatric commercials were probed together.

The results demonstrated that no confusion arose between formulations of their individual efficacy, i.e. Benylin Expectorant for adults, Benylin Paediatric for children; and indeed the two commercials appeared to act synergistically to promote the Benylin brand name.

## CONCLUSION

The first year of national TV advertising for Benylin was a major marketing and advertising success. Threatened by an unsettled market, the loss of prescription business by statute and the danger of an associated decline in the consumer perception of efficacy, the TV campaign for Benylin delivered increased brand share and sales.

The campaign also allowed the opportunity to promote several aspects of the Benylin profile which it had been impossible to do before. The consumer was motivated to purchase Benylin at the expense of all other brands because of the information contained in the advertising. The pharmacist was encouraged to recommend Benylin in return for the customers which the strong 'Only from your pharmacist' message in the commercials had delivered to the shop.

The mix of two Benylin presentations in two areas was successful and pointed the way to the 1986/1987 season's campaign. The double-weight experiment in Tyne Tees gives strong evidence of the power of advertising in a high frequency, continuous campaign for a self-medication product such as Benylin.

1985/1986 was a season in which the introduction of the Limited List posed a serious threat to the brand leader, Benylin. The advertising campaign developed in response to this threat did more than counterbalance it. While competitive volume fell by 3 per cent, advertising behind Benylin generated a volume increase of 11 per cent, a sterling increase of 23 per cent, and Benylin brand share increased to a sterling value of 34.7 per cent of the total market.

*The clear conclusion* is that the 1985/1986 Benylin advertising campaign was highly effective in increasing volume, sterling and brand share, so much so that exactly the same advertising strategy and executions have been maintained for the 1986/1987 season. Further gains for the brand are confidently expected.

## APPENDIX

### BENYLIN EXPECTORANT, 30-SECOND COMMERCIAL

| *VISION* | *SOUND* |
|---|---|
| Establish man coughing. | *Sfx* man coughing |
| Man fades slightly and woman establishes through as double image.<br>Man image pulses with coughing.<br>Woman leaves house. | Coughs need really effective medicine. |
| Woman reaches pharmacy, still in double image, goes into counter scene with pack. | Benylin Expectorant, the leading cough medicine for many years, is trusted by millions. |
| Arm with white sleeve takes pack from Benylin range on shelf, places on counter. | |
| Dissolves to computer terminal displaying information, with scientists viewing. | Recent trials with cough sufferers show yet again that Benylin Expectorant relieves coughs fast and effectively, with a warm, soothing taste.<br>Just what you need. |
| 'Proved' stamp comes down in front of pack. | Go to your pharmacist for Benylin Expectorant, proved really effective and available without prescription. |
| *Super up.* Benylin the No. 1 name for coughs. | |

Only from your Pharmacist.                    Benylin the No. 1 name for coughs.


WARNER-LAMBERT HEALTH CARE (logo)


## BENYLIN EXPECTORANT, 10-SECOND COMMERCIAL

| VISION | SOUND |
|---|---|
| Range of Benylin packs on shelf. Hand brings forward Expectorant pack. Cuts to shot of pouring Benylin on to spoon. | Benylin, the leading cough medicine for many years. |
| Cuts to 'Proved' sign lit up with range of packs behind. Cuts to computer screen with barchart. | Proved really effective . . . |
| Cuts to man taking Benylin | . . . . and available without prescription. |
| Cuts to range shot of Benylin. | Benylin, the No. 1 name for coughs. |

*Titles*: Benylin the No. 1 name for coughs.
Only from your pharmacist.


WARNER-LAMBERT HEALTH CARE (logo)


## BENYLIN PAEDIATRIC – 'MOTHER AND DAUGHTER'
## 30-SECOND COMMERCIAL

A gentle emotional commercial with soft photography and a relaxed pace. Shot mostly in close-up against soft intermediate backgrounds.

| VISION | SOUND |
|---|---|
| Interior. Night. | ½-second mute. Lyrical piano solo throughout. *Sfx* child coughing. |
| Girl (aged five or six) in pretty nightdress appears in doorway clutching a woollytoy. She coughs. | |

| | |
|---|---|
| Close up of mother (late 20s), reacting with concern. She is attractive with a kind but 'capable' face. | *Mv/o*<br>When a child coughs and coughs and can't settle down, it's an anxious time for Mum. |
| Mother comforting daughter. | She needs all the reassurance of Benylin Paediatric, specially formulated for children. |
| Close up of Benylin bottle as mother's hand picks it up. | |
| Cut to slow-motion shot of Benylin liquid pouring. | |
| Mother administers Benylin to child and then offers empty spoon to toy. | And so pleasant to take. |
| Interaction between mother and child. Child asleep in bed with toy. | Benylin acts fast and effectively, soothing inflamed tissues and gently relieving the cough. |
| Camera closes in on toy so that it fills the screen. | Now for sleep. |
| Pull pack from identical design on Benylin pack. Three other Benylin products in back-ground. | Benylin Paediatric, available without pre-scription. |
| *Super*<br>Benylin the No. 1 name for coughs.<br>Only from your pharmacist | Benylin, the No. 1 name for coughs. |

WARNER-LAMBERT HEALTH CARE (logo)

## ACKNOWLEDGEMENTS

The authors would like to thank A. C. Nielsen Company Ltd and Warner-Lambert Health Care for permission to use the sales data.

# 14

# The New Ford Granada – The Need to Succeed

## INTRODUCTION

Evaluating advertising's contribution to the launch of a new car presents more problems than would be encountered when evaluating a launch in many other markets. This paper does not concern itself with discussing those problems, which were covered generally in *Advertising Works* (1980) and referred to (in part) for the specific case of a new car launch in *Advertising Works 2* (1982). It begins from the premise that it is reasonable, given the difficulties of assessing the economic contribution of new car launch advertising, to evaluate that advertising against the tasks and objectives uniquely set for it. In this case, these objectives were primarily concerned with the building of awareness of the new car and the creation of favourable attitudes and a propensity to buy among the target audience. However, sales performance is not ignored.

The success of the new Granada since its introduction in May 1985 will be demonstrated in sales terms: both relative to the car it replaced and, in absolute terms, against the sales objective set at launch. However, this paper will mainly discuss the objectives set for the advertising, how those objectives came to be set and how successful the advertising has been in achieving them.

We believe that the Granada advertising was not only successful in achieving short-term objectives but also played a key strategic role in that it encouraged buyers and prospective buyers to reconsider the way they evaluated cars in the D/E sector. It did this by raising the salience of one particular aspect of the car's performance – safety – and pre-empted that attribute to the new Ford Granada. Thus a longer-term benefit – the creation of a substantiable competitive advantage – was achieved.

Thus, we believe, advertising played a key role in making Granada successful and continues to play an important role in *keeping* Granada successful. This paper sets out to demonstrate how and why.

## BUSINESS BACKGROUND

By May 1985, when the new Granada was introduced in Britain, Ford's share of the UK passenger car market had declined to 26.2 per cent (year to date) from an all-time high of 30.9 per cent in 1981.

211

The need for the new Granada to succeed and, importantly, to be *seen* to succeed was paramount. As well as losing market share in Britain, profit generated by the UK company had been in decline since 1979, and overall reputation as a manufacturer had been gradually eroded over the past four years. Moreover, competitive pressure had increased significantly over the past five years with imports taking an increasing share of the UK market and, on the 'domestic' front, General Motors – through its Vauxhall subsidiary – virtually doubling its market share from 8.8 per cent to 16.2 per cent in 1984.

The consumer, too, was beginning to show signs of a loss of confidence in Ford – albeit relative: Ford was still ahead of its major competitors in terms of overall image, but the gap had narrowed considerably. The introduction of the Sierra in 1982, although considered by many to be a bold step by Ford, produced uneasiness among some 'traditional' Ford buyers and prospective future buyers. As the first major Ford launch since Sierra, the new Granada had a particular job to do in terms of restoring some of the *confidence* lost by Ford – not only for the car-buying public, but also for the corporation itself.

The following section provides a business background specific to the Ford Granada and the market segment in which it competes (known in Ford terminology as the D/E or large car segment).

### The Ford Granada

The Ford Granada was first introduced by Ford in June 1977. In 1982 a 'facelift' model was introduced with various engineering and sheet metal changes. The all-new Granada, the subject of this paper, was introduced on 17 May 1985.

The Granada has traditionally been available in a range of levels (L, GL, Ghia and Ghia X) and with a range of engines (2.0, 2.3, 2.8, 2.8 injection and a diesel). In terms of price, Granada covered a spectrum from, at today's prices, £8 500, to around £16 000.

Since 1979, Granada's share of the total UK passenger car market has been declining – apart from a brief recovery in 1982 when the 'facelifted' model was introduced.

TABLE 1:   FORD GRANADA SHARE OF TOTAL MARKET (%)

|          | 1979  | 1980  | 1981  | 1982  | 1983  | 1984  |
|----------|-------|-------|-------|-------|-------|-------|
| Granada  | 3.04  | 1.92  | 1.70  | 1.84  | 1.35  | 1.33  |
| Memo:    |       |       |       |       |       |       |
| Total Ford | 28.29 | 30.70 | 30.94 | 30.49 | 28.97 | 27.90 |

Source: Ford/SMMT

TABLE 2:   COMPETITIVE SHARES (% of TM)

|              | 1979 | 1980 | 1981 | 1982 | 1983 | 1984 |
|--------------|------|------|------|------|------|------|
| Rover SD1    | 1.7  | 1.6  | 1.5  | 1.6  | 1.2  | 1.0  |
| Carlton      | 0.5  | 0.5  | 0.3  | 0.2  | 1.0  | 1.2  |
| Volvo 200/700| 1.5  | 1.4  | 1.4  | 1.4  | 1.4  | 1.4  |
| Memo:        |      |      |      |      |      |      |
| Granada      | 3.0  | 1.9  | 1.7  | 1.8  | 1.4  | 1.3  |

Source: Ford/SMMT

This is in part due to more general trends in the car market – notably that known as 'downsizing' i.e., the move away from big/expensive cars to smaller, more economical ones. However, the decline is also due in part to Granada's age and reputation (in the segment) versus competition.

### The D/E Segment

The D/E, or large car, segment has declined significantly over recent years, from 16.4 per cent of total market in 1978 to 10.4 per cent in 1981 and down to only 8 per cent in 1984.

*The Competition*

As with Ford overall, the major competition to the Granada comes from ARG and GM. The Rover SDI and Vauxhall Carlton/Senator range has provided the main 'domestic' competition. Of the imports, Volvo with the 200/700 series has provided the major volume competition.

*The Consumer*

Car buyers rarely fall into easily identifiable homogeneous groups. However, with the D/E segment in particular there are a number of common denominators. Firstly, many of the cars bought in this segment are 'business assisted purchases', i.e. paid for in part or in whole by a company rather than the individual. It should be recognised, however, that virtually all these individuals are offered a *choice* of company car – albeit a limited choice in some cases.

The second factor, and a somewhat less tangible one at that, is 'prestige' or 'status'. This is conveyed in part by the sheer size and price of products in this category, but it is also governed to a large degree by the manufacturer itself. For example, imports such as Volvo, BMW and SAAB tend to be rated higher on 'prestige' than domestic marques. On the domestic front, Rover, though rated below Granada as a product, has a higher reputation as a prestige marque.

In general terms, buyers in this segment are predominantly male, older (relative to the market in general) 35–55 years of age, and more up-market – largely ABC1.


## THE PROBLEM

The situation we faced coming up to the launch of the new Ford Granada can be summarised as follows:

— Overall passenger car market buoyant.
— Overall Ford share declining.
— Granada sales and share declining.
— Carlton share on the increase.

and

— Ford reputation declining.
— Granada getting 'long in the tooth'.

Yet this is simply a description of the situation we faced. Defining the problem was the next step.

The stated Ford marketing objective at launch was:

to successfully launch the new Granada and achieve a market share of 1.9% for the new car in its first full year in the market.

The problem stems directly from this objective.

— We had a totally new car to launch and early research indicated some evidence of rejection among existing Granada owners (many of whom preferred the traditional lines of the old Granada to the new hatchback shape).
— We had no Estate car derivative. With the 'old' Granada, the Estate version accounted for 15–20 per cent of total sales.

— The proposed model line up was similar to that of the old Granada and a change of name (to something other than Granada) had been approved for use across Europe.

To achieve the stated objective of a 1.9 per cent share from a base level of just over 1.3 per cent without an estate car, meant not only getting maximum conversion of existing owners (many of whom were 'nervous' about the new car), but also getting a substantial number of conquest sales.

Twelve months from launch, the agency, along with Ford of Britain marketing, instigated a fundamental review of the plans to take Granada to market.


## THE MARKETING SOLUTION

Substantial desk research, along with both quantitative and qualitative consumer research, suggested that the D/E segment was *not* a homogeneous whole. There were indications that consumers themselves (including fleet operators), either consciously or unconsciously, divided this area of the market into two or three subsections. These subsections were defined in terms of price, product characteristics (e.g. engine size) and 'status' of the cars. Moreover, there was evidence to suggest that the proposed model line up for the new Granada – based largely on that of the old – was not best placed to maximise volume potential within the segment. There were too many physical properties within the proposed range and there was too much overlap between models (on price, engine size and specification). This made life particularly difficult for fleet operators who were looking for a clear hierarchical structure to the range.

A greater concern, however, was that Granada's sales profile was out of kilter with that of the segment as a whole – particularly so at the lower end where volume is highest – as Table 3 shows.

TABLE 3:   PROFILE OF D/E SEGMENT SALES BY PRICE

|  | D/E | D/E excluding Granada | Granada |
|---|---|---|---|
| £ 6– 9 000 | 49.3 | 55.6 | 30.8 |
| £ 9–12 000 | 27.1 | 23.0 | 43.2 |
| £12–15 000 | 23.7 | 21.4 | 26.0 |

1983/84 Source: O&M

Although Granada performed well in the mid and upper segments, it lagged behind the market in the lower segment which, at that time, accounted for nearly 50 per cent of total D/E volume.

The overall conclusion was to market the new Granada to the three sub segments within D/E. The implications of this segmentation strategy were as follows;

1.  A reduction in the number of models in the range from 14 (proposed) to only *seven* at launch.
2.  A clear delineation between all models on price, engine size and specification.
3.  The retention of the Granada name in *Britain* and the addition of a new name, Scorpio, to the flagship model to help support the segmentation strategy and give added 'status' to this model.

4.  The 'cascading' of the Ghia and GL badges to the mid and lower segments respectively to support an 'added value' proposition in each.

This strategy was signed off by senior Ford management six months from launch and advertising development commenced.

## THE ADVERTISING SOLUTION

Again a considerable amount of development research was conducted to help us get to the right solution. In total, three stages of research were involved and a wide cross section of D/E prospects, fleet operators and Ford dealers were involved. The three stages covered:

1.  Positioning
2.  Ideas
3.  Executions

Two fundamental points emerged. Firstly, to position the new Granada as 'a significant improvement on the old' was most effective – both with current owners *and* non-owners. The Granada was seen very much as the 'benchmark' product in the D/E segment – even for non-owners who, though unlikely to consider the car then, used it as a means of comparison (the segment 'norm', if you like). By suggesting that the 'benchmark' had been improved significantly, non-owners felt they would fundamentally reassess Granada against what *they* thought was important. At the same time, current owners loyal to Granada took considerable reassurance from the thought that this was their car made better.

The second fundamental was that the advertising should recognise the needs and aspirations of the different sub segments identified in the marketing analysis, and present the car to them in terms of product *benefits*, rather than 'product' *per se*. With the new Granada we had a number of areas of interest that were product-based (anti-lock brakes were *standard* across the range, flush-fitting glass likewise). In advertising, these had to be presented in terms of what they delivered and not simply be a statement (no matter how interesting) of what they were.

The advertising objectives were defined as follows:

1.  To establish the new Granada as the 'benchmark' product in the D/E segment.
2.  To generate *immediate* awareness of, and interest in, the new car.
3.  To improve Granada's overall image such that it competes more effectively with competition.

At launch, two campaigns were developed: the main campaign, using press, TV and posters, introduced the GL and Ghia. A separate colour press campaign introduced the Scorpio derivative via up-market newspapers and magazines. The total budget for 1985 (May to December) was £3.75 million.

Two 60-second TV commercials, a poster and five separate colour press advertisements made up the 'mainstream' campaign. The Scorpio campaign consisted of two colour press treatments. A *range* of treatments was developed so that each important benefit area could be promoted singlemindedly – again research had shown that this approach was far more preferable to the 'catalogue' style used in much car advertising.

Scene from launch TV commercial

The campaign started on the evening of 16 May 1985 with both TV commercials, and a 10-second 'linking' commercial, dominating 'News at Ten' that evening and the following six evenings in most TV areas. TV support continued nationally for four weeks and the press continued over a three-month period with a heavy weighting towards the first six weeks.

Scorpio advertising broke two weeks after the launch in order to allow the main news (new car, new shape, etc.) to be established and then deliver its specific message to a more discrete audience.

## RESULTS

### Business

The specific share objective set for Granada was to achieve a 1.9 per cent share in its first 12 months in the market. Even with considerable supply problems in the six months following launch, this was achieved. In the twelve months from launch over 36 000 new Granadas were registered (total market 1 876 601), equivalent to a 1.9 per cent share. Furthermore, in 1986 Granada's share of the total UK market was 2 per cent for the full year.

Moreover, both total D/E segment registrations and D/E segment share of total new car registrations has increased since Granada launch, and though this was never a stated objective, it was hoped that the new Granada introduction would at least halt the long-term decline being experienced by the D/E segment as a whole. The period since Granada launch has seen a significant change in Ford's overall performance – both in terms of market share and profitability. Pre-tax profits increased from £60 million in 1984 to £160 million in 1985 (source: Ford annual report) and share has increased from 26.2 per cent in the first half of 1985 to 26.8 per cent over the same period in 1986. (Author's note: Ford finished 1986 with 27.4 per cent of the UK car market.)

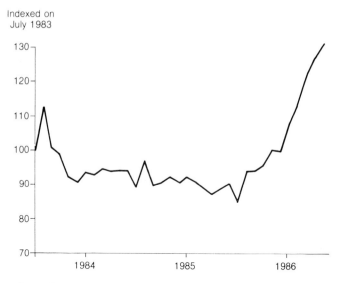

Figure 1. *Granada registrations (moving annual total)*

As was said in the introduction, the new Granada was looked upon not only as a potential success in its own right, but also as an important *catalyst* in reversing Ford's overall business performance.

### Advertising

The primary source of information used to measure achievement against objective is a continuous tracking study subscribed to by Ford (and a number of other major manufacturers) known as the 'RAP' Monitor (Requirement and Perception Monitor). This study reports

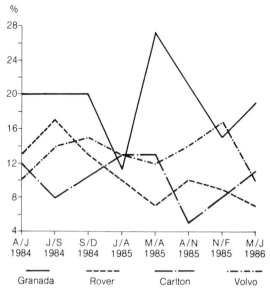

Figure 2. *Intention to purchase – 'next car'*

quarterly on a total sample base of 3 000 new car buyers and tracks purchase intention, advertising awareness and image dimensions (and their importance) in all sectors of the car market.

All three of the advertising objectives set at launch were met. The first two objectives were:

to establish the new Granada as the benchmark product in the D/E segment.

and,

to generate immediate awareness of and interest in the new car.

The following charts demonstrate that these objectives were met. Figure 2 (on page 217) shows 'intended next car purchase' scores for Granada and major competition. This shows the percentage of people within the segment *definitely* intending to buy a Granada as their next car. This is the measure against which we evaluated the first objective and, as can be seen, Granada's performance improved dramatically after the new car launch.

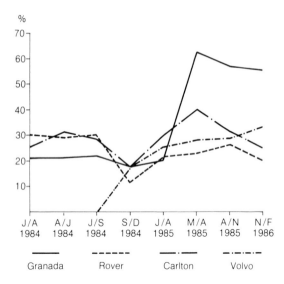

Figure 3. *Advertising recall*

Figure 3 shows the level of *awareness* generated by the advertising. The immediacy and scale of the improvements are clear from the chart.

In terms of monitoring *interest* levels, we used the percentage of D/E prospects prepared to consider Granada as their next car to assess this. As Figure 4 shows, the scores for Granada increased dramatically following the new car launch.

The third advertising objective set at launch was:

to improve Granada's overall image such that it competes more effectively with competition.

Granada's image, which was already strong on certain key dimensions with the 'old' car – notably comfort, proven record, luggage capacity and value for money – has improved

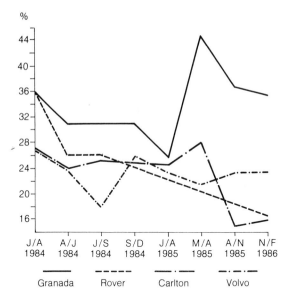

Figure 4. *Next car consideration*

dramatically on those dimensions rated most highly by D/E prospects, i.e. reliability, road-holding, safety and quality.

The following charts (Figures 5, 6, 7 and 8) show the extent of the improvement versus major competition on these key dimensions, and provides further support to the new cars' 'benchmark' status in the sector.

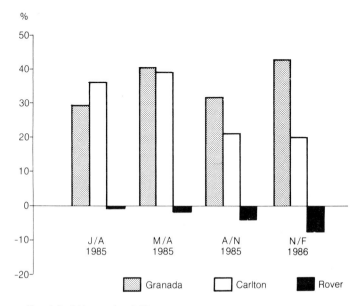

Figure 5. *Detailed image trends – reliability*

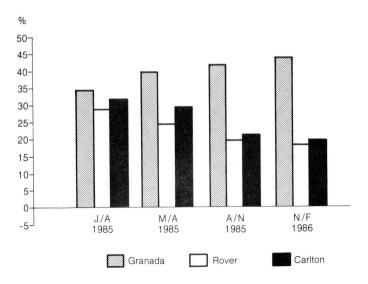

Figure 6. *Detailed image trends – roadholding*

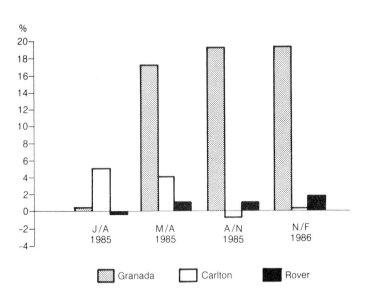

Figure 7. *Detailed image trends – safety*

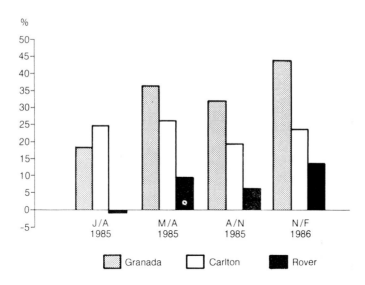

%

Granada     Carlton     Rover

Figure 8. *Detailed image trends – quality of finish*

The most significant improvement has been seen on the 'safety' dimension – a direct result, we believe, of Granada's inclusion as standard equipment of ABS brakes and high security locks. Furthermore, *safety* as a determining factor in new car purchase consideration in the D/E segment as a whole has moved up in the importance hierarchy to become second only to reliability.

## CONCLUSIONS

A large part of the success of the new Granada in terms of sales performance since launch, and marque imagery, must be attributed to the improvements made to the car itself. In the car market, fundamental reactions to and impressions of both manufacturers and models are based primarily on the products themselves. Advertising can only help shape these reactions and responses such that good cars are *seen* to be good cars and reacted to as such by as many potential prospects as possible.

Awareness *is* important because of the sheer number of cars, many of them relatively new, in the market. Image, too, *is* important because cars are, for most people, expected to reflect their own self-image and status as individuals.

Advertising played a major part in generating immediate and extensive awareness for the new Granada, and improving its image on *the* most important dimensions for buyers in this segment. Furthermore, by establishing safety as a (more) important criterion for the segment as a whole, and a major image strength for Granada, we have created a substantiable competitive advantage.

# 15

# Castlemaine XXXX Lager – The Role of Advertising in Building a Profitable New Brand

## INTRODUCTION

This paper charts the first phase of the launch of a major new brand into the growing and highly competitive UK lager market. Castlemaine XXXX first went on sale on draught in the Yorkshire and Central TV areas in May 1984. XXXX is now available nationally (from May 1986), but we shall concentrate on these initial launch areas where a full two-year run of data is available.

The main points we shall make relate to the *business* contribution made by XXXX advertising, and are that:

— The launch of XXXX has generated considerable incremental business for Allied Breweries.
— The advertising was fundamental to this success and – despite the large investment in advertising (over £5 million a year in national equivalent terms) – profits directly attributable to the advertising already exceed its costs.
— Advertising has fuelled the rapid creation of strong consumer franchise and so a secure base for future profit in the growing lager market.

Additionally we will describe a number of features of the launch which have been crucial to the brand's success, such as how:

— Advertising helped achieve the right positioning relative to Allied Breweries' other volume brand, Skol, and its main (consumer perceived) competitor, Foster's.
— Advertising was used in the NPD process to focus development of a totally integrated brand package (product, counter dispense unit, promotions, etc).
— The launch was carefully monitored to help maximise the effectiveness of on-going and future activity.

For the most part our case is supported by actual figures, but confidentiality dictates that sensitive sales-related data be indexed.

222

## PUTTING THE LAUNCH INTO CONTEXT

*Advertising in the Lager Market*

The standards required of lager advertising are extremely high, in part due to the sheer amount of competitive activity; in 1985 MEAL registered a total spend of £45 million spread across 34 brands, with 7 spending in excess of £2.5 million. Even more exacting are the standards imposed by the consumer – in no other market is involvement with advertising so intense, leading to extremes of appreciation and approbation.

Historically, few drinkers have discriminated between mainstream lagers in product terms. Brand preferences come from images which, in the lager market, are derived mainly from advertising. Young, frequent drinkers – the key target group – drink in on-licences among their peer group. The image projected by the advertising must not only appeal to the individual drinker, but it must also appeal to their friends. A heavy weight of advertising is also crucial in these terms, providing reassurance of a brand's success and popularity to the young drinker.

*Market Trends*

The intensity of advertising is not surprising given the size and growth of the market. The UK lager market is vast – almost £4 billion at retail value in 1986. Moreover, in an overall beer market which is at best static, lager is enjoying solid growth. Introduced on draught in the early 1960s, it grew steadily to 3 million bulk barrels in 1970, rising to 16 million barrels in 1985. Further growth of about 25 per cent is expected by 1990.

Growth comes from the steady flow of young drinkers with a strong preference for lager into the market. Drinkers tend to stick with lager as they grow older, and lager's overall market share (currently about 40 per cent) appears to be moving inexorably towards its share of young drinkers' consumption (about 70 per cent for under 25s).

In the 1960s each of the Brewers sold a single lager; standard strength brands like Skol, Carlsberg and Heineken. The newness and size of the market meant that one brand per pub was all that was required. 'Premium' draught lagers, like Lowenbrau and Stella Artois, were introduced in the 1970s. Standard lagers, however, still account for over 80 per cent of volume – premium brands being too strong for the extended 'sessions' in which most lager is drunk.

By 1980, the standard lager sector had grown to about 11 million barrels and could support more than one brand per pub. The emergent young drinker was open to something new, an alternative to brands they saw more as their father's than their own. The market was ripe for a new generation of lagers, especially the more developed southern market.

Watney, with its southern-based estate, explored this opportunity in 1981 with Foster's. The time was right and they delivered the right benefits; certainly new and different, but within the established values of the market (sociable, humorous, 'sharp', macho and credible). At the root of Foster's success was *Australia*, not only bringing the right lager values, but a new 'heritage' in a market previously dominated by brands explicitly or implicitly of Continental origins.

*A New Lager Brand – the Brewer's Dilemma*

The beer market differs from most branded markets in that the Brewers own the majority of on-licence outlets and so control the brands on sale (usually their own). The 'tied trade' accounts for about 55 per cent of on-licence beer volume, the 'free trade' (free houses, working men's clubs, etc. – some of which deal with a single Brewer) accounts for the rest.

The launch of a new brand – unless an *outstanding* success – can easily result in a reduction of overall profitability. Within the Brewers's tied outlets it requires a strong brand to increase overall volume sales; otherwise volume is simply cannibalised from other of the Brewer's brands, increasing overall operating costs without increasing income. Similar cannibalisation can occur in the free trade, unless the brand opens new accounts for the Brewer and performs well in multi-brewer accounts.

However, in a growing and developing market, a Brewer will inevitably lose out if it does not match changing consumer needs. Allied Breweries knew that their long-established standard lager, Skol, could not by itself realise the company's full potential in the developing market. On balance, they wanted a new mainstream lager to join Skol, but had exacting requirements for it.

### The Exacting Requirements for Business Success

To make overall business sense, the new brand must produce substantial volume (and profit) *over and above* that which would result from the continued marketing of the existing lager portfolio. This required a brand which would:

—  Have exceptional consumer appeal (not one which would be drunk simply 'because it's there').
—  Greatly enhance free trade performance by opening new accounts and taking sales from competitive lagers in multi-brewer accounts.
—  Build traffic in the tied (and solus free) trade by broadening the appeal of Allied's lager portfolio, especially to young, image-conscious session drinkers.

## THE N.P.D. PROCESS

### The Brief

In the quest for a new mainstream draught lager to meet the requirements outlined above, Allied Breweries briefed the agency in early 1983. The main direction given was the appeal of 'new' (non-Continental) heritages to younger drinkers, as demonstrated by the success of Foster's.

Though the brief was deliberately open in terms of which new heritage, at this early stage neither agency nor client felt that a second Australian brand was likely to be the solution. Australia had already been 'done', and well.

### Identifying the Brand

We first concentrated on screening the likely appeal of a large number of countries. An analysis of existing information was followed by a programme of extended group discussions with regular lager drinkers.

The volume objectives required a brand with broad appeal among younger (18 to 30) drinkers on a national basis. In these terms it very quickly became clear that – contrary to our preconceptions – Australia was far away the strongest available heritage.

Australia – or, rather, Australians – had all the right lager credentials:

—   (In)credible lager drinkers!
—   A tough 'macho' image.
—   More like us than any other country's inhabitants.

Foster's was well-known and liked via its advertising and, where available, trial. Australians would demand good lagers; because they are like us, we would like their lagers too. Crucially, being its 'national drink', Australia was expected to boast several good lager brands.

Though drinkers were highly interested in a second Australian lager, we needed a strong and distinctive appeal to avoid the risk of being seen as an inferior copy of Foster's by consumers (and the trade).

Castlemaine XXXX stood out on every count. It was one of the brands readily available to Allied Breweries through their (then) minority shareholding in its brewer, Castlemaine Tooheys. More importantly, it had an authentic, rugged, beery feel to it – from its name, the four Xs, the brash yellow and red livery, down to the proud representation of its brewery on its can design. No less important, XXXX was the best-selling brand in Australia.

Because of the crucial importance of advertising in the lager market, it was decided to explore the brand's potential by preparing rough advertising treatments for the next stages of consumer research. A second Australian brand, plus American brands, were also included in subsequent research, but these quickly fell by the wayside while XXXX evoked a strong consumer response at each stage.

### Developing the Advertising

For once in the lager market there was a real and relevant point of difference to work with – that XXXX was Australia's best-selling lager. However, our understanding of the relationship between lager drinkers, lager brands and their advertising suggested that a hard sales story would be unlikely to deliver the emotional values required. The single-minded proposition we briefed was therefore based upon the more 'human' angle of Australians' *preference* for XXXX, supported by the best-selling claim.

The strategy was also chosen with a prudent eye to long-term campaignability. A 'best-selling' campaign could be difficult to develop over time and, worse, could be a hostage to fortunes in Australia. In the event, the Australian sales picture became progressively unclear, and it was decided to drop the best-selling claim at the end of 1985. Because the campaign was not based upon it, this involved only minor alterations to the end sequence, and no change in consumer's response to the brand.

The creative brief was as follows:

*Purpose of the Advertising*

—   To launch a major new brand of lager.
—   To position XXXX as an authentic Australian lager for everyday session drinking.

*Target Audience*   All regular lager drinkers, focusing upon males aged 18 to 24 and belonging to the BC1 (C2) social grades.

Attitudinally, they will be a bit more positive, experimental, and 'on the ball' than the average lager drinker.

*Proposition*   Castlemaine XXXX is the lager most Australians prefer.

*Support*   Castlemaine XXXX is Australia's best-selling lager.

Additionally, the brief provided background on the values to which drinkers respond best in lager advertising, plus the obvious guideline to be totally distinct from the Foster's 'Hogan' campaign.

Two creative routes were developed and put into qualitative, then quantitative research. One – embodied by the 'Flying Doctor' script – became the focus for the launch advertising campaign and development of a totally integrated brand package.

The campaign idea relied on the 'outback' and its inhabitants: single-minded, hard-drinking characters who value XXXX above any other lager, and indeed anything else (their marriage, their friends, etc.). Each script was humorous, but in a very deadpan way. The common end sequence featured a draught pouring shot, the information that XXXX was Australia's best-selling lager, and the memorable campaign line:

AUSTRALIAN'S WOULDN'T GIVE A (CASTLEMAINE) XXXX FOR ANY OTHER LAGER

Authenticity was central to the creative approach and the films were shot in the Australian outback with Australian actors by an Australian director.

The launch package comprised six TV commercials; 'Flying Doctor', 'Wedding' and 'Rescue' (all 40 seconds), 'Jackaroo' (30 seconds), 'Divorce' and 'Surfer' (20 seconds). Additionally, two 48-sheet poster executions were used.

### *Developing a Total Brand Package*

Early in the NPD process we had a well-defined brand strategy and a *tangible* representation of it in advertising (notably a high quality animatic of the 'Flying Doctor' script) and the Australian brand livery. Everybody involved in the NPD process had a clear point of reference – Client; Agency; Design; Promotions and PR Agencies and, importantly, consumers involved in research to refine the draught product and the counter dispense unit (CDU).

Each element of the mix could relate to the advertising and in combination form a highly integrated package:

—   A draught product which met the high expectations aroused by the brand name and advertising (the UK brew uses Australian yeast and techniques but, like Foster's, is brewed at a lower gravity to meet UK requirements).
—   A CDU design reflecting the brash, 'macho' values of the advertising and imported Australian can.
—   A below-the-line package playing off the advertising and the XXXX *double entendre*.

Bruce: G'day, g'day. Is that the flying Doctor? Over.

Doctor: Copy you Bruce.

Billy is real crock Doc. He's sweating like crazy, temperature of 104°, he looks terrible. What'll we do? Over.

Give him a cold drink, the coolest thing in the house until I get to you. Otherwise.... well it could be real bad.

(Bruce open the fridge and finds just one can of lager)

Billy: What the Doc say Bruce?

(Bruce opens the can over his friend)

He said it's going to be real bad Bill.

v/o: Castlemaine XXXX is Australias best selling lager

In fact Australians wouldn't give a Castlemaine XXXX for any other lager.

'Flying Doctor' TV commercial

## THE LAUNCH STRATEGY

*Overall Philosophy*

In this market the chances of achieving major incremental volume would be slight without marketing activity at least on a par with leading brands in the market. The early stages would be crucial as considerable consumer impact is required to engender interest, the right expectations, and trial – and so rapidly build sales to maintain trade confidence. Considerable investment had been made in research, film production, brewing equipment, CDUs and coolers. It would have been short-sighted to put this at risk with a shoestring marketing budget.

*Area Selection and Roll-Out*

Brewing and distribution logistics make area launches the norm for draught beers. Confidence in XXXX was high, and its introduction was viewed more as a rolling launch than an area test market. There was, though, a degree of prudence, and the initial launch areas were as carefully monitored as any test market. This gave the opportunity to identify any problems and optimise the mix quickly, and before subsequent roll-out.

Two major areas were selected: the Yorkshire and Central TV areas, serviced by Allied Breweries' Joshua Tetley and Ansells local trading companies. These areas account for around a quarter of market volume and a third of Allied Breweries' lager volume. They offered a good distribution base, reasonable typicality, and freedom from new brand activity within the company.

The imported cans were on sale in these areas (with supporting POS materials) from December 1983. Draught XXXX went on sale in late May 1984 and is now national (Table 1).

This shows that XXXX was launched into two limited areas *without TV advertising support*: Tyne Tees and Bristol. These will feature later in our analysis of the advertising contribution to the brand's success.

TABLE 1: CASTLEMAINE XXXX AREA LAUNCH TIMETABLE

| Product on sale | TV area |
|---|---|
| May 1984 | Yorkshire |
| | Central |
| | Tyne Tees (pockets of distribution, no TV) |
| May 1985 | London |
| July 1985 | Bristol area (no TV support) |
| October 1985 | Granada |
| May 1986 | Scotland (STV and Grampian) |
| | Border |
| | Tyne Tees (TV support) |
| | HTV |
| | Anglia |
| | TVS |
| | TSW (little available distribution, no TV support) |

*Media Strategy*

TV was the obvious choice as our main medium. For a mass market product, TV is unequalled in terms of intrusiveness, ability to establish a brand personality, and status. No less important, it is the market norm and what consumers and trade expect.

To create a big brand, we had to be seen to behave as one. TV was planned with the intention of at least matching the (expected) weight of leading competitors, and to be the heaviest advertiser in the market when on air. In broad terms, this has been achieved in the two years since the launch.

Posters were an important secondary medium, giving an almost continuous presence in ad-

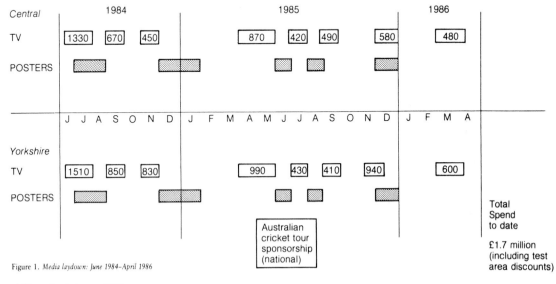

Figure 1. *Media laydown: June 1984–April 1986*

* 30-second equivalent men TVRS
** heavyweight 48-sheet poster package
Figure 2. *Media laydown: June 1984–April 1986*

vertising and reaching light TV viewers. XXXX is tailormade for posters: a simple, memor-able campaign line, plus the 'fastest' brand livery possible. You could see the yellow and red a mile away!

The copy rotation plan for the six films made pre-launch was the result of careful research. 'Flying Doctor', 'Wedding' and 'Surfer' ran in the first two bursts, with a steady rotation of the six films after that. In Spring 1986, the first of a batch of six new films began to appear, inter-mixed with existing films.

### Other Key Factors

Early distribution was targeted at the top 25 per cent of accounts: those with the greatest chance of supporting two standard lagers and building incremental custom. The free trade focus was on outlets where Allied Breweries had no lager listing. Though a similar strength, XXXX was generally sold at a 2p per pint premium over Skol (and competitors' standard lagers).

The below-the-line package was strong, using the intrusive red and yellow livery and feeding off the advertising. XXXX was an attraction and exterior pub 'dressing' – bunting, banners, window posters – was used extensively to help draw in new customers.

## THE CONTRIBUTION OF ADVERTISING – SALES EFFECTS

### Brand Performance Overview

Before isolating the advertising contribution, it is salutory to consider XXXX's overall impact on Allied Breweries' business.

Sales have exceeded expectations. With substantial new distribution/areas coming on-stream during summer 1986, a national brand share of about 5 per cent looks likely by late 1986.

TABLE 2:   LATEST XXXX BRAND SHARES (FEB/MARCH 1986)

| TV Area | Launch Date | Volume Share (Draught Lager) % |
|---------|-------------|--------------------------------|
| Central | May 1984 | 6.7 |
| Yorks | May 1984 | 4.9 |
| London | May 1985 | 5.1 |

Source: Stats MR Retail Audit; Total On-Licence

In the growing lager market a 5 per cent share equates with annual sales of over 600 000 barrels, worth over £150 million at retail prices.

In the nature of the trade, some substitution against other Allied Breweries' beers was in-evitable. Substitution analyses were conducted in both Central and Yorkshire in 1984 and 1985, comparing overall volumes between XXXX stockists and non-stockists, pre- and post-launch. These consistently show about 50 per cent of XXXX volume to be totally *incremental* to the business. BMS data show the particularly strong performance in the free trade where considerable non-substitutional volume has come from the many new lager accounts opened for Allied by XXXX (Table 3).

TABLE 3:   ALLIED BREWERIES' LAGER MARKET SHARE GROWTH (INDEXED)

*Allied Breweries' Market Share of Midlands and Yorkshire Regions combined –
Low/Medium Gravity Lagers*

|  | Pre-launch Qtr I 1984 ( = 100) | 18 months from launch Qtr IV 1985 |
|---|---|---|
| Total trade | 100 | 111 |
| Tied trade | 100 | 106 |
| Free trade | 100 | 124 |

Source: BMS. The Beer Market Survey is compiled by an independent third party from the sales returns of 7 major brewers, between them accounting for about 75 per cent of Great Britain's beer volume. BMS regions do not conform exactly with TV areas, but the two launch TV areas fall within the Midlands and Yorkshire BMS regions.

Two years from launch, Allied Breweries have a brand which in the next year will generate *incremental* (i.e. allowing for substitution) retail sales of about £80 million directly attributable to the brand. The gross contribution to profit on this incremental sales value is several times the projected media spend (about £7 million). And this ignores profits generated indirectly (e.g. profits on food, wines and spirits, etc.) due to increased custom in the tied trade, and profits on other brands gaining free trade distribution 'on the back of' XXXX.

### *Isolating the Sales Effects of the Advertising*

The overall profitability of new brands can generally be quantified, but it is seldom possible to *quantify* advertising's contribution. Econometric modelling of sales associated with different advertising weights requires years of data (by definition not available for a new brand) and the only available technique is some sort of area test. In advertising-led markets like lager, launching into significant areas with no or low support rarely makes business sense, despite its benefits for evaluation.

With XXXX we were fortunate to have two 'naturally occurring' area tests. The Newcastle-upon-Tyne and Bristol areas had 'pockets' of Allied Breweries' accounts which could benefit from XXXX, but presence across the respective TV areas was insufficient to make TV support financially viable. XXXX was launched without TV support, more on business grounds than a conscious desire to mount a test, but these areas are reasonable non-advertising controls: workable numbers of accounts, selected on the same criteria as Yorkshire and Central, benefiting from the same heavy below-the-line package but with no advertising, except for limited poster and cinema support (totalling £10 000 in Newcastle and £4 000 in Bristol). The Tyne Tees launch was on the same timescale as Yorkshire and Central; Bristol launched a year later.

Table 4 compares sales between the two TV areas and two non-TV areas.

TABLE 4:   TV AREAS Vs. NON-TV AREAS

|  | TV AREAS | NON-TV AREAS | |
| --- | --- | --- | --- |
|  | Yorks/Central Average | Tyne Tees | Bristol |
| *Total Allied lager sales* (indexed) |  |  |  |
| Pre-launch year ( = 100) (12 months to April 1984: 1985 in Bristol) | 100 | 100 | 100 |
| Launch year 1 (12 months to April 1985: 1986 in Bristol) | 113 | 101 | 105 |
| Launch year 2 (12 months to April 1986) | 117 | 97 | n/a |
| *XXXX share of all Allied lager sales* | % | % | % |
| Launch year 1 | 14 | 7 | 21 |
| Launch year 2 | 24 | 16 | n/a |
| *XXXX distribution as a % of all Allied accounts (average over year)** |  |  |  |
| Launch year 1 | 24 | 9 | 30 |
| Launch year 2 | 44 | 21 | n/a |

* Based on accounts, not turnover
Source: Allied Breweries

The differences between overall Allied Breweries' performance in TV and non-TV areas cannot be attributed to other market or marketing factors and clearly demonstrate the value of TV advertising to total sales. In Yorkshire and Central, XXXX became a major attraction drawing considerable additional custom into stocking outlets, and resulting in a major uplift in *total* sales. In non-TV areas, despite good distribution and sales levels (especially in Bristol), XXXX apparently failed to draw in new customers and its sales were largely substitutional. We shall see later that in non-TV advertised areas, XXXX lacked the status and salience among consumers required for a brand to build additional pub traffic.

These data suggest that virtually all the *incremental* business produced by XXXX is due to the investment in TV advertising. In Yorkshire and Central combined, XXXX has sold over 200 000 barrels since launch, and we know that over 100 000 have been incremental. Advertising investment in these areas to April 1986 (about £1.7 million) is less than a third of the gross profit contribution on incremental volume; *the advertising has already generated profits considerably over its cost.*

While this is gratifying, advertising's greatest contribution is the strong base built for *future* profit – a secure and growing distribution base and brand franchise in a growing market. The next section, which looks at consumer effects – how the advertising has worked – also shows the strength of XXXX's franchise.

## THE CONTRIBUTION OF ADVERTISING – CONSUMER EFFECTS

*Overview*

XXXX advertising has made an extraordinary impact on consumers in terms of memorability, take-out and involvement.

Advertising awareness in advertised areas is consistently the highest in the market. Weight – matching the leading market spenders — is important, but the crucial difference is sheer creative power. Millward Brown model TV advertising awareness against advertising weight ('adstock') for all major lager brands on their syndicated continuous tracking survey. For each brand/campaign they calculate two measures of advertising effectiveness:

Awareness Index    Effectively the increase in advertising awareness delivered by an incremental 100 TVRs.

Base Level    The residual base of awareness towards which levels decay exponentially when a brand is not advertising (for a new brand a measure of ability to enter consumers' 'long-term memory').

XXXX has the highest Awareness Index in the market:

TABLE 5:  COMPARATIVE MODELLING STATISTICS (ENGLAND/WALES)

|  | Awareness Index | Base Level |
|---|---|---|
| XXXX | 10 | 13 |
| Market average (19 draught brands covered) | 4.4 | 8.3 |
| New brand average (XXXX, Fosters, Oranjeboom, Tennents Pilsner, John Smiths Lager) | 6.6 | 7.8 |

Source: Millward Brown, January 1986

Content recall of the advertising is detailed, and drinker involvement exceptional. Here is a quote from the report on qualitative research conducted in Yorkshire and Central nine months after launch:

> We found complete recall of all the ads, and respondents were willing and clearly enjoyed giving a complete account of the story of 'Flying Doctor' and 'Wedding'. Part of the enjoyment of the ads was their ability to be relived in the pub.

> The image which the campaign has created is of an authentic Australian lager, drunk by genuine Australians who know a good lager . . . Castlemaine is seen as a true export of Australia, despite knowledge that the product is UK brewed.
>
> (Winstanley, Douglas & Partners, February 1985)

There can be no doubt that the advertising has figured large in drinkers' relationship with the brand.

*Rapid Development of a Consumer Franchise*

The launch in Yorkshire and Central was monitored via specially commissioned consumer tracking research running continuously from May to December 1984. A baseline measure of 300 interviews was taken in each area in the two weeks between the product going on sale and the first TV advertising. From then, weekly samples of 75 were interviewed, building to matched samples of 300 per month, per area. The sample comprised regular lager drinkers aged 18 to 30 years of age.

Table 6 summarises the rapid growth of XXXX's standing in Yorkshire and Central on all key measures:

— Advertising awareness.
— Brand salience.
— Brand image (on product-related and user-related dimensions).
— Trial and drinker commitment.

TABLE 6:　THE RAPID GROWTH IN XXXX'S FRANCHISE FROM LAUNCH

| | | Yorks/Central average Weeks from commencement of advertising: | | |
| | Baseline (May '84) | 1–8 (June/July) | 9–16 (Aug/Sept) | 17–24 (Oct/Nov) |
| XXXX ratings | % | % | % | % |
|---|---|---|---|---|
| *Advertising awareness* | | | | |
| TV | * | 47 | 69 | 64 |
| Posters | 8 | 33 | 43 | 40 |
| *Brand awareness* | | | | |
| Spontaneous | 11 | 30 | 38 | 37 |
| Spontaneous after new brand prompt | 22 | 58 | 63 | 59 |
| Prompted | 38 | 77 | 89 | 94 |
| *Brand image (among those aware of XXXX)* | | | | |
| Strong in alcohol | 21 | 23 | 28 | 27 |
| Particularly refreshing | 23 | 27 | 33 | 30 |
| Particularly good flavour | 17 | 22 | 27 | 25 |
| Particularly good quality | 16 | 21 | 25 | 27 |
| Suitable for sessions with the lads | 26 | 33 | 37 | 36 |
| Appeal particularly to younger people | 18 | 30 | 37 | 32 |
| A bit different from most | 27 | 27 | 35 | 32 |
| *Identification as Australian* | 30 | 74 | 90 | 91 |
| *Usage* | | | | |
| Ever tried | 23 | 39 | 52 | 58 |
| Drink regularly | 10 | 16 | 22 | 22 |
| Drink most often | 2 | 4 | 8 | 8 |

Source: Ad Hoc Launch Tracking Survey

By autumn 1984, XXXX was already among the leading brands in each area on most consumer measures. Table 7 shows its standing relative to its main Allied countermate, Skol, and its main consumer-perceived competitor, Foster's. XXXX's brand standing compares favourably with the longer-established Foster's. Importantly, it has carved out a distinct position from Skol, developing a much younger drinker profile and playing a complementary role within the Allied brand portfolio.

TABLE 7:   BRAND STANDING COMPARED WITH FOSTER'S AND SKOL

*(Yorks/Central average: weeks 17–24 from commencement of advertising – i.e., Oct/Nov 1984)*

| Brand ratings | Skol % | XXXX % | Foster's % |
|---|---|---|---|
| *Advertising awareness* | | | |
| TV | 30 | 64 | 43 |
| Posters | 22 | 40 | 12 |
| *Brand awareness* | | | |
| Spontaneous | 67 | 37 | 31 |
| Spontaneous after new brand prompt | 67 | 59 | 38 |
| Prompted | 99 | 94 | 95 |
| *Brand image (among those aware of brand)* | | | |
| Strong in alcohol | 7 | 27 | 24 |
| Particularly refreshing | 38 | 30 | 29 |
| Particularly good flavour | 23 | 25 | 24 |
| Particularly good quality | 26 | 27 | 25 |
| Suitable for sessions with the lads | 41 | 36 | 33 |
| Appeal particularly to younger people | 39 | 39 | 38 |
| A bit different from most | 4 | 32 | 28 |
| *Identification as Australian* | n/a | 91 | 94 |
| *Usage* | | | |
| Ever tried | 86 | 58 | 67 |
| Drink regularly | 39 | 22 | 20 |
| Drink most often | 19 | 8 | 7 |

Source: Ad Hoc Launch Tracking Survey

### The Consumer Effect of Not Advertising – the Bristol Test

When XXXX was launched without TV support in the Bristol area, it was decided to monitor the consumer implications of not advertising (as well as sales). Similar research to the original Launch Tracking Survey was commissioned for the first 24 weeks of the launch, and direct comparisons of consumer response in TV and non-TV areas can now be made (Table 8).

This comparison explains the failure of XXXX to build major incremental volume in the Bristol area and is a stark reminder of the potential power of television. Without TV advertising, XXXX is a respectable brand, rather than the major attraction which can help build overall business. In Bristol, XXXX was much less top-of-mind and did not inspire the drinker commitment found in the TV areas. Brand image is similar in character, but weaker on all counts, especially in its appeal to younger drinkers.

TABLE 8:  XXXX IN CENTRAL/YORKS Vs. BRISTOL – COMPARISON OF KEY
CONSUMER MEASURES

*Based upon weeks 17–24 from launch*

|  | Central/Yorks Average % | Bristol % |
|---|---|---|
| *Advertising awareness* | | |
| TV | 64 | 10 |
| Posters | 40 | 21 |
| | | |
| *Brand awareness* | | |
| Spontaneous | 37 | 14 |
| Spontaneous after new brand prompt | 59 | 28 |
| Prompted | 94 | 68 |
| | | |
| *Brand image (among those aware of XXXX)* | | |
| Strong in alcohol | 27 | 23 |
| Particularly refreshing | 30 | 23 |
| Particularly good flavour | 25 | 18 |
| Particularly good quality | 27 | 18 |
| Suitable for sessions with the lads | 36 | 29 |
| Appeal particularly to younger people | 39 | 25 |
| A bit different from most | 32 | 29 |
| | | |
| *Usage* | | |
| Ever tried | 58 | 42 |
| Drink regularly | 22 | 6 |
| Drink most often | 8 | 2 |

Source: Ad Hoc Launch Tracking Survey

## OPTIMISING FUTURE PERFORMANCE

Thorough continuous monitoring of brand and advertising made the above analysis of advertising's contribution possible, but more importantly has already contributed to the brand's development and profitability:

— Providing confidence for an accelerated area roll-out.
— Refining the optimum launch mix for subsequent new areas.
— Refining copy rotation.
— Providing guidance for the development of further executions (for example, six have already been added to the first six).
— Increasing media planning efficiency.

The contribution made by various research companies – Hudson, Payne, Iddiols; Winstanley Douglas; John Nolan; Millward Brown – has been tremendous. Continuous evaluation of brand, advertising and profit performance can be cost-effective in its own right.

## CONCLUSIONS

We have demonstrated how advertising has helped achieve the difficult objective of generating genuinely incremental sales in the lager market. It has done so effectively and profitably.

Success to date, and the establishment of a firm base for future profit, is the result of getting *all* the key elements right – careful planning, followed by a bold launch (both in terms of scale and creative executions), guided by thorough and continuous monitoring. The case of XXXX shows how powerful advertising can be when it is part of a strong and integrated marketing package.

# 16

# Kensington Palace

## INTRODUCTION

This paper sets out to describe how Doyle Dane Bernbach addressed the problem of how to promote the Royal Palaces in the care of The Department of the Environment, and how the advertising developed and paid for itself through the incremental visitors – and thus entrance fees – which it generated.

## BACKGROUND

At the beginning of 1984 the Government set up a new body called 'The Historic Buildings and Monuments Commission' (English Heritage) to look after most of the historic houses, castles, monuments in the country, which had previously been in the care of the Department of the Environment.

Six so-called 'Royal Palaces' were left in the care of the Department of the Environment. They are:

1.  The Tower of London.
2.  Hampton Court.
3.  Kensington Palace.
4.  Kew Palace.
5.  Osborne House.
6.  Banqueting House, Whitehall.

Prior to setting up the commission, any marketing/promotion of these buildings had been done on an ad hoc basis. It now became the aim of the Department of the Environment to produce a cohesive marketing strategy for 'the six'.

*Corporate vs. Individual Promotion*

The option existed to promote the palaces jointly on a 'corporate' platform or singly. The latter was felt to be the better approach.

238

1.  There was no readily understandable way accurately to group the buildings. While they
    were commonly referred to in The Department as Royal Palaces – one (the Banqueting
    House) is actually only part of a building; Osborne is more a country house than a
    palace.

    A corporate terminology could mislead the consumer.
2.  There was no major unifying link between the buildings. They all had, at one time, been
    associated with Royalty, but to a varied extent; some (Kew Palace, the Banqueting
    House) could not justifiably be promoted on this platform.
3.  Little could be said about each separate building in an advertisement for them all.
4.  The buildings differed widely in

    —  Level of awareness.
    —  Present number of visitors.
    —  What they offer.
    —  Potential to accommodate increased numbers.
    —  Opening times.
    —  Accessibility.

Client, COI and agency believed it made better sense to examine each in more detail as
potential advertising subjects.

## THE OPPORTUNITY FOR INDIVIDUAL PROMOTION

### The Tower of London and Hampton Court

Both buildings needed little promotion, as they already had high awareness among tourists,
and attracted large numbers of visitors.

### Kensington Palace

This building offered immediate potential for an increase in visitor levels.

—  It had strong links with present-day royalty.
—  It was conveniently sited in Central London.
—  It had the Court Dress Collection on permanent display.
—  It offered considerable scope for increasing awareness that it was open to the public, so
   putting it on the tourist map.

### Kew Palace

Again, there was limited awareness of the building, and the fact that it was open to the public.
However, it was felt that less potential existed as an advertised site:

—  There was nothing sufficiently compelling about the building's history, current-day
   attraction, or architecture to make it a major tourist attraction.

— As such, major advertising might well raise expectations to a level at which they would not be fulfilled.
— The location was less convenient for tourists.

### Banqueting Hall, Whitehall

Again, while current awareness was low, its historical and current-day connections did not provide sufficient potential for development as a major tourist attraction.

### Osborne House

The location of this building made its promotion rather a different proposition to that of other palaces. While each of the other five might be promoted effectively to a localised and sizeable target audience in London, the location of Osborne House on the Isle of Wight gave this palace less potential for increasing visitor numbers.

### Overview

It was agreed that Kensington Palace was the building with greatest potential for generating increased visitors at the low level of funding available, and that all efforts should be put behind this single site.

## ADVERTISING STRATEGY

### Target Audience

This falls into two distinct categories:

— Tourists to London, both from overseas and of domestic origin.
— London and home counties residents.

Based on previous 'dipstick' research it was agreed that, of the two categories, the first one would be the most important as it appeared that the majority of visitors to Kensington Palace were tourists to London.

### Objective

The advertising objective that was set was to create awareness of Kensington Palace and its attractions, and persuade the target audience to visit the site.

### Proposition

Kensington Palace ranks among the most interesting places to visit in London.

*Supports*

— Court Dress Collection.
— State Apartments.


*Executional Guidelines*

Two executional guidelines were set. Firstly, in view of how the key target audience has been defined, the execution would need to be both clear and simple, enabling as many people as possible to understand its message. Secondly, it was felt that it was desirable to show both where the Palace was situated and when it was open.


## MEDIA STRATEGY

The complete range of media were assessed against a number of criteria:

1. Mass coverage of all adults – both from overseas and the UK.
2. Coverage of the key campaign period at an acceptable weight. This campaign was to vary from normal campaigns in so far as tourists are a continuously moving target audience. Usually a campaign is aimed at a segment of adults who can be reached in a variety of ways – for example, through their regular readership of a paper or magazine, or via posters in their area of abode. Thus, to a certain extent, the number of people is fixed, and coverage and frequency can be built up against that fixed market. The number of tourists, however, is not fixed, as some leave, more arrive and the number coming and going varies across the year.

   Therefore, the advertising would not only need to cover as much of the prime tourist season as affordable in order to ensure the broadest possible coverage but would also have to be maintained at a relatively heavy weight as there was very limited time to build coverage and frequency.
3. Regional flexibility.
4. Cost effectiveness against the target audience.


*Media Plan*

The agency recommended a plan that was a combination of London Transport tube cards and four sheet posters. Research from a number of sources (BTA, TGI and London Transport's own research) showed that the tube would provide high coverage of tourists as well as reaching a large number of people who live in and around London. Furthermore, the fact that people are in effect 'contained' in the enclosed environment of the tube while they are travelling on it increases the opportunity they have of seeing the tube card, and also allows them the time to take in the necessary details (where the Palace is and what are the opening times).

The posters, a specially designed tourist package, were used to upweight the prime tourist and high turnover stations both in terms of places of interest and British Rail stations. An additional upweight was included to cover stations close to the Palace.

Due to the low level of funding available and the previously agreed requirement to maintain a relatively heavy weight, the campaign was limited to July and August, when there are the highest number of visitors to London. Indeed, it was only possible to afford posters for one month, so August was chosen, again because it had a higher number of visitors.

# ·KENSINGTON·
# ·PALACE·

Open daily 9am – 5pm
(Sundays 1pm – 5pm)

# · VISIT THE STATE APARTMENTS ·
# ·AND COURT DRESS COLLECTION·

Department of the Environment.

Issued by the Department of the Environment and the Central Office of Information 1985. Printed in UK for Her Majesty's Stationery Office. Dd 8831460 ENV 8908180

## THE RESULTS

The results were extremely encouraging. Admission figures were significantly up on the previous year (by over 25 000); in fact, they set new records for Kensington Palace.

TABLE 1:   ADMISSIONS FOR KENSINGTON PALACE

| 000s | 1984 | 1985 | % Increase |
|------|------|------|------------|
| July | 15.9 | 24.8 | + 56.0 |
| August | 16.2 | 26.6 | + 64.2 |
| September | 13.3 | 19.1 | + 43.6 |
| TOTAL | 45.4 | 70.5 | + 55.3 |

Source: DOE

Not surprisingly, August was the month which showed the largest increase in admissions as this was the period during which both the tube cards and the poster ran. Furthermore the effect of the advertising was likely to be subject to a 'time-lag'. It would take time for people to see it, for it to register and then for people to act on it. (However, in the case of Kensington Palace, this time-lag would be relatively short as tourists would only be in the country for a limited period.) Interestingly, September (by when the advertising was officially meant to have finished) also showed a significant increase in admissions. This increase was probably due to two key factors: the 'time-lag' effect of the advertising (as previously described) and the fact that many of the tube cards and posters were not taken down or replaced until a later date.

## CONSUMER RESEARCH

During the campaign period it was agreed that some relatively small-scale consumer research would be conducted among visitors to Kensington Palace.

The objectives of this research were:

1.   To find out where visitors to Kensington Palace came from.
2.   To find out how they came to know about Kensington Palace.
3.   To find out how they travelled to Kensington Palace.

The results were to be used to help in planning future activity for Kensington Palace, and secondly they were to be used as a guide to assessing the effectiveness of the advertising. The research was conducted between the 15 and 21 July, and 17 and 25 August. Sample sizes obtained were 230 and 229 respectively.

The research showed that the overwhelming majority of visitors during this period were foreigners (94 per cent). This confirmed the necessity for making the execution clear and simple, so that as many people as possible would understand it.

Respondents were asked where they had heard about Kensington Palace. (It should be noted that no specific questions were asked about their source of awareness of the fact that Kensington Palace was open to the public, or what had prompted their visit.)

TABLE 2:   Q: WHERE DID YOU HEAR ABOUT KENSINGTON PALACE?
(SPONTANEOUS)

|  | TOTAL | 15–21 July | 17–25 August |
|---|---|---|---|
| Poster on Underground station/tube card | 12.5 | 8 | 17 |
| Poster in Kensington Gardens | 11 | 6 | 16 |
| Guide book | 23.5 | 28 | 19 |
| Leaflet | 11 | 13 | 9 |
| Friends | 13 | 11 | 15 |
| Always known | 29 | 30 | 28 |

Source: Consumer Research

The results show that 12 per cent of people spontaneously mentioned the advertising as their source of knowledge. This is very high, given the general nature of the question and people's tendency not to mention advertising. Looking at the results over the two periods they also show the build-up of the effect of advertising.

On a prompted level the scores for the advertising increase again reflecting the build-up of the effect.

TABLE 3:   Q: WHAT GUIDES/LEAFLETS/ADVERTISING HAVE YOU SEEN FOR
KENSINGTON PALACE?

|  | % TOTAL | 15–21 July | 17–25 August |
|---|---|---|---|
| Underground tube card | 32.5 | 27 | 38 |
| Underground poster | 24 | 23 | 25 |
| Historic Royal Houses (DOE) | 37.5 | 40 | 35 |
| Kensington Gardens poster | 44 | 50 | 38 |
| Visitors Guide to Central London (LT) | 43.5 | 45 | 42 |

Source: Consumer Research

Looking at the mode of travel used to get to the Palace confirmed the appropriateness of the media chosen, as the majority of people came by foot or tube.

TABLE 4:   Q: HOW DID YOU TRAVEL TO KENSINGTON PALACE?

|  | TOTAL | 15–21 July | 17–25 August |
|---|---|---|---|
| Foot | 65.5 | 72 | 59 |
| Tube | 36 | 30 | 42 |
| Bus | 7.5 | 8 | 7 |
| Car | 2 | 1 | 3 |

Source: Consumer Research
(Note: No question was asked as to whether they had used London Transport
in the last week.)

## MEASURING THE EFFECTIVENESS OF THE ADVERTISING CAMPAIGN

### Method

While the raw data of admission figures were an indication that the campaign had been successful, it was agreed that an evaluation of the effect of the advertising should be undertaken. The process by which this was achieved was, firstly, to produce an estimate of what the admissions would have been without any advertising, then to subtract this figure away from the actual number of admissions. The resulting figure then provided an estimate for the number of admissions that have been generated by the advertising.

In estimating what admissions would have been, the first stage was to hypothesise what, if any, variables other than advertising would have affected admissions. We hypothesised that the key variable was the number of visitors to London, in so far as it would be expected that if the number of visitors went up, then the number of people visiting Kensington Palace would go up. Then, by assuming that the same proportion of these additional visitors would know about and visit the main tourists sites, it was hypothesised that visitors to Kensington Palace would go up by the same percentage as the number of visitors to London.

### Application

Using figures from the London Visitor and Convention Bureau on the number of visitors to London, and figures on admissions to another key London tourist site, but one that did not receive any advertising support (in this case Hampton Court) as a control (which should confirm our second assumption), it was possible to construct the model of the expected increase in admissions not due to the advertising.

As a further control we looked at the non-advertised and advertised periods.

TABLE 5: PERCENTAGE INCREASE 1984–1985

|  | Jan–June | July–Sept |
|---|---|---|
| Visitors to London | + 16.8 | + 5.2 |
| Admissions to Kensington Palace | + 16.2 | + 55.2 |
| Admissions to Hampton Court | + 11.6 | + 11.4 |

Source: London Visitor and Convention Bureau DOE

This data confirmed our hypotheses. Admissions during the non-advertised period to both Kensington Palace and Hampton Court were in line with the increase in visitors to London. During the advertised periods, admissions to Hampton Court and visitors to London also went up roughly in line, but admissions to Kensington Palace increased significantly more. However, as there was some variation between the percentage increase in London visitors ( +5.2) and admissions to Hampton Court ( +11.4) it was decided that both figures should be used to provide a 'high' and 'low' estimate.

The next stage was therefore to take the admission figures for Kensington Palace for 1984 and multiply them by one plus the percentage increase figures which would give us the estimate for admissions had there been no advertising.

i.e.    (a)   1984 Admissions × 1.052

      (b)   1984 Admissions × 1.114

Admissions to Kensington Palace during the July–September period 1984 were 45 400 and therefore the two estimates were:

(a)  47 760
(b)  50 575

Subtracting these two figures from the actual number of admissions to Kensington Palace July–September 1985 gave the estimate for the increase that was attributable to the advertising.

Our estimates were therefore:

(a)  22 740
(b)  19 925

### Cost-Effectiveness

The next stage was to use these results to prepare an evaluation of the cost-effectiveness of the campaign. To do this, we multiplied the estimated increase in admissions due to the advertising by the average price of admission (i.e. accounting for the proportion of concessionary tickets sold) and then subtracted the known cost of the advertising from this figure. This calculation demonstrated that the incremental admissions generated had more than paid for the cost of the advertising – in the case of the 'high' estimate by as much as 20 per cent more and in the case of the 'low' estimate by 5 per cent more.

It should be noted that, for this campaign, this cost-effectiveness calculation is much simpler that it would be for many other campaigns as what was being promoted here was a service and not a product, and that therefore there were no additional costs involved with the increase in admissions. (There was no need to produce extra goods or indeed to take on extra people to staff Kensington Palace).

Furthermore, if anything, the calculation may be an underestimate of the cost-effectiveness as it does not take into account the additional revenue, and profit, which were generated at the Kensington Palace souvenir kiosk from the increased number of visitors.

## IMPLICATIONS FOR FUTURE CAMPAIGNS

Given this excellent result there seems no reason why, given similar support, Kensington Palace should not once again prove a potent attraction.

There are a number of reasons for this view:

— The universe is likely to be new.
— Visitors to London, at the time of original planning for 1986, were again expected to the high.
— Among the visitors to Kensington Palace foreign visitors dominate admissions. Given this bias with the new universe, it seems more immediately productive to concentrate resources in this area.

However, in the plans for 1986 it was recommended that in addition to the London Transport tube cards and four sheet posters there should be a selected package of four sheet posters in the vicinity of the Palace. This recommendation was based on the consumer research that highlighted the proportion of visitors who arrived on foot, and the hypothesis was that this should help encourage 'impulse visitors' who are strolling in the vicinity.

# 17
# Cymalon – A Successful Relaunch

## INTRODUCTION

This paper details the successful advertising relaunch of Cymalon, an over-the-counter medical treatment for the symptoms of cystitis, from Sterling Health. It explains how a change in the media used, and a refining of the creative strategy in the second year of the brand's life, dramatically improved consumer sales of the product.

## BACKGROUND

### Sterling Health – the Company

Sterling Health is the consumer medicine marketing arm of the Sterling-Winthrop Group Limited, a subsidiary of Sterling Drug Inc. of the USA. The company is involved in the marketing of non-prescription drugs and health care products, through both pharmacy and grocery outlets in the UK.

### What is Cystitis?

Cystitis is an inflammation of the urethra and bladder lining. It is one of the most common complaints suffered by women and is a particular problem to those of child-bearing age. Although little known and rarely discussed, it is estimated that 50 per cent of all women will suffer from cystitis at least once in their life. In this country around 1.7 million women suffered 3.7 million attacks last year.

The main symptoms of cystitis are:

1. An urgent and frequent need to pass water, and
2. dysuria – pain and discomfort when doing so.

Other symptoms can be feverishness and nausea, and pain in the lower back and abdomen.

In most cases cystitis is caused by a relatively minor bacterial infection which creates inflammation of the bladder lining and urethra. This inflammation is irritated by the normal acidity of urine, and so the painful symptoms are generated. While cystitis is not a serious complaint, it is a very uncomfortable and upsetting problem which can cause embarrassment.

247

*The Opportunity*

Three-quarters of all cases of cystitis in the UK in 1983 were treated by a trip to the GP. Doctors usually prescribed antibiotics to treat the infection and encouraged the sufferer to drink plenty of fluids to keep their urine dilute, and so reduce the irritation and pain. The attack normally cleared up in a few days.

While antibiotics are invariably prescribed in case there is a bad infection, the common bacteria causing cystitis can also be eliminated in most cases by changing the ph value (acid/alkaline nature) of their environment. These bacteria are fastidious in their choice of breeding ground and a change from acid to alkaline conditions will inhibit their growth. Theoretically, most women could treat themselves by controlling the acidity of their urine. However, lack of understanding led women almost invariably to consult their GP on each occasion, and for the GP in turn to prescribe antibiotics.

Qualitative research conducted by Sterling Health had shown, however, that there was a growing dissatisfaction with the need to consult often unsympathetic GPs for an inevitable repeat prescription. This research, done in the early 1980s, showed that for the majority of sufferers, and the frequent sufferers in particular, the convenience of self-treatment had enormous appeal. Sterling Health therefore felt there was potential for a new self-medicating cystitis treatment for women.

*What is Cymalon?*

Cymalon is the first structured treatment for the symptoms of cystitis. It was developed for the UK by Sterling Health to take advantage of this apparent market opportunity for a self treatment. While it was given a General Sales Licence (GSL), theoretically allowing it to be sold in any type of shop, the DHSS felt that it should be sold only through pharmacists.

Cymalon is a structured course of treatment that alters the ph balance of urine, making it more alkaline and so unfavourable to common cystitis bacteria. More immediately, it relieves the pain of acid urine on the inflamed bladder and urethra.

The course is made up of six sachets of powder (the active ingredient being sodium citrate) which are taken over a 48-hour period. Each sachet is mixed in a glass of water to make a pleasant-tasting drink. Also within the pack of Cymalon there is an information leaflet which helps the sufferer understand what cystitis is and how it can be treated.

Although other products were available before Cymalon, they are all P licence (pharmacy only) medicines which can only be sold under the supervision of a registered pharmacist and are not available for self-selection. They also taste very unpleasant, which does nothing to encourage repeat usage. Quantitative research showed that these remedies were not well used: only 10 per cent of the attacks were treated with them and brand awareness was very low; even among frequent sufferers it was only between one per cent and four per cent (Gallup Omnibus).

## THE LAUNCH OF CYMALON IN 1984

Cymalon was lauched to the chemist trade in January 1984 and sold in well. The brand was introduced to consumers with an advertising campaign in women's press during March–June 1984. This was a relatively heavyweight campaign achieving 80 per cent coverage of women

21 to 44 years old who were the defined target market. It was produced by the brand's previous advertising agency.

*Results from the Initial Launch Campaign*

After the initial selling-in success, ex-factory sales showed no appreciable uplift as a result of the consumer advertising. Although the brand had achieved good sterling distribution throughout the country, average sales stayed low and began to drop by early 1985.

Brand awareness was low at 5 per cent (July 1984 Gallup) though improved to 16 per cent when respondents were prompted with the pack. Gallup also showed there was no dissatisfaction among those who had tried the product: repeat purchase was, therefore, not the problem. Sterling Health became concerned that trade dissatisfaction with the slow offtake would soon lead to de-stocking. The high expectations for the brand had clearly been disappointed.

## THE RELAUNCH OF CYMALON IN 1985

Gold Greenlees Trott took over the advertising of the brand in November 1984. In order to clarify our own understanding of cystitis and to check the strategy, we carried out a qualitative research study among both chronic and infrequent sufferers.

Our main findings were:

1. Almost all sufferers felt immense relief at being able to discuss their problem openly since it was a subject that was not normally talked about, even among friends.
2. Sufferers were surprised to find out how common their complaint was – they had felt themselves to be isolated in their suffering.
3. The most disabling aspect of cystitis was the pain, and while an attack lasted, the urgent need was to find relief from this pain.
4. While it was agreed that self-treatment would be a convenient release from repeated trips to the GP very few seemed convinced that an attack involving pain could be solved without a doctor's visit. The most natural thing would be to fall back on trips to the doctor.
5. Awareness of Cymalon was not only low, but almost no-one could pronounce it (we pronounce it Sigh-ma-lon). Clearly a difficulty with the name did not aid the consumer's confidence and, more fundamentally, it is difficult to remember words which are hard to pronounce.

*Our Learning*

Our research findings highlighted two important facts:

1. Pain was the single most important discomfort to sufferers of cystitis. To convince consumers that they could ease the pain was the most motivating aspect of self-treatment. The proposition needed to be singleminded.
2. Previous advertising had underestimated how difficult it was to modify behaviour, even though there was a clear desire by sufferers to find a way to relieve their pain themselves.

The sufferers needed to make a quantum leap in their thinking in order to seriously consider self-treatment.

Before considering how our learning helped us develop the creative work it is important to look at the media option we chose, as this was crucial in achieving the impact the brand needed.

### The Media Answer

To be successful the new advertising strategy required national support for the brand to build awareness and trial quickly. We also wanted media that would help us build confidence in the brand and the self-treatment route, i.e. reassure sufferers it was a common complaint and self-treatment was not a risk.

After discussion with the IBA it was agreed that TV advertising was acceptable for Cymalon. On the budget available, TV-AM was capable of delivering national coverage at an acceptable advertising weight. Televison not only gave us far greater impact than we could have achieved in any other medium, but we felt that it helped to give the advertising the authority it required to be accepted and acted upon by cystitis sufferers.

## ADVERTISING OBJECTIVE AND STRATEGY

### Advertising Objectives

Within the bounds of the sensitive nature of cystitis suffering:

1. To increase awareness of Cymalon among current cystitis sufferers.
2. To position Cymalon as the self-treatment for cystitis sufferers.

### Target Audience

The target audience were women aged between 20–34 years who were experienced enough sufferers of cystitis to be capable of self-diagnosis of the symptoms. We did not want to encourage initial self-diagnosis (which should always be directed through a doctor) and so were not interested in telling women how to recognise cystitis.

### Proposition

At last, relief from the pain of cystitis whenever you need it.

### Support

1. Cymalon neutralises the acidity of urine and so relieves pain and discomfort.
2. Cymalon can be bought from any chemist.
3. Cymalon is all that is necessary to bring relief in the majority of cystitis cases and will not mask the symptoms of more severe cases, in that if the pain persists after 48 hours a trip to the doctor is recommended.

*Executional Guidelines*

Cymalon advertising should be seen as an important announcement, not to be confused with a cosmetic or trivial feminine product.

*Tone*

Reasuring and informative.

*The TV Commercial*

In the commercial a piece of acid-sensitive paper is dipped into uric acid and turns red: this symbolises the pain of cystitis. Cymalon is then poured into the uric acid, and its neutralisation is illustrated via the acid-sensitive paper returning to its original colour: this symbolises the relief of the pain.

Creative development research showed that this was an arresting and powerful demonstration of the benefits of Cymalon, which did not overstep the boundary of good taste.

*The Media Plan*

To date, two bursts of advertising have run on TV-AM. There has also been an up-weight test in the Harlech TV region on ITV1 and Channel 4.

| | | | | | | | | | | |
|---|---|---|---|---|---|---|---|---|---|---|
| TV-AM | | | | | | | | | TV-AM | |
| 518 TVRs | | | | | | | | | 395 TVRs | |
| | | | | | | | | | HTV | |
| | | | | | | | | | 400 TVRs | |
| JULY | AUG | SEPT | OCT | NOV | DEC | JAN | FEB | MAR | APRIL | |
| 1985 | | | | | | 1986 | | | | |

All ratings are against women aged 20 to 34 years. Less than £250 000 was spent on media in 1985. This was also the case on TV-AM and HTV in 1986.

## THE RESULTS OF THE RELAUNCH

The first burst of TV-AM advertising in July/October 1985 was so successful that the campaign was continued in 1986. Details of the results to date are given below. The main measurements used were Nielsen Audits of the chemist trade and attitude and awareness tracking carried out by Gallup Omnibus.

*Sales Volume*

After the first burst of TV advertising in July/October 1985, sales showed a significant upswing – see Figure 1. The response to the advertising was so dramatic that Sterling Health could not keep up with the demand and factory supply problems caused temporary out-of-stocks in the trade. Although sales dropped away slightly once the advertising ended, a much

This is a beaker of uric acid.

This is a piece of acid sensitive paper.

It's acid in your bladder that causes the pain of cystitis.

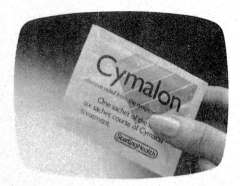

But now there's a treatment you can buy from the chemist – Cymalon.

Cymalon neutralizes the acid and eases the pain.

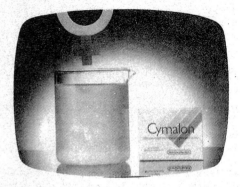

When you get cystitis.
Get Cymalon, from Sterling Health.

higher level than previously was maintained. The second burst of TV early in 1986 lifted sales back up towards the previous peak.

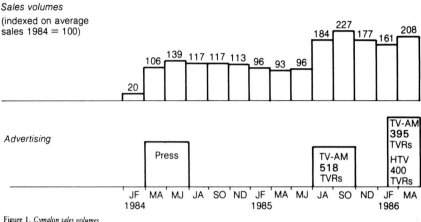

Figure 1. *Cymalon sales volumes*
*Sources:* sales volumes – Nielsen
        advertising – GGT

The price of Cymalon has remained constant to prescription charges throughout the period covered in Figure 1.

### Awareness

Attitudes towards cystitis and awareness of Cymalon and other cystitis treatments have been monitored by a Gallup random omnibus among 1200 women.

Figure 2 shows a very dramatic increase in spontaneous brand awareness for Cymalon since the TV advertising started. Television has clearly removed the problem of pronouncing and

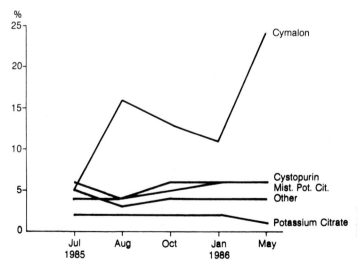

Figure 2. *Spontaneous brand awareness*
Source: Gallup 85/86

remembering the brand name. No other brand comes anywhere near Cymalon's level of awareness.

Prompted brand awareness (Figure 3) has tripled since the beginning of the TV campaign. Nearly half of all cystitis sufferers now claim to have heard of Cymalon. Given that TV-AM only reaches about 50 per cent of the target market, prompted awareness of 48 per cent is a very pleasing result.

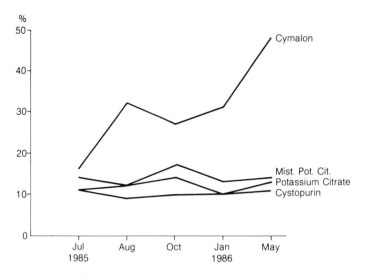

Figure 3. *Prompted brand awareness*
Source: Gallup 85/86

Both spontaneous and total advertising awareness have also increased significantly among all sufferers (Figure 4).

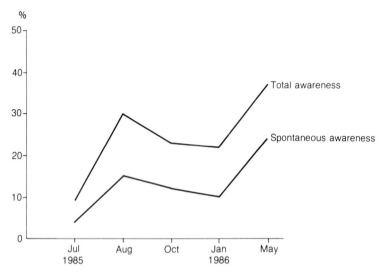

Figure 4. *Advertising awareness of Cymalon*
Source: Gallup 85/86

*Harlech TV Test*

Although TV-AM proved to be a very successful medium for Cymalon, it has limited cover of the target market as the station's overall reach is still relatively low. Only 50 per cent of women aged 20 to 34 years of age will have had the opportunity to see the Cymalon commercial so far.

We were interested to find out what the effect of increasing coverage would be. Consequently, we ran a test in the Harlech area on ITV1 and Channel 4 alongside the TV-AM campaign in 1986. The results have been extremely encouraging. Table 1 compares Harlech and total UK sales. Year-on-year sales in the up-weighted area are up significantly on the country as a whole.

TABLE 1:   YEAR ON YEAR CHANGE (85/6)

|  | Jan/Feb | Mar/Apr |
|---|---|---|
| *Sales Volume* | | |
| UK | + 67% | +125% |
| Harlech | +122% | +258% |
| *Weighted average sales* | | |
| UK | + 59% | +105% |
| Harlech | + 80% | +180% |

Weighted average sales is a Nielsen measure of volume sold per store adjusted to 'average' store size.

These results lead us to believe the only thing that has been restricting the sales of Cymalon on a national basis is the limited cover of our target market we have been able to achieve on TV-AM.

## CONCLUSIONS

It is clear from the evidence in this paper that advertising has been effective in establishing the Cymalon brand after its faltering beginnings. Sales to date are very encouraging and the Harlech test suggests that further growth can be achieved by switching the advertising to ITV1 and Channel 4 in the future.

This case history demonstrates very clearly the importance of the media choice. It also endorses the philosophy that you do not always need huge budgets to make advertising work. In this instance TV-AM offered us outstanding value and conversion against the target market for the relatively small budgets available. For any new product, building awareness and trial is critical. For Cymalon we had the additional problems that sufferers were not aware that self-treatment of cystitis was an option open to them and, even when they were, many were unconvinced it could work. Using a medium as powerful as television helped solve that problem: it added credibility and weight to our message. The other important factor in the success of the advertising was the creative execution. It was a simple, straightforward demonstration that left no room for doubt that the product worked. The message that Cymalon removed the pain of cystitis came through loud and clear.

# 18

# Paul Masson California Carafes: 'They're really jolly good!'

## INTRODUCTION

The success of Paul Masson California Carafes since their launch in the summer of 1980 in itself provides a fascinating and powerful case history. The purpose of this paper however is to demonstrate advertising effectiveness in a specific phase of that period. That phase is a crucial one for many products, namely the period after initial launch when the original momentum of consumer and trade 'novelty' is no longer sufficient to propel the brand forward, and competitive pressures are building. It is also the case that in a rapidly growing market (such as table wines) no new product stays 'new' for very long. Thus after two years in the market the Paul Masson California Carafe was an established wine product.

This paper is about the re-evaluation of that brand's position in the market – particularly with regard to other branded wine ranges – and the impact that re-evaluation had on advertising. Above all, however, it is about the power of advertising in building brand values that defended the brand from severe generic and own-label competition, and maintained sales growth momentum at a time when other brands had begun to suffer.

## BACKGROUND

Seagram Distillers internationally are the largest wine and spirits company in the world. Very few of their international brands (eg Chivas Regal, Captain Morgan, Mumm, Paul Masson, 100 Pipers etc) carry the Seagram name however. In the UK, the Seagram company is unusual in two respects. Firstly prior to the launch of Paul Masson, its UK turnover was almost entirely (95 per cent) based on spirits. Secondly, unlike most of its competitors, Seagram had no tied distribution either in the on- or off-trade.

Paul Masson Vineyards (California) is a wholly owned subsidiary of Seagram Distillers and Paul Masson is a major brand of wine in the US market – though by no means market leader. Paul Masson himself was a Frenchman who emigrated to California in the 1870s, taking with him vine roots from Burgundy and establishing vineyards some of which, ironically, later provided the cuttings for the replanting of French vineyards in the late 19th century after fungal plagues had destroyed the native French vines.

## THE UK OBJECTIVE

Given Seagram UK's lack of tied distribution, having a strong branded property is critical to be able to sell in effectively to the trade. For the same reason, a product failure, particularly in a growth sector could be extremely damaging to company reputation. Secondly, given the above, and the bias in Seagram's UK business towards spirits (a sector in decline since 1978), it was crucial for Seagram to have a *big* brand – one that would contribute fully to a shift in the company's business base away from spirits and into wine. The criteria for success were therefore long-term rather than short-term; essentially, to establish and maintain a high-volume branded wine property in the UK market.

## THE PRODUCT

A Californian, non-vintage, blended table wine in 1-litre, resealable, non-returnable carafes, available in red, medium sweet white and rosé. A dry white variant was added to the range in the summer of 1983, nationally, although this has had only minor significance to date (less than 20 per cent sterling distribution, less than 7 per cent of sales volume).

## THE UK WINE MARKET

The UK wine market has been growing at between 10-15 per cent per annum since 1975. It is characterised by a plethora of, in effect, unbranded generic wines, a strong own-label sector, and a relatively small though highly profitable branded sector (approximately 15–20 per cent of total). As wines have become more widely available, so they have become more accessible to more people and also cheaper. The traditions of wine have broken down to the extent that the 'new wine majority', though still up-market in bias, are relatively unfettered by the attitudes of their parents. Wine is increasingly an informal drink – both privately and socially. Importantly, however, new drinkers continue to enter the market every year. Volume growth therefore comes from increasing penetration as well as increasing frequency.

## LAUNCH AND ROLL-OUT 1980–82

Initial research conducted prior to the launch had indicated a number of key issues that were to shape our strategic and creative thinking at that time:

1. Whilst reactions to the wine itself were generally good, the pack (a 'given') aroused some perceived price and disposability problems amongst consumers.
2. Interest in California origin, however, was high.
3. Despite the obviously rich creative area of 'the Paul Masson story', research indicated that consumers could find this area boring.
4. More important was the need for strong branded reassurance especially to less frequent/new drinkers.

In addition we were conscious of the potential presence of a number of 'me-too' competitors waiting in the wings, and hence:

(a) the implicit danger of focussing on packaging;
(b) the competitive threat from pursuing a generic or 'origin' route;
(c) the need to sell the wine itself;
(d) the need for strong branding.

In order to address these last two points, a presenter route was developed since, with the right person, such a route could give credibility and reassurance on wine values, whilst at the same time offering the opportunity for a unique branded property. The chosen presenter was Ian Carmichael, and a script was developed. Given the desire to use the presenter route to the full and the reduced requirement for informational content, TV was the medium chosen for maximum impact in the key pre-Christmas (1980) period, which is traditionally a highly 'cluttered' time for drink advertising.

Paul Masson California Carafe was launched onto the UK market in the London area in the summer of 1980 and supported with TV advertising at minimal weight (180 TVRs) in that area pre-Christmas 1980. Consumer acceptance was high, and the brand was rolled out nationally during 1981. In the pre-Christmas 1981 period, advertising support was extended into five other areas, at weights of between 200 and 400 TVRs.

As a branded range, Paul Masson California Carafe faced competition from three key directions:

1. Other branded ranges (e.g. Nicolas, Hirondelle, Don Cortez).

2.  Individual branded wines (e.g. Blue Nun, Mateus, Lutomer, Black Tower).
3.  Own-label and generics.

Whilst these distinctions were less clear-cut in the consumer's mind, it was clear from early post-launch research that Paul Masson California Carafe was most closely compared with the 'other branded ranges' outlined above. Equally clear, was the fact that these branded ranges were themselves the sector most under threat, particularly from the growth of own-label. Such has been the impact of own-label that these ranges were already in decline in 1981. If Paul Masson California Carafe was not to follow the same pattern, it was crucial that the brand should distinguish itself from the field.

It has been a clear objective at the launch stage to brand the product strongly rather than to rely on the generic origin appeal of California. The original advertising had achieved this, but the task was now to protect that branded position. The position at the beginning of 1982 can best be summarised in tabular form (see Table 1). The pre-Christmas period is a crucial one for the wine market and especially for branded wines,

TABLE 1:   PAUL MASSON PERFORMANCE 1980-81

|  | 1980 | 1981 | %± |
|---|---|---|---|
| Paul Masson California Carafe case sales (index) | 100 | 250 | +150 |
| *pre-Christmas period:* | | | |
| total market sales (million units) | 30.1 | 37.4 | + 24 |
| Paul Masson California Carafe brand share | 0.5* | 1.0 | +100 |
| Hirondelle ⎫ | | | |
| Nicolas      ⎬   brand share | 10.0 | 8.1 | − 19 |
| Don Cortez ⎭ | | | |

* estimate

Source: Seagram UK

Nielsen (Grocers & Specialists)

TABLE 2:   CONSUMER AWARENESS AND TRIAL 1980-82 (Base: adult wine drinkers)

|  | Jan 1981 | | Jan 1982 | | | |
|---|---|---|---|---|---|---|
|  | London | Southern | London | Southern | Trident | Granada |
| pre-Xmas adult ratings: | 182 | 0 | 270 | 227 | 379 | 0 |
| advertising awareness (prompted): | %<br>28 | %<br>3 | %<br>34 | %<br>18 | %<br>42 | %<br>7 |
| brand awareness (total): | 48 | 21 | 58 | 42 | 71 | 40 |
| trial: | (28)* | (23)* | 28 | 19 | 31 | 17 |
| repeat (% of trialists): | 42 | 38 | 61 | 64 | 55 | 73 |

* Boosted sample, not comparable with 1982 data.

Source: Gordon Simmons Research Tracking Studies

since the branded sector – normally around 15 per cent of total – increases its share in December to around 17–18 per cent. In the light of this phenomenon, the performance of the other branded ranges was very disappointing.

However, Seagram could take little comfort from their own performance since the majority of the improvement 1980–81 had been as a result of increased distribution for the brand. Whilst the first two years' advertising has been highly effective in terms of consumer awareness, trial and repeat purchase (see Table 2), it was clear that if the Paul Masson California Carafe brand were not, in 1982 and beyond, to go the same way as its competitors, there would have to be a fundamental reassessment of the brand's positioning and advertising.

## THE SITUATION IN 1982

A number of key factors are worth stating at this point since they largely formed the basis for our re-evaluation of the opportunity.

1. Branded ranges were clearly under threat and seemed likely to continue to decline.
2. Individual brands, whilst strong, also appeared to have peaked in share terms.
3. The growth of own-label products was continuing.
4. The launch of the *Le Piat* brand on TV pre-Christmas 1981 seemed to be going very well.
5. Seagram did not have unlimited funds to support the brand, especially in the light of the deteriorating £/$ exchange rate and the need to maintain price at a competitive level.

Our examination of the market at this time was very broad ranging and embraced the following elements.

### *Analysis of TGI Data on Brand Repertoires and Usage*

Using this data source, we were able to 'map' the wine market on two key dimensions. Firstly, we examined indices of brand share amongst heavier vs. lighter drinkers (the horizontal axis on Figure 1), and secondly the indices of above and below average usage according to most-often usage occasion (the vertical axis on Figure 1). In confirmation of these patterns we were also able to examine the duplication of brand usage (repertoires) amongst all drinkers, thus establishing the degrees of 'overlap' between the different brands. Figure 1, therefore, maps the market in terms of the 'clusters' of brands about the two axes according to usage. Because Paul Masson was not a TGI-listed brand at that time however we had to turn to our own tracking study data to establish the position of our brand within this map.

### *Analysis of Tracking Study Data*

Analysis of this source with regard to both type of user and usage occasion suggested not only the appeal of the brand to both experienced/heavier and inexperienced/lighter

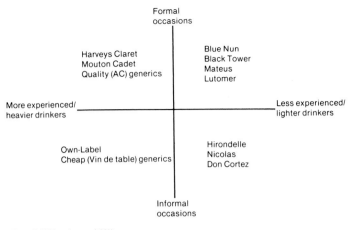

Figure 1. *TGI market map (1982)*
*Source:* TGI

drinkers, but also its ability to fulfil a dual role as an informal occasion brand for the former segment, and as a formal occasion brand for the latter segment (see Table 3).

TABLE 3:   DRINKING OCCASIONS: PAUL MASSON CALIFORNIA CARAFE
              BUYERS 1981

|  | heavier drinkers % | lighter drinkers % |
|---|---|---|
| *formal occasions* | | |
| dinner party | 12 | 21 |
| Xmas/New Year | 5 | 16 |
| *informal occasions* | | |
| drinking at home | 59 | 49 |
| informal party | 17 | 10 |

Source: Gordon Simmons Research 1982 Tracking Study

Thus in positioning terms, and using the same axes as in the TGI analysis, Paul Masson seemed to 'span' the market in a way that no other brand did. Figure 2 indicates diagrammatically the nature of this unique positioning.

## Qualitative Research

The large amount of qualitative research conducted at this time provided us with substantial attitudinal confirmation not only of the usage patterns and repertoires outlined above but also of Paul Masson California Carafe's almost unique position in being capable of appealing to different types of consumer. In so doing, it enabled us to understand the 'critical balance' between on the one hand offering branded reassurance to less experienced drinkers, whilst on the other hand not being patronising, and at the same time providing sufficient wine 'credentials' to make the brand 'legitimate' to the more experienced

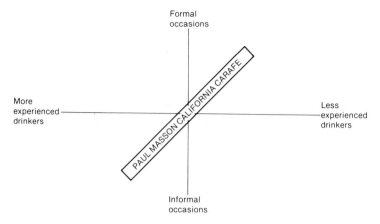

Figure 2. *Masson market positioning*

drinker. This was a balance that we felt most other brands had failed to achieve and hence had accounted for their more narrow appeal and actual usage by segments of consumers within the total market.

## OBJECTIVES AND STRATEGY 1982

### *Market Objectives*

1. To maintain brand share growth despite the pressures on branded ranges in general.
2. To reinforce the brand's position *vis-à-vis* own-label.
3. To make the brand robust in the face of competitive launches/relaunches.
4. To maintain rate-of-sale increases even when distribution plateaued.

### *Advertising Objectives*

1. To reflect the balance of formal and informal usage, and hence appeal to both experienced and inexperienced drinkers.
2. To reinforce the Paul Masson branding.
3. To build wine 'credentials' for the brand.

In addition, it was an important objective at the time for both the agency and Seagram UK to use advertising cost effectively within a limited budget, but at the same time to be able to demonstrate the differential effectiveness of that advertising.

### *Target Audience*

ABC1 (C2) wine drinkers 25–40, both inexperienced and experienced (though not connoisseurs).

*Brand Positioning*

Paul Masson California Carafes are better-than-average quality, California wines, suitable for both formal and informal occasions.

Although the target audience and brand positioning statements had changed only in their definition of types of drinkers and types of occasions since 1980, the thinking that lay behind this change, out-lined under marketing and advertising objectives above, had moved on significantly.

The role for advertising had in effect been redefined from one primarily concerned with launching the brand (ie building awareness and trial), to one of maintaining the brand through positioning it in such a way that it was less vulnerable to both market forces and competitive threats than any other. It was this redefinition, we believed, that would be crucial to the brand's continued success.

## ADVERTISING DEVELOPMENT AND SUPPORT 1982–84

The original commercial developed for the launch in 1980 had featured Ian Carmichael introducing the wines with a high degree of scepticism. The setting had been a fairly formal one and the featured variant was the red. Our earlier (1980–81) research had confirmed the effectiveness of this commercial in terms of branding and presenter. Our re-evaluation however, had stressed the need for a balance with informal occasions (and hence, more usually, white wine), the need to reinforce the 'Paul Masson' element within the name and to build wine 'credentials' for the brand without boring consumers with detailed product information.

The second film therefore, designed to run in rotation with 'Jolly Good', was 'Grabbed'. Here the setting was an outdoor/informal one, the featured wine was white and Carmichael speaks of Paul Masson having been making wines since 1852. In every respect therefore the two executions are complementary.

The two commercials went on air together for the first time nationally pre-Christmas 1982, at area weights that ranged between 150 and 350 adult ratings. In 1983 support was given to the brand for the first time mid-year in a limited number of areas at low weights (150–400 adult ratings), and pre-Christmas 1983 the brand was again advertised using the same two commercials, but this time only semi-nationally at area weights between 120 and 320 adult ratings.

This period 1982–84, therefore, is the central focus of this evaluation. Let us now go on to examine in detail what the advertising achieved.

## THE RESULTS

In assessing the brand and the contribution of advertising, it has always been recognised that sales and share have been the two key measures. Whilst consumer research on attitudes and behaviour had been valuable in monitoring progress and particularly in shaping strategic direction, as already demonstrated, the focus in this section is on identifying the relative performance of the brand in sales and share terms both vs. other brands, and between advertised and non-advertised areas.

*VISION*

Open on Ian Carmichael in a very British drawing-room.

On a table stand some carafes, one of which he picks up and shows to camera. We see carafes in CU.

Cut back to presenter. He raises an eyebrow.

He gives a look of mild disbelief at the words he is using ... which increases in incredulity to the point of distaste.

He pours himself a glass of wine from the carafe he's holding, then sips some.

He obviously likes what he has tasted.

Cut to three pack shot and *super: Paul Masson's California Carafes.*

*SOUND*

*Ian Carmichael:* I was first introduced to Paul Masson's California Carafes by some California chaps.

Paul Masson I was told have a fruity white that you can really relate to. A rose that's got its act together. And a red that knows where it's coming from .... man.

I decided to try them all the same.

And I must say – they're really jolly good.

*American VO:* Paul Masson's California Carafes. They're really ... jolly good.

| VISION | SOUND |
|---|---|
| Open on the harbour of a small fishing port, somewhere on the south west coast of England | |
| | *SFX:* Motor boat, seagulls and sea sounds. |
| It is late afternoon. | |
| A medium-sized cruiser is slowly making its way into port. | |
| As the camera closes in, we see the skipper at the wheel and another crew member. | |
| Reclining on the after deck with a Carafe is Ian Carmichael. | |
| He talks to camera. | *Ian Carmichael:* I was chatting to some Californians recently about Paul Masson's California Carafes. |
| Camera closes in on Ian as he gestures towards the Carafe. | Paul Masson, they informed me, has been laying fine wines on people since 1852. |
| As he talks, we close in on his pouring out some wine. | Try a Carafe, they suggested and see how it 'grabs' you, man. |
| Cut to Ian's face registering wry amusement. | Though somewhat wary of being grabbed by a bottle of wine I decided to give it a whirl. |
| Ian takes a non–committal gulp. Then grins to camera. | And I must say, they're really jolly good. |
| Cut back to pack shot of 3 Carafes<br>*Super: Paul Masson's California Wines.* | *Male VO:* Paul Masson's California Carafes. They're really jolly good. |

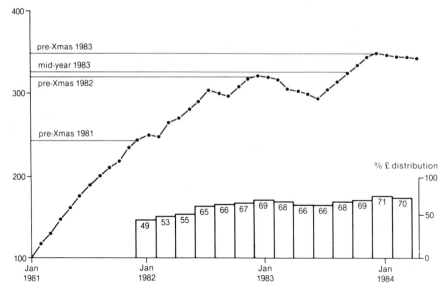

Figure 3. *Index of Paul Masson California Carafe ex-factory case sales (MAT) : year to Jan 1981 = 100*
Sources: Seagram UK, Nielsen (Grocers & Specialists)

In the simplest terms, the brand has been a success (see Figure 3). Brand sales have increased consistently across the period even after distribution plateaued in mid 1982.

Particularly impressive have been:

1.  The consistent improvement year-on-year in the pre-Christmas period.
2.  The mid-year achievement in 1983; higher than any previous pre-Christmas peak.

In tandem with this has been the continued development of the brand's consumer franchise. Although tracking study data collected in January 1983 and 1984 was based on a different sample design, and (in 1984) analysed only on a national basis (and hence not comparable with 1981 and 1982), Table 4 indicates quite clearly the development of consumer knowledge and increasing trial of the brand over the 1982–84 period. It also demonstrates increasing frequency of purchase amongst repeat users within the growing overall penetration of the brand and during the peak pre-Christmas period.

TABLE 4:    PAUL MASSON CONSUMER PERFORMANCE 1982-84
(NATIONALLY) (Base: all UK wine drinkers)

|  | Jan 1983 | Jan 1984 |
| --- | --- | --- |
| advertising awareness (prompted) | 31 | 40 |
| brand awareness (total) | 49 | 61 |
| ever bought | 18 | 25 |
| repeat buyers | 10 | 11 |
| (of which) bought in last month | 41 | 47 |

Research: PHD Research Tracking Studies

In addition, qualitative research conducted at regular intervals throughout the period continued to suggest not only advertising's role in the development of a highly distinctive brand personality, but also in positioning the brand as acceptable on a number of usage occasions, and against both sectors of the target audience. This too has been confirmed quantitatively (see Table 5). Within this, however, were the marketing and advertising objectives met?

TABLE 5:   DRINKING OCCASIONS: PAUL MASSON CALIFORNIA CARAFE REPEAT BUYERS JAN 1983

|  | heavier drinkers % | lighter drinkers % |
|---|---|---|
| *formal occasions:* | | |
| dinner party at home | 29 | 38 |
| dinner party away from home | 46 | 47 |
| Christmas/New Year | 22 | 22 |
| *informal occasions:* | | |
| drinking, at home without friends/guests | 61 | 43 |
| weekends/meals at home without guests | 11 | 7 |

Source: PHD Research Tracking Study

Table 6 demonstrates that the marketing objective of maintaining share, despite pressures against brands generally, was met. Paul Masson California Carafe share rose in the pre-Christmas 1982 period to 1.4 per cent, making it the sixth biggest brand in the market. More importantly, it maintained this position in 1983 at a time when the other three branded ranges experienced severe decline, and even the individual brands dropped back.

TABLE 6:   BUILDING BRAND SHARE WHEN OTHER BRANDS IN DECLINE

|  | Dec-Jan 1980-81 % | Dec-Jan 1981-82 % | Dec-Jan 1982-83 % | Dec-Jan 1983-84 % |
|---|---|---|---|---|
| Paul Masson | 0.5* | 1.0 | 1.4 | 1.4 |
| Hirondelle | 4.8 | 3.9 | 3.3 | 2.1 |
| Nicolas | 2.0 | 1.5 | 1.2 | 0.8 |
| Don Cortez | 3.2 | 2.7 | 2.1 | 1.6 |
| Blue Nun | | | 1.9 | 1.8 |
| Black Tower | | | 1.1 | 0.9 |
| Lutomer | | | 3.6 | 3.3 |
| Mateus | | | 1.4 | 1.2 |

* estimate

Source: Nielsen (Grocers & Specialists)

**TABLE 7: ADVERTISED VS. NON-ADVERTISED AREAS**

| brand shares: | Dec–Jan 1982–83 | | Dec–Jan 1983–84 | |
| --- | --- | --- | --- | --- |
| | national | Wales, West, Westward | national | Wales, West, Westward |
| Paul Masson | 1.4 | 1.2 | 1.4 | 0.8 |
| Hirondelle | 3.3 | 3.6 | 2.1 | 1.7 |
| Blue Nun | 1.9 | 1.9 | 1.8 | 1.7 |

Source: Nielsen (Grocers & Specialists)

Whilst competitive price differentials across the period 1982–83 were almost entirely consistent, and distribution between the two periods relatively static for all brands, advertising support for Paul Masson however was not. One area (Wales, West, Westward) received no support in 1983 although it had received support in 1982. If brand performance in Wales, West, Westward is compared to the national performance, the picture in Table 7 emerges. From this analysis it can be seen that Paul Masson California Carafe performed significantly worse in the non-advertised area than in the rest of the country. With all other factors remaining constant, advertising was the only variable within the mix that changed. Furthermore, if one examines all four identifiably separate Nielsen areas* and compares sales performance for the full year 1983 vs. 1982, Table 8 emerges. This relationship is shown graphically in Figure 4. Together with the share data described earlier it provides clear evidence of the role and effectiveness of advertising in sustaining and building the brand in both share and sales terms across the period.

**TABLE 8:    1983 VS. 1982 (YEAR TO FEB–MAR FOLLOWING)**

| | Sales ±% | TVRs ±% |
| --- | --- | --- |
| London | + 13 | + 50 |
| Southern | + 28 | + 122 |
| Wales, West, Westward | − 6 | − 100 (ie no support in 1983) |
| Lancashire | − 8 | − 22 |

Source: Nielsen (Grocers & Specialists)
       AGB

Turning to the second and third marketing objectives, Table 9 illustrates further the 'robustness' of the Masson brand – not only did it maintain share, but it did so in the face of further severe encroachment on the branded sector by own-label and the continued success of Le Piat. Here, too, this was not the case in Wales, West and Westward, where Le Piat share reached only 1.6 per cent in December–January 1983–84, yet as we have seen, Masson share dropped back from 1.2 per cent to 0.8 per cent. Once again, therefore, in the context of contrast price differentials and a static distribution position, Masson's 'robustness' can really only be explained in terms of advertising support and strategic/ creative 'edge' over the competition.

---

* Nielsen tables combine Midlands & Anglia, Yorkshire & Tyne Tees, Scottish & Grampian TV areas, all of which received differential levels of support.

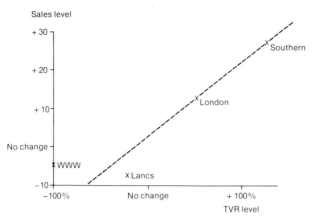

Figure 4. *1983 vs. 1982 year to Feb–Mar following*

TABLE 9:   ROBUSTNESS IN THE FACE OF COMPETITIVE LAUNCHES AND THE GROWTH OF
             OWN LABEL

|  | Dec–Jan 1982–83 % | Dec–Jan 1983–84 % | Brand Share %± |
|---|---|---|---|
| Paul Masson | 1.4 | 1.4 | n.c. |
| other branded ranges* | 6.6 | 4.5 | −2.1 |
| individual brands** | 8.0 | 7.2 | −0.8 |
| Le Piat | 2.0 | 2.7 | +0.7 |
| All others (generics & own label) | 81.9 | 83.9 | +2.0 |

\* Nicolas, Hirondelle, Don Cortez
\*\* Blue Nun, Black Tower, Lutomer, Mateus
Source: Nielsen (Grocers & Specialists)

Finally, what about rate of sale? From an examination of the sales performance, effective sterling distribution and, hence, rate of sale, across the period 1982 vs. 1983, quite clear comparisons can be made between the major competitive brands. From this analysis, it can be demonstrated that in 'real' terms, rate of sale for Paul Masson California Carafe increased by 10 per cent across the period. This performance was significantly better than the other branded ranges (which declined between 16 and 33 per cent), and better even than any other individual brand except Blue Nun, whose rate of sale increased by 24 per cent largely because distribution for that brand fell back 10 points. As a measure of consumer offtake, this is yet another indicator of the strength of the Masson franchise vs. the competition.

Once again, it is worth pointing out that in the only identifiable non-advertised area in 1983, Wales, West and Westward, not only did Paul Masson California Carafes' effective distribution actually fall by 2 per cent but rate of sale even through that reduced base dropped by 19 per cent, on a par with the other branded ranges.

It will be recalled that the advertising objectives for the brand, as well as relating to content (already addressed), also included the proviso that the advertising should be cost effective within a limited budget, while at the same time being capable of demonstrating differential effectiveness. Taking differential effect first, we have referred already to the 'special case' of Wales, West and Westward having received no support in 1983. In addition, Granada was the only identifiable area to receive support pre-Christmas 1983 but not mid-year. To compare performance between these we also need to examine an area which received support in both periods. We have selected Southern as that area, on the basis of comparable total market sales, distribution and population levels. Figure 5 illustrates the relative performance of the three areas over the 1983 period. From this it

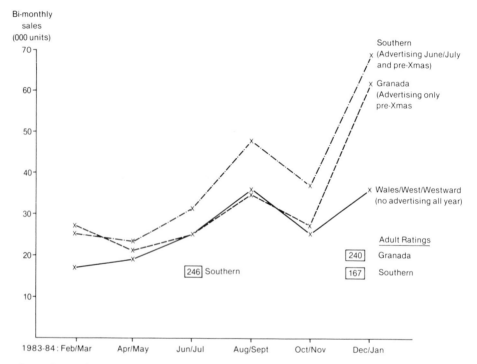

Figure 5. *Relative performance in advertising areas and control*
*Source:* Nielsen (Grocers and Specialists)

can be seen that whilst all three areas start roughly on a par in sales terms in February–March, the situation changes significantly across the year. Granada (advertised only pre-Christmas) follows the same sales pattern as Wales, West and Westward for every period until December–January, when it pulls ahead dramatically. Southern, on the other hand, appears to respond well to advertising in the June–July period and that improvement is maintained across the rest of the year, effectively 'distancing' Southern from the other two areas for the second half of the year. This then is the clearest possible illustration of discernible and differential advertising effectiveness between different levels of support in three comparable areas.

Turning now to cost effectiveness of advertising, Table 10 examines the adspend of the four major TV spenders amongst the established brands in 1983. Taking ratecard

TABLE 10:    COST-EFFECTIVE ADVERTISING EXPENDITURE VS. COMPETITION 1983
(YEAR TO FEB–MAR 1984)

| | TV and press £000 spend (ratecard) | £ million sales | advertising as % of sales |
|---|---|---|---|
| Paul Masson | 614 | 6.34 | 9.7 |
| Hirondelle | 1069 | 10.41 | 10.3 |
| Mateus | 952 | 5.43 | 17.5 |
| Black Tower | 1000 | 4.52 | 22.1 |

Source: MEAL
       Nielsen (Grocers & Specialists)

expenditure on TV and press and comparing this with sterling sales of the brands it can be seen that not only was Paul Masson California Carafe advertising effective, it was also *cost effective* vs. other brands.

The true expenditure picture is even more interesting. Taking the whole period of the brand's existence (1980–84) the *actual* expenditure behind the brand has yet to exceed £1 million in total. Yet over that period the brand's sales have been well in excess of one million cases (12 million bottles). Advertising support therefore has amounted to less than £1 per case (7–8p per bottle) which at current prices represents less than $2\frac{1}{2}$ per cent of retail value.

Finally, it is perhaps worth restating that the advertising achievement has been one not only of distinctive branding, but of effective *positioning*. It is through its achievement of the 'critical balance' referred to earlier (neither too patronising nor too 'product story' – based for inexperienced drinkers; not too lightweight in wine credentials for the experienced drinker), that the advertising has positioned the brand desirably to both sectors of the market.

The final table (Table 11) illustrates precisely the nature of that achievement. From the most recently available TGI data it can be seen that Paul Masson California Carafe has established itself not only amongst a more even spread of users, but also across a broader spectrum of usage occasions than any of its mainstream competitors.

TABLE 11:    BRAND PROFILES (1984) BY DRINKER TYPE AND USUAL DRINKING OCCASIONS

| | Paul Masson % | Black Tower % | Blue Nun % | Nicolas % | Don Cortez % | Hirondelle % | Sainsbury's % |
|---|---|---|---|---|---|---|---|
| *drinker:* | | | | | | | |
| heavy | 32 | 20 | 9 | 25 | 15 | 15 | 18 |
| medium | 46 | 46 | 36 | 38 | 35 | 36 | 38 |
| light | 21 | 30 | 52 | 34 | 48 | 46 | 41 |
| *occasion:* | | | | | | | |
| at home | 86 | 69 | 60 | 83 | 72 | 68 | 72 |
| at other people's home | 25 | 26 | 21 | 21 | 19 | 22 | 22 |
| in restaurant | 29 | 33 | 39 | 40 | 24 | 27 | 25 |

Source: TGI 1984

## EVALUATING THE ACHIEVEMENT

Undoubtedly, in the first two years of the brand's life, advertising played a key role in building awareness and trial of the product as well as trade acceptance. Without a tied distribution network this would have been very difficult without advertising. But what of the period under discussion here: the third and fourth years of the brand's life?

The preceding analysis has demonstrated the importance of the re-evaluation of the brand and the role of its advertising in 1982. What was summarised briefly in the way of research (see pages 260–262) was in fact a highly intensive exercise covering many months.

The results however appear to have justified that effort. By comparing the performance of Paul Masson California Carafe to other brands (especially other branded ranges) and, where possible, between advertised and non-advertised areas, it has been demonstrated that against a background of consistent competitive price differentials and distribution strengths, advertising has achieved the following:

1.  Maintenance of brand share and hence sales growth when other brands (including those advertised at heavier weights) were declining in the face of a growing own-label sector and a significant competitive launch (Le Piat). This 'robustness' has been shown not to have been the case in a non-advertised area over the same period.
2.  Maintenance of rate-of-sale growth when a distribution plateau had been reached. Again, not the case in the non-advertised area.
3.  Clearly differentiable sales effect across a full year in three areas; one receiving no advertising at all, one receiving advertising pre-Christmas only, one receiving advertising mid-year and pre-Christmas.
4.  Cost-effective support for the brand compared to levels of support for competitive brands and cost-effective support for the brand in real terms, amounting to an advertising to sales value ratio of less than $2\frac{1}{2}$ per cent.

For Seagram (UK) Ltd, the success of Paul Masson California Carafe has been a major achievement. Wine products now account for over 40 per cent of company turnover compared to less than 5 per cent in 1979. With the continued decline of spirits this has had a significant impact on company profitability. Not only is Paul Masson California Carafe now still the number six brand in the UK market, it is actually brand leader in the in-litre-size sector and second only to Mateus in rosés. Furthermore, the credibility gained with the trade as a result of the success of Paul Masson California Carafe ensures a sympathetic response to Seagram wine products in the future.

For Paul Masson in California, the UK now represents the biggest export market for Carafes in the world, in fact only some 100,000 cases less than US sales. It also represents a firm foundation for both themselves and Seagram UK to launch other Paul Masson products into the UK in the future.

# 19

# How Advertising Helped Mazda (UK) to Sell a More Profitable Model Mix

## INTRODUCTION

The purpose of this paper is to demonstrate how advertising has contributed to the business success of Mazda cars in the United Kingdom. It will encompass the particular problems that Mazda face in the United Kingdom:

— The development of a business strategy to counter those problems.
— The identification of the role for advertising.
— Case histories demonstrating the effectiveness of advertising across a number of criteria.

Finally, it will explore other aspects of the total market marketing mix in order to demonstrate that these factors could not have enhanced the apparent advertising effect markedly.

## BACKGROUND

### A One Per Cent Marque

Mazda are limited by the Japanese Automotive Manufacturers Association (JAMA)/Society of Motor Manufacturers and Traders (SMMT) gentlemen's agreement to only one per cent of the UK passenger car market. Since neither the SMMT nor any of the major car manufacturing companies project the car market to grow significantly or consistently year by year, increased volume cannot be a Mazda objective. Thus, any increase in profitability must be achieved within the constraint of selling a largely fixed volume product.

Nor do Mazda have the opportunity of significantly altering the basic model line up. Mazda, in the UK, are a franchise operation and have a restricted opportunity to develop their own product. They are importers of several models, two of which account for 82 per cent of their business: the 323, which competes in the 'C' (or medium-sized family hatchback sector), and the 626, which competes in the 'CD' (or larger family saloon/hatchback sector). Unfortunately for Mazda, these two sectors are in gradual decline: in 1982 they represented 63.5 per cent of new car sales, and in 1985 they accounted for 59.6 per cent. Furthermore, Mazda have no model in the 'supermini' and diesel car sectors which are the two fastest growing sectors.

The 'C' and 'CD' sectors are the most highly competitive and are the sectors in which *all* the volume manufacturers have at least two models.

### A Market-place which Suffers from Over-capacity

Total volume over the last few years has been relatively buoyant. This has, however, been matched with the much documented over-production of the UK and Europe. This over-production has led most manufacturers to try to increase their share by discounting; the whole tenor of the market-place has been one of ever-reduced margins. Since Mazda are limited to one per cent they cannot attempt to increase share. Yet the environment in which they are operating is one in which the public expect discounts. Maintaining or increasing revenue in such circumstances is clearly a difficult task.

### The Need to Increase Revenue

There is a more fundamental problem for Mazda than market discounting. As an importer from Japan, Mazda in the UK have a far greater need for increased revenue than do those franchises who manufacture in the UK or in Europe. Mazda in the UK pay for their product in yen and sell their product to their dealers in sterling. Since late 1982, the yen/sterling exchange rate has fallen dramatically from over 450 yen to the pound in late 1982, to around 350 yen to the pound in 1983, to just over 300 yen in 1984, to around 220 yen at the time of writing. Given this impact on supply costs, it is crucial that Mazda increase revenue from their fixed volume.

## THE BUSINESS STRATEGY

Given the constraints of a one per cent limit on volume, little control over the basic products being imported and increasing supply prices with a continuing over-supplied market, Mazda had little choice in their business strategy.

Since all vehicles offer Mazda a similar structure and percentage of profit, the more expensive the vehicles that they sell, the greater will be their revenue. Mazda, therefore, embarked on a plan of trying to alter the mix of the models that they sell, i.e. they planned to sell more 626s than previously, fewer 323s than previously and, within the individual models, to sell the more highly specified derivatives. In addition, there was also the objective of increasing total prices as far as the market would allow.

## TOWARDS THE ROLE FOR ADVERTISING

In assessing the role for advertising, agency and client investigated the *typical* car-buying process, the process by which *Mazda owners* had come to purchase their vehicle and the nature of existing Mazda owners. From this investigation emerged what advertising had to achieve . . . and further analysis of the car-buying process highlighted *how* advertising might achieve this.

*An Analysis of how People Typically Buy Cars*

Three key findings emerged from a detailed analysis of how people come to a decision about the car they are going to buy, namely:

— In the volume sector people buy *models* not *marques* (i.e. they go out to investigate Escorts, Golfs and 323s, not Ford's, Volkswagen's or Mazda's).
— They draw up a mental *shopping list* of possible models. They begin to gather information and arrive at some provisional candidate models.
— Finally, they visit the showrooms. Here the car itself and the persuasiveness of the salesman influence the decision.

*How Mazda Owners Come to Buy their Cars*

Quantitative and qualitative research revealed that many Mazda owners had not followed this typical process. Many of the existing owners (*42 per cent*) had 'discovered' Mazda models on the recommendation of a friend or relation. And while 'word of mouth' is a means of selling that would be the envy of many manufacturers in many markets, it is clearly not a sufficient nor a precise enough mechanism given the cut-throat nature of the market-place and Mazda's objectives.

A further *35 per cent* of Mazda owners had come across their Mazda by serendipity. Stories ranged from a man who had popped out to buy a lettuce and had glimpsed a 626 in a showroom and fallen in love with it, to a lady who had called a mini-cab and was so impressed with the 626 that came to pick her up that she went out and bought one the following day!

Figure 1 illustrates the closed cycle of Mazda owners repurchasing (on which volume had been largely dependent) with the seemingly random and limited introduction of non-owners to the car.

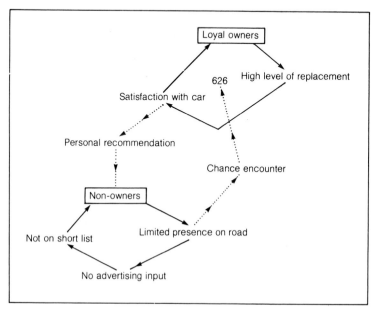

Figure 1. *Diagram illustrating the cycle of Mazda owners re-purchasing, and the 'random' link that operated to introduce non-owners to the marque*

Only 23 per cent of Mazda owners had bought their vehicle as a result of the typical car buying process. One positive factor that emerged was the strength of the Mazda models themselves. Once potential purchasers were brought face-to-face with the vehicle they thought very highly of it. This was validated by a series of car clinics commissioned by the agency. They would clearly do well in the showroom situation.

Where Mazda needed to improve was not at the final decision but at the input end. Low awareness meant that they were simply not getting on enough shopping lists.

### Loyal but Ageing Customers

This was shown by that fact that much of the showroom traffic that did exist was from existing Mazda owners. The Mazda models are much loved by their owners and Mazda had, and have, a very high level of loyalty from their existing owners. However, quantitative research suggested that these owners were ageing and were, as a result, more likely to trade down in specification or even down from the 626 to the 323.

### What Advertising Had to Do

From this analysis it emerged that the role for advertising was to place Mazda models on more shopping lists in order to generate more showroom traffic (demand) and, ultimately, provide increased opportunities for the dealers to sell high specification and more expensive models.

### How Should the Advertising Work?

Having identified *what* the advertising had to do, the issue became *how* should it be done.

At this stage we returned to the model of the typical car buying process. As outlined above, Mazda models were failing to get on as many shopping lists as they should have done. The reason for this was a lack of awareness as to the *kind* of cars that Mazda made. If potential customers did not know that the 323 was in the family hatchback sector, they could not be expected to place it on a shopping list along with the Escorts, Golfs, etc. Similarly, if they did not know that the 626 was in the medium-sized car sector they would be unlikely to place it on their shopping list along with the Cavalier, the Montego, the Sierra, etc. Thus the role for advertising emerged as 'Making the Mazda models famous in their respective classes.'

If this could be achieved then it was hypothesised that the following model of the *contribution of advertising* to Mazda's business strategy would take place.

Make the models famous

↓

Educate the public as to what kind of car they are

↓

Increase interest, inclusion on more shopping lists

↓

Deliver more showroom traffic

↓

Allow the opportunity to alter the model mix

## MEDIA SELECTION AND CREATIVE DEVELOPMENT

Given the need to *make the models famous*, the advertising itself would need to be highly in-trusive. This had implications for both media and creative strategies.

### Media Selection

Television was selected as the advertising medium, not only for its intrusiveness and its proven ability to generate rapid awareness but also because it was a high profile, public medium which would motivate the dealerships by developing a pride in selling a television-advertised car marque. This latter aspect, although relatively intangible, was found to be vital in further stimulating the sales effectiveness of an advertising campaign.

The timing of the television campaign reflected the *seasonality of new car sales*, with peaks in late spring and August, and varying *costs of television air-time* over the year.

The television medium is, however, cluttered with a large amount of advertising for competitive motor cars – most of whom have substantially larger budgets (they are selling a far higher volume of vehicles). For example, MEAL records almost £200 million being spent on car advertising in 12 months ending April 1986. Ford and Austin Rover's total advertising budgets are both in the region of £30 million for this period.

Clearly, if Mazda (on a total budget of £2½ million in 1985 and £3 million in 1986) was going to gain a significant share-of-mind, the need for intrusiveness would be crucial.

### Advertising Development

The requirements to generate *increased interest in the Mazda models* (showroom traffic) by '*making the models famous in their respective classes*' focused the advertising development process in three areas.

— *making the models famous* – required the advertising itself to be noticeable and distinctive. To make the models thought about far more than their share-of-road would dictate required the advertising to look very different from that of all other cars.
— *in their respective classes* – necessitated a clear indication of the category in which each model competed.
— *generate increased interest* – the identification of an intriguing and potentially motivating aspect or feature of the model which could be dramatised and provoke consumers to find out more details about the cars themselves.

Table 1 summarises the development process that was followed in producing two TV execu-tions for both the 626 and the 323.

### Creative Executions for the 626

The Mazda 626 is one of at least 20 cars in its sector: it does not excel in any one particular attribute nor is it particularly deficient. Extensive qualitative research, however, had

TABLE 1:   ADVERTISING DEVELOPMENT FOR 626 AND 323

| Advertising requirement | Execution for 626 | Execution for 323 |
|---|---|---|
| *'Making the models famous' | 'Dancing Man': visual focus on an annoyed new car buyer | 'Boxes': visual focus on large boxes being raised one over another |
| | 'Moving Stunt': dramatic film of Mazda driving over two cars | 'Toy Car': Miniature models of competitive cars used throughout the film |
| * 'In their respective classes' | 'Cavalier/Montego' used as category descriptor | Variety of well-known competitive cars referred to, including Golf |
| * 'Generate increased interest' | Superior to Mercedes and Porsche in road tests | *Boxes:* more interior space than Rolls Royce |
| | | *Toy Car:* more head and legroom than any car in its class |

indicated that the facts that the Mazda 626 had come top in a *German* magazine road test that included the *Mercedes 190* and had been voted by United States motoring journalists as the *top imported car* ahead of a long list which included the *Porsche 944* were intriguing and potentially motivating to buyers of new 'CD' sector cars.

In clearly portraying the 'class' in which Mazda 626 competed, research had indicated that using such details as engine capacity, body shape or size or the descriptor 'medium-sized family car' were either meaningless or confusing. Price was a good indicator of the type of car but there were practical constraints in using this reference in long-term advertising. The most effective descriptor was reference to the well-established cars in the sector. In developing this comparative approach, research provided guidelines on how not to make the advertising appear to be 'knocking' the other cars in its sector. If the advertising was felt to be 'knocking', it was likely to alienate, rather than motivate, its target audience.

Two complementary executions were developed. 'Dancing Man' was visually distinctive as car advertising and used the idea of a recent new car buyer who was annoyed at not having seen the Mazda 626 prior to making his purchase. The emphasis of this commercial was a clear identification of the cars with which the Mazda 626 was comparable.

'Moving Stunt' laid greater emphasis on the intriguing road test claims for the Mazda 626 by filming the car driving over the roofs of a Porsche and a Mercedes while they were driven along.

The end-line, 'You'll be amazed at a Mazda', was common to both executions and embodied the pleasant surprise that consumers would have on 'discovering' the Mazda and its many qualities.

A storyboard of 'Moving Stunt' is shown opposite.

## MAZDA 626
## "MOVING STUNT"

MVO: In a German road test...     ...one car beat the Mercedes 190.     In America, the coupé version...

beat the Porsche 944.

And yet it's in the same price range as, say, a Cavalier or a Montego.     The 626. You'll be amazed at a Mazda.

### *Creative Executions for the 323*

As with the 626 in its class, the 323 is a highly competitive, all-round family hatchback in a sector of at least 20 models. A detailed examination of the car and its competitors, however, revealed that the 323 had more interior space than any competitor.

Qualitative research revealed that this was potentially motivating to the two car-buying sectors to whom hatchbacks are most likely to appeal. *Young families* found space appealing as they are often carrying around the paraphernalia that accompanies young children wherever they go. The *older 'retired'* sector also found space (particularly head and rear passenger leg-room) motivating since this offered them the prospect of increased comfort for themselves and their passengers.

As with the 626 development, it was still important to communicate the 'class' in which the 323 competed. It seemed that the most effective way of doing this in the 323's sector was to communicate that it was in the same sector as the well-known Volkswagen Golf.

Two complementary executions were developed. 'Boxes' was visually distinctive since the first twenty seconds of the commercial featured large boxes being raised one over the other to demonstrate the 'amazing' fact that, while a Rolls Royce was larger on the outside than the 323, the 323 was larger when it came to interior room. Positioning the car in its class was achieved by utilising the memorable 'dropping' sequence from a previous Golf commercial

## MAZDA 323
## "BOXES"

**MVO:** This is the outside of a Rolls Royce Corniche...   ...which is bigger than...   ...the outside of the new Mazda 323,   But this is the inside of the 323...

...which is bigger than...   the inside of the Rolls Royce   Yet the Mazda 323 range costs less then the Volkswagen Golf range. **JAPANESE MAN:** That's amazing!   **SFX:** CRASH!! **MVO:** No, that's a Mazda

The new 323 family hatchback.   You'll be amazed...   ...at a Mazda

and turning it into a visual joke. The 323 was actually dropped on top of a Japanese who was 'amazed' that the 323 range costs less than the Volkswagen Golf range. The storyboard is shown above.

The second execution concentrated more single-mindedly on placing the car in its class and demonstrated the fact that when you 'add head and leg-room together' the Mazda 323 beats every other car in its class. Visual impact was achieved by demonstrating this fact, using miniature models of the competition. A presenter placed those models that had less headroom than the Mazda on his head and those that had less leg-room by his feet. The Volkswagen Golf joke was taken one stage further by dropping a model Golf on the presenter's head. The storyboard is shown opposite.

## HOW WAS THE ADVERTISING MONITORED?

The model of the role of advertising in enabling Mazda to sell a more profitable model mix had hypothesised that the following process had to be achieved:

## MAZDA 323
## "MODEL CARS"

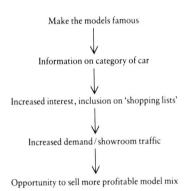

MVO: In case you haven't seen the Mazda 323, it's got...

...2.7 inches more combined legroom than a Golf...

...and 5½ more than an Astra

The 323 also has 2½ inches more combined headroom than a Renault 11...

...and 3½ inches more...

...than a Honda Civic.

In fact, add head and legroom together, and the Mazda 323 beats...

...any other car in its class

Including the Golf

SFX: CRAAASH!

MVO: You'll be amazed...

...at a Mazda.

Make the models famous

↓

Information on category of car

↓

Increased interest, inclusion on 'shopping lists'

↓

Increased demand / showroom traffic

↓

Opportunity to sell more profitable model mix

Having set up this hypothesis of the role of advertising in the marketing of Mazda cars, it was not sufficient solely to monitor the company's business performance to evaluate the validity of the hypothesis. It was important to monitor the intermediate stages in the purchase process to judge if the process was working in the way that it was posited.

Three different research methodologies were utilised to assess the effectiveness of the advertising.

TABLE 2:　OUTLINE OF RESEARCH PROGRAMME TO MONITOR THE PROCESS AND RESULTS OF THE ADVERTISING

| Role of advertising in decision-making process | Consumer research variable | Consumer research methodology |
|---|---|---|
| Noticeability of advertising | Advertising awareness | Omnibus |
| Increased top-of-mindness of model | Awareness of relevant Mazda model ⎫ | research among motorists |
| Establish model in relevant sector of market | Awareness of Mazda 626 in correct competitive category | (Omnicar) |
| Inclusion on candidate shopping list | If about to purchase, which models would be interested in finding out more about ⎭ | |
| Enquiry at Mazda dealer | Showroom traffic | Observational research at sample of Mazda dealerships |
| Increased level of demand for fixed volume of cars | Changes in proportion of sales of higher specification models. Changes in list price. | Desk research on sales and price data |

*Omnicar*　Sample Survey's monthly omnibus survey of 1000 motorists was commissioned immediately prior to, and after, bursts of television advertising. From this data source the target audience sub-sample of *purchasers of new 'C' or 'CD' sector cars* was analysed.

*Showroom Traffic Monitor*　A regular count of members of the public making an enquiry about new Mazda vehicles was conducted every second or third Saturday between January to July 1985 and December 1985 to June 1986. Initially, a sample of six showrooms was selected to be representative of high, medium and low volume dealerships. As this research technique had never been used previously, the first period of data collection was experimental. It was learnt that the *absolute number* of customers being identified could often be small, imposing limitations on statistical confidence in the data. In November 1985 the sample was revised to comprise 12 medium-high volume dealerships. While this was recognised as not being representative of the entire dealer network, it did provide a more reliable data base. Direct comparability of this set of data with the previous set was not possible.

*Model Sales and Price Data*　Model sales data was obtained from SMMT who compile detailed new car registration data obtained from the Department of Vehicle Licensing at Swansea. Price data for Mazda and competitive models in 1984 and 1986 were obtained from the relevant month's issue of *What Car*.

## DID THE ADVERTISING WORK?

### *Generating Showroom Traffic*

Table 3 summarises the changes in the key indirect measures used to assess the *process* by which the advertising was intended to work. The net result of increases in the level of showroom traffic for both the 626 and 323 linked with increases in levels of advertising and marque awareness, attribution to correct market sector and increased level of inclusion on potential shopping lists, seemed to validate the model of how advertising could work.

TABLE 3: SUMMARY OF KEY INDIRECT VARIABLES USED TO MONITOR THE PROCESS BY WHICH THE ADVERTISING WORKED FOR MAZDA 626 AND 323

| Role of Advertising in Decision Making | Consumer Research | Pre (Dec 1984) | Post (July 1985) | % Change |
|---|---|---|---|---|
| *Mazda 626* | | | | |
| Noticeability of advertising | Advertising awareness | 2 | 15 | + 650 |
| Increase top-of-mindness of model | Spontaneous awareness | 6 | 15 | + 150 |
| Establish model in relevant sector | Attribution of model to correct sector | 20 | 32 | + 60 |
| Inclusion on candidate shopping list | Models interested in finding out more about | 3.8 | 6.0 | + 57 |
| Enquiry at Mazda dealers | Showroom traffic (index) | 100 | 130 | + 30 |
| *Mazda 323* | | *Pre (Dec 1985)* | *Post (May 1986)* | |
| Noticeability of advertising | Advertising awareness | 5 | 20 | + 300 |
| Increase top-of-mindness of model | Spontaneous awareness | 4 | 14 | + 250 |
| Establish model in relevant sector | Attribution of model to correct sector | 22 | 27 | + 20 |
| Inclusion on candidate shopping list | Models interested in finding out more about | 1 | 6 | ( + 500) |
| Enquiry at Mazda dealer | Showroom traffic (index) | 100 | 225 | + 125 |

The relationship between these indirect measures is examined in the following sections.

## Model Awareness

A necessary prerequisite of increasing the level of interest in Mazda 626 and 323 shown by the target audience was to increase their top-of-mind awareness that Mazda produced family cars. This spontaneous awareness measure was obtained in response to the question:

Thinking of medium-sized family cars, which manufacturers come to mind?

There are several factors which can influence the level of mentions a manufacturer receives:

ownership (current and previous), presence on the road, strength of dealership network, news coverage, new car launch and advertising. Over the period of the 626 campaign (January to July 1985) and 323 campaign (December 1985 to April 1986), with the exception of advertising, these factors were either constant for Mazda (e.g. ownership, presence on the road) or non-existent (news coverage, new car launch). Advertising activity, and the model awareness generated by it, were the only significant variables. As Figure 2 demonstrates, there was a clear relationship between these two factors.

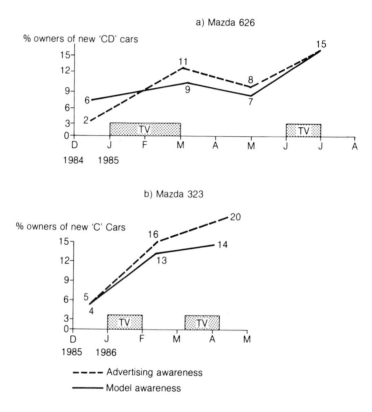

Figure 2. *The relationship between prompted advertising awareness and model awareness for Mazda 626 and 323*

## Candidate Shopping List

Increased *awareness of the Mazda models* in their *respective sectors*, allied to the dramatisation of an intriguing and motivating aspect of the car's achievement or attributes would, we hypothesised, generate consumer interest in finding out more about the 626 and 323. On the macro-level this was evaluated on Omnicar by tracking responses over time to the question:

If you were thinking of buying a new car which of the models on this list would you be interested in looking at or finding out more about?

Given the complex nature of the decision-making process, it was not expected that the advertising would prompt a purchase decision. Instead, it was hypothesised that it would prompt consumers to acquire more information in order to help make their decision. Figure 3 demonstrates that there was a clear relationship between advertising, model awareness and levels of interest.

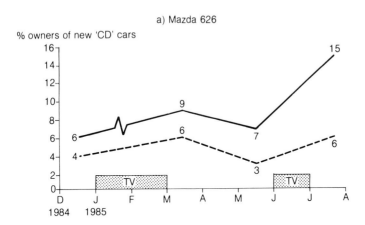

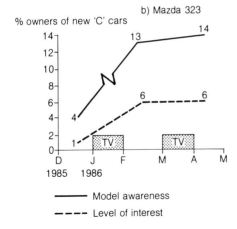

Figure 3. *Relationship between advertising, model awareness and level of interest for Mazda 626 and 323*

## Customer Enquiries at Showrooms

Changes in actual interest in finding out more about Mazda 626 and 323 (showroom traffic) occurred in response to advertising which had produced increases in marque awareness (Figure 4). The changes in customer enquiries must also be related to general seasonality. However, confidence in the positive contribution of advertising is obtained from the observations that the most *marked* increases were recorded within the first two to three weeks of the start of each burst. It is unlikely that market seasonality alone would result in such immediate changes.

It might be argued that it was disappointing to see increases in showroom enquiry levels for the 626 and 323 which were markedly less than the increases in model awareness. However, this is not surprising when one considers the infrequent nature of car buying. If the car

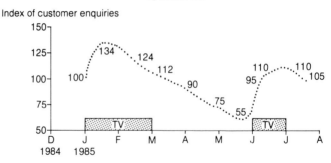

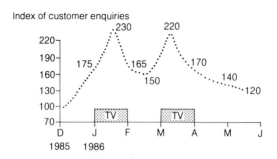

Figure 4. *Relationship between advertising and level of customer enquiries at showrooms*

purchase cycle is between three and four years (say 40 months), and the purchase consideration period is around three months then, while the advertising is *impacting* on all new car owners and being recalled by a proportion of those potential purchasers, only about 8 per cent (3/40) are likely to be *in the market at that time*. Figure 5 illustrates this point schematically.

On this basis an increase of 30 per cent for the 626 is very creditable and there is clearly likely to be a long 'tail' of long-term benefit as more of the informed public are considering buying a car.

Moreover, not only did the *absolute level* of traffic increase with advertising but also its *characteristics* changed in comparison with non-advertised periods:

— Increased proportion of enquiries from owners of cars other than Mazda.
— Younger profile of enquiries.
— Proportion enquiring about 323 and 626 models changed reflecting advertising emphasis.
— Markedly increased proportion of enquiries claiming to have seen Mazda advertising.

This further supported the hypothesis that advertising, and not seasonality alone, was responsible for increasing showroom enquiries.

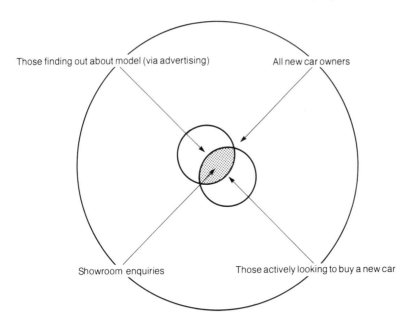

Figure 5. *Schematic diagram of relationship between all new car owners, those interested in finding out about a model and those actively in the market*

*Altering the Model Mix*

*Balance of 626 and 323 Sales* As already established, the end objective of the advertising was to change Mazda's model mix in favour of the more expensive and higher specification models. Table 4 demonstrates the change in model mix in favour of the 626 – increasing from 43 per cent of total passenger car sales in 1983 and 1984 (prior to advertising) to 47 per cent of the sales mix in 1985 and a target of 48 per cent for 1986.

TABLE 4:   MAZDA 323 AND 626 MODEL SPLIT (EXCLUDING ESTATES)

|  | 1983 % | 1984 % | 1985 % | 1986 (Target) % |
|---|---|---|---|---|
| 323 | 56.9 | 56.3 | 53.1 | 52.2 |
| 626 | 43.1 | 43.7 | 46.9 | 47.8 |
|  | 100 | 100 | 100 | 100 |

Source: Mazda

*Balance of Model Derivative Sales for the 626 and the 323* In 1985 there was a significant decrease for the 626 in the proportion of 1600cc model sales compared with average of 1983/84. Table 5 demonstrates that the forecast for 1986 is of an even smaller proportion accounted for by the cheaper 1600cc models. At the same time as sales of the standard 2-litre model are increasing, the launch of the fuel injected 2-litre models will result in total 2-litre sales accounting for 71 per cent of 626 sales in 1986 compared with 51 per cent in 1984.

TABLE 5:   BREAKDOWN OF MODEL DERIVATIVE SALES OF MAZDA 626

|                       | 1983 % | 1984 % | 1985 % | 1986 (Target) % |
|-----------------------|--------|--------|--------|-----------------|
| 1600cc                | 41     | 42     | 37     | 23              |
| 2 litre (carburettor) | 49     | 51 ⎫   | 55     | 57 ⎫            |
| 2 litre (fuel injected)| –     | –  ⎬ 58| 1      | 14 ⎬ 77         |
| Coupe                 | 10     | 7  ⎭   | 7      | 6  ⎭            |
|                       | 100    | 100    | 100    | 100             |

Similar changes in model derivative sales for the 323 are planned, with the share target for 1500cc and 1600cc fuel-injected models increasing from *22 per cent* in 1985 to *48 per cent* in 1986, which reflects the start of advertising support at the end of 1985. This does coincide with the introduction of 1600cc fuel-injected derivative in late 1985 but, nevertheless, sales of the 1500cc models are planned to increase from *21 per cent* to *37 per cent* without a new model introduction (Table 6).

TABLE 6:   BREAKDOWN OF MODEL DERIVATIVE SALES OF MAZDA 323

|        | 1983 % | 1984 % | 1985 % | 1986 (Target) % |
|--------|--------|--------|--------|-----------------|
| 1100cc | 2      | 2      | 2      | 1               |
| 1300cc | 73     | 77     | 76     | 51              |
| 1500cc | 25     | 21     | 21     | 37              |
| 1600i  | –      | –      | 1      | 11              |
|        | 100    | 100    | 100    | 100             |

The changing pattern of Mazda sales, with increases in the proportion accounted for by the more expensive, higher profit derivatives – both *within* each model and *between* the 626 and 323 ranges – clearly would lead Mazda to generate significantly increased revenue from their fixed share of the market. Unfortunately, it is not possible to evaluate the actual revenue generated as Mazda's trading terms vary by dealership according to the volumes sold by, and the status of, each dealer in the network.

*Increasing Model Prices*

For Mazda, the achievement of their key business objective of altering the model mix in favour of more profitable models would be devalued if they did not increase their model prices at least in line with key competition. Increasing their prices *ahead* of the competition, however, would be indicative of a further relative increase in the company's revenue. Table 7 documents the achievement of this subsidiary objective over the period of the advertising activity by comparing changes in list prices of key Mazda models with those of the key competitors which consumers use as benchmark cars in each category.

Table 7 documents the achievement of this objective for 626 and 323 respectively.

TABLE 7: COMPARISON OF PRICE INCREASE FOR MODEL DERIVATIVES IN MAZDA 626 AND 323 RANGES WITH THOSE FOR COMPARABLE COMPETITIVE CARS

|  | November 1984 £ | June 1986 £ | % Increase |
|---|---|---|---|
| *A: Mid-Range Model Derivatives* | | | |
| Mazda 1.6 LX | 6199 | 7174 | 15.7 |
| Austin Montego 1.6 GL | 6875 | 7948 | 15.6 |
| Ford Sierra 1.6 GL | 7281 | 8124 | 11.6 |
| Vauxhall Cavalier 1.6 GL | 7076 | 8104 | 14.5 |
| *B: Top Range Model Derivatives* | | | |
| Mazda 626 2.0 GLX | 7149 | 8449 | 18.2 |
| Austin Montego 2.0 HL | 7195 | 8298 | 15.3 |
| Ford Sierra 2.0 GL | 7734 | 8513 | 10.1 |
| Vauxhall Cavalier CD | 8819 | 10226 | 16.0 |

*Mazda 323*

|  | November 1984 £ | June 1986 £ | % Increase |
|---|---|---|---|
| *A: Mid-Range Model Derivatives* | | | |
| Mazda 323 1.3 LX | 4799 | 5624 | 17.2 |
| Austin Montego 1.3 L | 5419 | 6050 | 11.6 |
| Ford Escort 1.3 L (3dr) | 5397 | 5930 | 9.8 |
| Vauxhall Astra 1.3 L | 5282 | 6146 | 16.0 |
| *B: Top-Range Model Derivatives* | | | |
| Mazda 323 1.5 GT/GLX | 5499 | 6749 | 16.4 |
| Austin Montego VDP | 6995 | 8066 | 15.0 |
| Ford Escort XR3i | 7035 | 7854 | 11.6 |
| Vauxhall Astra 1.6 SR | 6265 | 7266 | 16.0 |

## CONCLUSIONS

In pursuing a more profitable business strategy, it was hypothesised that the role for advertising was to increase awareness of, and interest in, the 626 and 323 in their sectors of the market. At the information gathering stage of the decision-making process this would result in an increase in the level of consumer interest in the models and subsequently lead to consumer enquiries at dealerships.

Figure 6 graphically illustrates that this process was achieved. Whereas the total number of new car buyers in the 'C' and 'CD' sectors remained essentially static at 1.1 million in any given year, during the course of the advertising the number of those motorists who

— were aware of Mazda advertising,
— had top-of-mind awareness of Mazda as a model,

— were aware of in which category the Mazda models competed,
— were interested to find out more about a Mazda model.

    . . . all increased considerably.

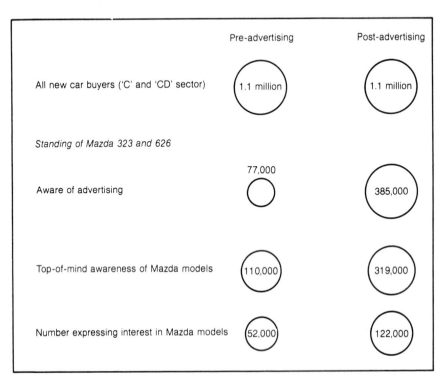

Figure 6. *Illustration of increase in number of new car buyers aware of and interested in Mazda 626 and 323 as a result of the advertising*

     The research programme demonstrates that this process was achieved successfully and that the level of customer enquiries increased in response to the advertising. Once the potential customer had entered the showroom, it was the responsibility of the sales management to sell the car. The model mix and list price data demonstrate that, by increasing demand, advertising is enabling Mazda to sell its fixed volume more profitably.

## LESSONS LEARNED

1. Model specific advertising is necessary as this reflects the way in which consumers buy mainstream family cars. Thus the launch of the new model 323 was supported by a 323 specific campaign as opposed to extending the 626 campaign.
2. TV advertising for Mazda needs a relevant, single-minded focus and should avoid the temptation of listing different facts and specifications. Advertising for 323 has focused on its plentiful interior space and has resulted in a high level of customer enquiries in 1986.
3. TV is proven to generate rapid and a high level of response. In more detail:

— Minimum 'strike rate' of TVRs identified.
— Incremental effect most noticed at beginning of burst suggests testing a platform of an increased number of shorter bursts in the future.

4. Research indicated that 'Moving Stunt' was the film that had more impact and showed greater potential to increase customer enquiries. This commercial was used exclusively for 626 in 1986.
5. Research confirms the low incidence of potential buyers in the population. Thus on-site showroom surveys are as important a part of the monitoring process as are conventional face-to-face interviews with the motorist.
6. Given Mazda's limitation to one per cent market share, there may be a 'ceiling' to the levels of a model awareness and potential interest for the 626. Research needs to continue to monitor these aspects to assess when the existing strategy has achieved the optimum and therefore when the need arises to identify a fresh role for advertising.

## APPENDIX: SOME REASONABLE QUESTIONS TO ASK

Advertising has played a significant part in Mazda's changing business strategy in the last 2 years. It has been the element of the marketing mix that has developed most markedly over this period – but it is important to question the role of the other elements.

The *dealer network* has changed slightly in the last two years with the termination of a number of less efficient outlets and the appointment of more aggressive and enthusiastic dealers. Mazda argue, however, that it has been easier to attract new enthusiastic dealers because of the higher and more dynamic profile which the marque is developing. Advertising is, in part, responsible for this development.

Temporary *bonusing to dealers* and discounting to *customers* has been an increasingly used method of maintaining volumes in the 1980s and can have a significant impact in the short-term (i.e. monthly sales). However, their impact upon sales in the long term is questionable. Furthermore, Mazda believe that they have to use these tactics far less often than most of their competitors. This is, perhaps, endorsed by the massive 'discounted price' campaigns that Ford and Austin Rover ran during the period in question. Mazda ran no such campaigns.

The *car brochure* is an important tool to help 'close the sale'. Mazda's are revised to continue to project their models in the most favourable light. Clearly, the brochure becomes important only *after* the potential customer has entered the showroom and, as such, cannot contribute to an increase in the level of customer enquiries.

Mazda take part in a limited amount of *sports sponsorship* which receives TV coverage. The effect of this is to keep Mazda's name top-of-mind in the way that it is one of the objectives of TV advertising. In the past this sponsorship may have acted in a vacuum as consumers were not entirely sure what the name 'Mazda' represented. TV advertising will have helped to make sponsorship more effective as more people are aware of Mazda as a manufacturer of family cars.

# 20

# Alphabites: How Advertising Helped Birds Eye Develop the Added-Value Potato Products Market

## INTRODUCTION

This paper sets out to show the effectiveness of advertising in the launch and continued development of Birds Eye's Alphabites. Alphabites were launched in the North of England in July 1984, followed by national extension in January 1985. They are small pieces of mashed potato, shaped into the letters of the alphabet.

The support for this case rests on:

— An immediate sales response to advertising support.
— The longer-term volume generated by advertising.
— The role of advertising in achieving high levels of awareness and trial.
— The highly successful positioning of the product.

While the sales trend of any new product might be expected to be upward, and given that novelty products may well be more responsive to advertising, this case demonstrates a remarkably high level of responsiveness and a very consistent level of responsiveness of the brand to advertising support over three distinct periods.

Within a year of launch, Alphabites had become a profitable £4½ million brand, at r.s.v., with a 15 per cent share by value of the added-value potato products market at the end of 1985. On this basis, Birds Eye continued to dominate the sector, achieving a peak 52 per cent share of the market by early 1986.

## BUSINESS BACKGROUND

### The Frozen Potato Market

The total frozen potato market, including chips, was worth £133 million in 1984 when Alphabites were launched. The bulk of the market was then (and still is now) frozen chips, which accounted for 88 per cent of the volume in 1984.

The total market had shown rapid growth in the late 1970s and at the beginning of the 1980s, primarily stimulated by the success of oven chips. The market showed significantly faster growth than total frozen food sales, and by 1984 accounted for 18 per cent of total frozen food sales.

However, frozen chips had increasingly become a commodity market, whereas Birds Eye's expertise lay in added-value products, which utilised a technological edge. On this basis the company made the decision to concentrate their resources behind the development of added-value potato products.

### The Added Value Sector

Between 1980 and 1984 the frozen potato products sector grew by 88 per cent in volume. In 1984 it represented 12 per cent of the total frozen food market by volume and 18 per cent by value, reflecting the premium which products in this sector could command.

The sector had comprised a number of small volume (traditional) premium-priced products such as potato croquettes, potato fritters and bubble and squeak, i.e. frozen equivalents of traditional potato products. These products had received very little marketing support, and the sector had been relatively static in volume until 1980. Birds Eye had held market leadership in the early 1980s, with an average one-third of the market by volume. The real breakthrough was the launch of Birds Eye Potato Waffles in 1980, with full marketing support. The development of Waffles was based on innovatory extruded potato technology. This extrusion technology meant that Birds Eye had a unique technological edge. The combination of this technological superiority and creative concept development enabled Birds Eye to produce revolutionary, shaped, mashed potato products. Birds Eye's marketing strategy in this sector was to develop a range of products over time, each with a unique positioning. On the basis of the success of Waffles, the company launched a spin-off product in 1983. This product was Mini-Waffles, which gained incremental volume outside the Waffles franchise.

At the end of 1983 Birds Eye's sterling share stood at a healthy 49.6 per cent. However, inevitably as the chip market moved more and more down the commodity route, the added-value nature of the potato products market made it increasingly attractive. As a result the market became more active and competitive, most particularly with the entry of own-label Waffles. By July 1984, due to this activity, Birds Eye's share of the market had dropped to 42.3 per cent by value.

In mid 1984 the task was clear. The company's objectives were to defend Waffles in the face of growing competition and to bring forward the launch of a second major product in this dynamic and profitable sector, aimed at a different segment of the market.

### The Role of Alphabites

The company's objectives for the new launch were:

> To exploit further and develop the potato products sector, by creating a strong new brand alongside our established Waffles offering a product which will have a very different personality.

The new product clearly had to be capable of expanding the market by bringing in new users, and be positioned so that the likelihood of straight substitution for Birds Eye Waffles was minimised.

## DEVELOPING THE PRODUCT

A number of alternative product concepts were examined in an initial piece of quantitative research among 400 housewives. Potato letters clearly emerged as the most promising concept for development, against the given objectives.

The initial research identified an extremely high level of appeal for the concept. In addition the research findings indicated:

1.  That Potato letters held strong appeal for current non-users of frozen potato products as well as current buyers, i.e. it had the potential to grow the market.
2.  That the concept was especially well received by younger housewives (25 to 35 years of age) with young children, and had very strong appeal to children, i.e. it offered a specific niche opportunity within the market, with a distinct appeal from Waffles, which has a very flat demographic profile.

To assess the potential appeal and positioning of the product in more depth, qualitative research was conducted among C1C2 housewives with children under 10 years of age.

The core of the appeal of the product to mothers lay in the offer of a combination of good, basic food (a quality, potato alternative) and a high level of novelty appeal. A number of alternative names were explored at this stage, and the name Alphabites emerged as most successfully conveying this essential balance. A final in-home test of the product was carried out in March 1984 to ascertain potential levels of trial, product acceptability, pricing and likely frequency of purchase. On all counts the findings were extremely positive.

On this basis, the decision was made to launch the product in July 1984, with an initial test period in the North of the country, where potato products had been traditionally stronger.

Two pack sizes were to be introduced:

```
12oz pack        69p
1¼lb pack      £1.32p
```

## MARKETING OBJECTIVES

In the light of the decline in Birds Eye's brand share in early 1984, the targets set for the launch of Alphabites were specifically related to rebuilding the company's dominance of the sector:

1.  To gain a 10 per cent sterling brand share for Alphabites.
2.  In line with the company's strategy to build its strength in the sector through the development of products targeted and segmented differently, it was important to ensure that any brand share gain from Alphabites was not directly at the expense of existing products. As such, a second objective was set that called for a 50 per cent potato products value share for Birds Eye. This would require a net gain from Alphabites of 8 percentage points, setting the substitution target at 20 per cent.

## DEVELOPING THE ADVERTISING

On the basis of previous evidence of the advertising responsive nature of Potato Waffles, and of the overt novelty appeal of the product, the need for advertising support to maximise the potential of the product was clear.

The advertising strategy is set out below.

### The Role for Advertising

1. To create awareness and trial of Alphabites.
2. To attract new users to the category.
3. To build a distinctive identity for the product.

### Target Audience

Research had clearly identified our target purchasers but had also confirmed the substantial appeal of the product to children. On this basis, the advertising had to communicate successfully at two levels:

— Younger mums (25 to 34 years of age) with children under 12, who are looking for new ideas to feed the children.
— Children under 12 who are attracted by the novelty and play appeal of the product.

### The Proposition

Birds Eye Potato Alphabites are a new fun way of eating potatoes for children.
Supporting facts:

— tasty, letter-shaped potatoes make mealtimes more interesting.
— delicious, crispy outside and soft, fluffy potato inside.
— easy three-way cook: oven, grill or fry.

### The Creative Execution

The creative execution that Lintas developed was a 30-second commercial which very successfully combined communication of the novelty and play value aspects of the product to children, with effective communication of the convenience and ease of cooking to mothers.

The voice-over used a nursery rhyme style, while the visuals showed children eating Alphabites. The Alphabites themselves were used to spell out in words how versatile, fun and convenient they are, while also showing them to be proper, serious food being eaten at mealtimes, and not simply as a snack.

# BIRDS EYE/WALLS – ALPHABITES

('Playschool' piano music throughout)

FVO:  'A' is for Alpha      'C' for yourself        'D' is for dinner
       'B' is for Bites     that they taste just right    'E' is for eggs

'F' is for Fish Fingers   'G' they taste great     Crisp golden potato
or even frogs legs !     'H' Hot on a plate      From 'I' through to 'O'

With bacon and burgers  Our 'P's' and our 'Qs'    Oven Baked . . .
and bangers they go     You can take them as read

Fried or Grilled      New from Bird's Eye so   And called Alphabites,
They go up to 'Z'      you can't buy better     'cos each one's a letter

## THE CAMPAIGN/MEDIA

### Rationale for Television

Television was selected rather than other media because:

— The target audience of children and mothers could be reached very effectively with careful programming.
— The fun, play values of the product could be most successfully communicated by the moving images of television, while still conveying the more serious messages of versatility and 'real food' values.
— Experience with Waffles showed that television was a highly effective medium in building up awareness quickly among the target market.

### Launch Planning

A minimum of 500 TVRs was taken as a prerequisite for the launch campaign on the basis that this would achieve high net coverage, and reach a high proportion of the target audience (on a basis of) ensuring a minimum of one opportunity to see per week for a period of four weeks.

Since Alphabites were to appeal directly to children as well as their mothers, the buying brief was that 25 per cent of the money should be targeted directly through children's programmes.

### Advertising Support

Alphabites have been supported with advertising over three distinct campaigns. The details of each are shown in Table 1.

Following the successful launch in the North, further creative development was conducted to establish whether the concept of Alphabites could be successfully communicated in a 20 second version of the film.

TABLE 1:  MEDIA ALLOCATION FOR ALPHABITES, 1984–86

|  | Area timing | Spot length | Spend (MEAL) £000 | Average TVRs achieved |
|---|---|---|---|---|
| *Phase 1* | North |  |  |  |
| 1984 Northern Launch | 30/7–2/9 | 30 seconds | 492 | 680 |
| *Phase 2* | South |  |  |  |
| 1985 Southern Extension | 28/1–10/3 | 20 seconds | 494 | 725 |
| *Phase 3* | Network |  |  |  |
| 1986 National Campaign | 17/1–23/2 | 20 seconds 10 seconds | 689 | 700 |

An effective 20 second cut down version of the commercial was produced and shown during the Southern campaign. Additionally, work between Lintas and Birds Eye in other product areas had indicated the effectiveness of using a combination of a 30-second/20-second establishing film and a 10-second reminder. On this basis, for the national campaign, a combination of the 20-second film and a 10-second reminder were shown.

The effectiveness of this strategy in maximising media expenditure is shown by the fact that 725 TVRs were achieved in the south with the 20-second, compared with 680 TVRs in the North eight months earlier, with the same level of spend in the South where TV costs are relatively higher. Each of these campaigns has been evaluated, in order to show the consistent effectiveness of advertising support for the brand.

## EVALUATION OF RESULTS

### 1. Influence of other variables

No other variables can be identified which would have had a major influence on the sales figures achieved over the periods examined. In particular distribution and pricing have been closely assessed.

(a) *Distribution*  Following a slower build-up of distribution in the North, distribution has been at very consistent level.

Total GB Distribution
Store distribution £ Sterling weighted

| | | |
|---|---|---|
| 1984 | November* | 42% |
| 1984 | July | 55% |
| 1984 | November | 52% |
| 1985 | March | 49% |
| 1986 | April | 49% |

*Regional only
Source: RBL Forecast: Storecheck

(b) *Pricing*  The manufacturer's list price had remained unchanged since launch. An assessment of AGB data on average price paid by the consumer indicates only marginal pricing fluctuations, none of which correlate in any way with the periods of advertising support.

### 2. Sales Results

Ex-factory sales data have been used throughout the analysis, as the most consistent and robust source. The sales patterns recorded at the time of each campaign are clearly demonstrated in Figures 1, 2 and 3.

In each instance, sales demonstrated a sharp uplift of up to two and half times the levels of sales prior to advertising. Sales consistently remained above the pre-advertising levels once the advertising had ended.

The continuous pattern of sales since launch is shown in Figure 4. The peaks in sales at the time of advertising on each of the three occasions is clearly demonstrated.

All share data quoted in the following analysis are AGB sterling figures. Table 2 shows the shares achieved by Alphabites and by Birds Eye in total from launch to March 1986.

Index based on pre-advertising sales (cycle 7) = 100

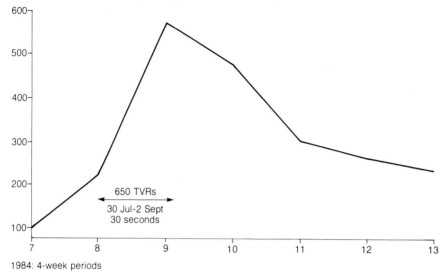

1984: 4-week periods

Figure 1. *The Northern launch*

Index based on pre-advertising sales (cycle 1) = 100

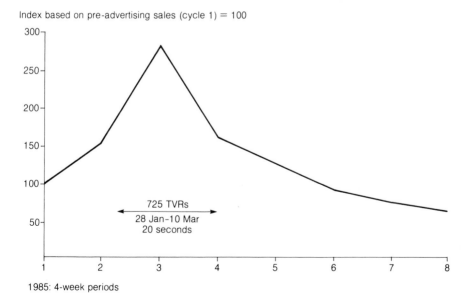

1985: 4-week periods

Figure 2. *The Southern Extension – South only*

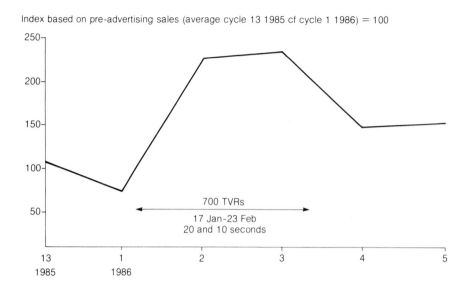

Figure 3. *Network campaign*

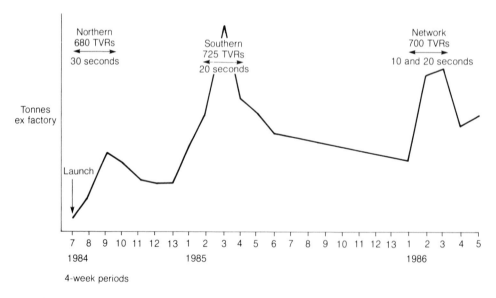

Figure 4. *Sales from launch to present*

*Phase 1: North*   By the end of 1984, Alphabites have achieved a 6.6 per cent value share of the market, equivalent to 11.8 per cent on a national basis (given that the North accounted for 56 per cent of Birds Eye potato products sales). Alphabites had, therefore, in effect surpassed its 10 per cent share objective within five months.

By the end of 1984, Birds Eye's total sterling share of potato products had increased to 45.5 per cent (AGB 24 w/e Dec 1984).

*Phase 2: South*   In 1985, Alphabites first full national year, Alphabites achieved a 15.1 per cent share of the total potato products market.

At the year end, in a market which grew by only 2 per cent, Birds Eye's market share reached 49.1 per cent, peaking at 54 per cent during the Alphabites advertising.

*Phase 3: National*   In the first 12 weeks of 1986, Alphabites achieved an 18.2 per cent share of the market, which actually represented a higher share from the one product than the closest competitor's total brand share. The peak attained during advertising was a 20 per cent sterling brand share.

This took Birds Eye's cumulative market share to its highest ever at 51.7 per cent.

TABLE 2:   BRAND SHARES ALPHABITES AND BIRDS EYE POTATO PRODUCTS

|  | Alphabites sterling brand share % | Birds Eye potato products sterling brand share % |
|---|---|---|
| January–June 1984 | – | 42.3 |
| July–December 1984 | 6.6   (11.8*) | 45.5 |
| 1985 | 15.1 | 49.1 |
| January–March 1986 | 18.2 | 51.7 |

\* National equivalent

Source: AGB

### 3.   *The Role of Advertising in Building Awareness/Trial*

Two usage and attitude surveys were conducted. The first was after the Northern launch, in November 1984, and the second was after the Southern launch in July 1985.

Total awareness amongst housewives with children had, in both cases, attained highly satisfactory levels. The results are shown in Table 3.

TABLE 3:   ALPHABITES: AWARENESS AND TRIAL

| % | Nov 1984 N | July 1985 N   S |
|---|---|---|
| Total awareness | 71 | 55   64 |
| Of those aware: ever bought | 27 | 30   31 |

Source: SRA U&A

It should be noted that the 1984 study was conducted two months after the advertising ended, and the 1985 study five months after the advertising ended in the South, which may account for the lower level recorded in the South. The tail-off in awareness in the North to 55 per cent by July 1985 is clearly indicative of the role of advertising in prompting awareness of the product.

Levels of trial of the product amongst those aware were also high at 27 per cent and 31 per cent in the North and South respectively. Trial rose only a further three percentage points between November and July in the North, without advertising support. Clearly, high levels of awareness and trial had been achieved, but how was the advertising working in terms of more specific communication?

The evidence from the U&A Study carried out in the North indicates that the advertising was communicating the strategy successfully. The product attribute statements shown in Table 4 received the most positive ratings overall, but were particularly high amongst those spontaneously aware of the product, who may be assumed to be more likely to have seen the advertising. The actual level of agreement for these attributes was extremely high.

TABLE 4:   USAGE OF, AND ATTITUDES TO, ALPHABITES

| Base | Spontaneously aware | Total aware |
|------|---------------------|-------------|
| My children would like them | 4.61 | 4.55 |
| More convenient than ordinary potatoes | 4.45 | 4.45 |
| Just the thing for childrens' meals | 4.29 | 4.44 |

Rating of statements on 1–5 score (1 = disagree strongly, 5 = agree strongly).

Source: SRA Alphabites U&A November 1984

### 4.   The Effective Positioning of the Product

The demographic profile of Alphabites clearly reflects the success of the brand's positioning against younger housewives with children (see Table 5).

TABLE 5:   DEMOGRAPHIC PROFILE OF ALPHABITES

| Housewives % | Alphabites | All potato products | Waffles |
|--------------|------------|---------------------|---------|
| Age | | | |
| 16–24 | 7 | 5 | 6 |
| 25–34 | 46 | 24 | 28 |
| 35–44 | 27 | 26 | 29 |
| 45–64 | 14 | 32 | 32 |
| 65 + | 6 | 13 | 5 |
| With children | 84 | 51 | 60 |
| Without | 16 | 49 | 40 |

(AGB 12 w/c March 1986)

This profile indicates that the successful niche positioning for the product was achieved because of having a very different appeal from Waffles. The product's unique and successful appeal, beyond existing users of potato products, is further shown by the fact that in 1985, overall, 57 per cent of Alphabite buyers bought no other convenient potato products.

The extent of this clearcut positioning for the product clearly reflects the advertising strategy.

## SUMMARY

The success of Alphabites and the effective role of advertising in achieving that success are clear from:

— The significant immediate and longer-term increases in sales both during and after advertising support. No other significant variables have been identified.
— As a result, Alphabites over-achieved its target of 10 per cent share by value of the potato products market, reaching 15.1 per cent share in 1985. In the first quarter of 1986 the brand achieved an 18.2 per cent share. In terms of Birds Eye's share of the total potato products market, sterling share had risen from 42.3 per cent in July 1984 to 51.7 per cent in the first three months of 1986. The results have well exceeded the original objectives.
— The high levels of awareness and trial attained for the product.
— The distinctive positioning of the brand as communicated in the advertising, reflected in the marked demographic skew to younger housewives with children, and the brand's high proportion of solus users.
— The effectiveness of advertising in this case ultimately rests on the fact that the advertising expenditure has been quickly recouped by the sales generated. In the case of the 1986 campaign, the advertising will have been paid for within four months after the end of the campaign.

# Index